GW01339191

A REBEL BOOK

Editing: Prem Lolita
Design: Bhaven, Deva Harito
Typesetting: Deva Radhika
Production: Anurag Spersa

Printing: Thomson Press (India) Ltd.

Published by Tao Publishing Pvt. Ltd.,
50 Koregaon Park, Pune 411001 MS, India

Copyright © 1976 Osho International Foundation, www.osho.com
Copyright © all revisions 1953-2006 Osho International Foundation
First edition 1976 as *Come Follow Me,* Volume 1
Second edition 2000 as *Come Follow To You 1*
Reprinted 2006
All rights reserved
Printed in India

Osho is a registered trademark of Osho International Foundation, used under license.

For more information: www.osho.com

ISBN 81-7261-109-9

Osho comments on excerpts from The Holy Bible
(The Authorized King James Version, Red letter Edition with Dictionary)
The World Publishing Company (Cleveland and New York).

OSHO

Come Follow To You

Extemporaneous talks given by Osho
in Gautama the Buddha Auditorium,
Pune, India.

Come Follow To You

Reflections
on
Jesus of Nazareth

◆ I ◆

OSHO

Contents

Grace To Grace page 1

My Way Is Via Positiva page 31

And Lo, The Heavens Opened page 59

I'm Simply Mirroring Jesus page 91

The Kingdom Of God Is At Hand page 121

6 You'll Never Forget The Jokes *page 151*

7 Have Mercy And Not Sacrifice *page 181*

8 I Treat Jesus As A Poet *page 213*

9 Let The Dead Bury Their Dead *page 241*

10 Open The Door *page 273*

Preface

I AM ABSOLUTELY FOR THE INDIVIDUAL. I CAN SACRIFICE every society and every religion and every civilization – the whole history of mankind – just for a single individual. The individual is the most valuable phenomenon, because the individual is part of existence.

You will have to drop your fear. It has been imposed on you; it is not natural. Watch every small child: he accepts himself perfectly; there is no condemnation, there is no desire to be anybody else. But everybody, as he grows, is distracted. You will have to gather courage to come back to yourself. The whole society will prevent you; you will be condemned. But it is far better to be condemned by the whole world than to remain miserable and phony and false and live a life of somebody else.

You can have a blissful life and there are not two ways, only one single way. This is: you have just to be yourself, whatever you are. From there, from that deep acceptance and respect for yourself, you will start growing. You will bring flowers of your own – not Christian, not Buddhist, not Hindu – just absolutely your own, a new contribution to existence.

But it needs immense courage to go alone on a path leaving the whole crowd on the highway. To be in the crowd one feels cozy, warm; to go alone, naturally one feels afraid. The mind goes on arguing within that, "the whole of humanity cannot be wrong, and I am going alone." It is better just to be part of the crowd because then you are not responsible if things go wrong.

Everybody is responsible. But the moment you depart from the crowd you are taking your responsibility in your own hands. If something goes wrong, you are responsible.

But remember one very fundamental thing: responsibility is one side of the coin and the other side is freedom. You can have both together or you can drop both together. If you don't want to have responsibility, you cannot have freedom, and without freedom there is no growth.

So you have to accept responsibility for yourself and you have to live in absolute freedom so that you can grow, whatever you are. You may turn out to be a rosebush, you may turn out to be just a marigold flower, you may turn out just to be a wild flower that has no name. But one thing is certain: whatever you turn out to be, you will be immensely happy. You will be utterly blissful.

Osho
Satyam Shivam Sundaram

Chapter 1

Grace
To Grace

**Osho,
the first
words of
the Gospel
according to
John read:**

1. In the beginning was the Word,
   and the Word was with God, and
   the Word was God.

3. All things were made by him
   and without him was not any thing made
   that was made.

4. In him was life;
   and life was the light of men.

5. And the light shineth in darkness;
   and the darkness comprehended it not.

6. There was a man sent from God,
   whose name was John.

7. The same came for a witness,
   to bear witness of the Light,
   that all men through him might believe.

8   He was not that Light,
    but was sent to bear witness of that Light.

11 He came unto his own,
    and his own received him not.

12 But as many as received him,
    to them gave he power to become
    the sons of God, even to them
    that believe on his name.

14 And the Word was made flesh, and
    dwelt among us,
    (and we beheld his glory, the glory
    as of the only begotten of the Father),
    full of grace and truth.

16 And of his fullness have all we received,
    and grace for grace.

17 For the law was given by Moses,
    but grace and truth came by Jesus Christ.

I WILL SPEAK ON CHRIST, BUT NOT ON CHRISTIANITY. Christianity has nothing to do with Christ. In fact, Christianity is anti-Christ — just as Buddhism is anti-Buddha and Jainism anti-Mahavira. Christ has something in him which cannot be organized: the very nature of it is rebellion and a rebellion cannot be organized. The moment you organize it, you kill it. Then the dead corpse remains. You can worship it, but you cannot be transformed by it. You can carry the load for centuries and centuries, but it will only burden you, it will not liberate you. That's why, from the beginning, let it be absolutely clear: I am all for Christ, but not even a small part of me is for Christianity. If you want Christ, you have to go beyond Christianity. But if you cling too much to Christianity, you will not be able to understand Christ. Christ is beyond all churches.

Christ is the very principle of religion. In Christ all the aspirations of humanity are fulfilled. He is a rare synthesis. Ordinarily a human being lives in agony, anguish, anxiety, pain and misery. If you look at Krishna, he has moved to the other polarity: he lives in ecstasy. There is no agony left; the anguish has disappeared. You can love him, you can dance with him for a while, but the bridge will be missing. You are in agony, he is in ecstasy — where is the bridge?

A Buddha has gone even farther away. He is neither in agony, nor in ecstasy. He is absolutely quiet and calm. He is so far away that you can look at him, but you cannot believe that he is — it looks like a myth, maybe a wish fulfillment of humanity. How can such a man walk on this earth so transcendental of all agony and ecstasy? He goes too far away.

Jesus is the culmination of all aspiration. He is in agony as you are, as every human being is born – in agony on he cross. He is in the ecstasy that sometimes a Krishna achieves: he celebrates; he is a song, a dance. And he is also transcendence. There are moments, when you come closer and closer to him, when you will see that his innermost being is neither the cross nor his celebration, but transcendence. That's the beauty of Christ: there exists a bridge. You can move toward him by and by, and he can lead you toward the unknown – and so slowly that you will not even be aware when you cross the boundary, when you enter the unknown from the known, when the world disappears and God appears. You can trust him, because he is so like you and yet so unlike. You can believe in him, because he is part of your agony; you can understand his language.

That's why Jesus became a great milestone in the history of consciousness. It is not just coincidental that Jesus' birth has become the most important date in history. It has to be so. Before Christ, one world; after Christ, a totally different world has existed – a demarcation in the consciousness of man. There are so many calendars, so many ways, but the calendar that is based on Christ is the most significant. With him something has changed in man; with him something has penetrated into the consciousness of man.

Buddha is beautiful, superb, but not of this world; Krishna is lovable, but still the bridge is missing. Christ is the bridge, hence I have chosen to talk on Christ. But always remember, I am not talking on Christianity. The Church is always anti-Christ. Once you try to organize a rebellion, the rebellion has to be subsided. You cannot organize a storm – how can you organize a rebellion? A rebellion is true and alive only when it is a chaos.

With Jesus, a chaos entered into human consciousness. Now the organization is not to be done on the outside, in the society; the order has to be brought into the innermost core of your being. Christ has brought a chaos. Now out of that chaos you have to be born totally new, an order coming from the innermost being – not a Church but a new man, not a new society but a new human consciousness. That is the message.

And these words from the gospel of St. John…you must have heard them so many times, you must have read them so many times – they have become almost useless, meaningless, insignificant, trivial. They have been repeated so many times that now no bell rings within you when you hear them. But these words are tremendously potential. You may have lost the significance of them, but if you become a little alert, aware, the meaning of these words can be reclaimed. It is going to be a struggle to reclaim the meaning …just as you reclaim a land from the ocean.

Christianity has covered these beautiful words with so many interpretations that the original freshness is lost – lost through the mouths of the priests who are simply repeating like parrots without knowing what they are saying, without knowing, without hesitating, without trembling before the sacredness of these words. They are simply repeating words like mechanical robots. Their gestures are false, because everything has been trained.

Once I was invited to a Christian theological college. I was surprised when they took me around the college. It is one of the greatest theological colleges in India. Every year they prepare two hundred to three hundred Christian priests and missionaries there – a five-year training. And everything has to be taught: even how to stand in the pulpit, how to speak, where to give more emphasis, how to move your hands. Everything has to be taught. But then everything becomes false, then the person is just making empty gestures.

These words are like fire, but through centuries of repetition, parrot-like repetition, much dust has gathered around the fire. My effort will be to uncover them again. Be very alert because we will be treading on a well-known path in a very unknown way, treading on very well-known territory with a very different, totally new attitude. The territory is going to be old. My effort will be to give you a new consciousness to see it. I would like to lend you my eyes so that you can see the old things in a new light. And when you have new eyes, everything becomes new.

Listen:

> In the beginning was the Word,
> and the Word was with God, and
> the Word was God.

The Upanishads can feel poor, the Vedas can be jealous:

> In the beginning was the Word.

What does it mean when the gospel says 'in the beginning'? Christians have been interpreting it as if 'in the beginning' means that there was a beginning. They have been using and interpreting these words 'in the beginning' as if they show something about the beginning of time. But without time how can there be a beginning? To begin, time will be needed in the first place. If time was not in existence, then what do you mean by 'in the beginning'?

'In the beginning' is part of time and cannot precede time, so 'in the beginning' does not mean that there was a day when God created the world. That's absolutely foolish. 'In the beginning' is just a way of speaking. 'In the beginning' does not mean in the beginning at all, because there has never been a beginning – and there can be no end. God is eternal, his creativity is eternal. It has always been so and it will always be so.

Because of these words 'in the beginning', much controversy has continued for centuries. There have even been foolish priests and bishops who have tried to fix the exact date: four thousand four years before Christ, on a certain Monday, the world started. And what was God doing before that? Eternity must have preceded it – four thousand years is nothing. What was he doing before that? Not doing anything at all? Then why suddenly on a certain date did he start the creation?

It has been a problem, but the problem arises because of a wrong interpretation. No, 'in the beginning' is just a way of speaking. One has to start from somewhere, the gospel has to begin from somewhere. Life is eternity, life never starts from anywhere, but every story has to start and every scripture has to start. Arbitrarily we have to choose a certain word and you could not choose better: in the beginning. 'In the beginning' simply says that we don't know.

But from the very beginning, if there was any beginning, God has been creative. Let me try to say it in a different way: God is creativity. You can even drop the word 'God'. In fact the gospel itself does not want to use the word 'God'. *In the beginning was the Word, and the Word was with God, and the Word was God.*

In the beginning was the Word. What word are you talking about? What is this word? Somebody who has known truth knows well that to name God is futile – there is no name, no definition, and all words are small, they cannot contain the whole. 'The word' is simply a way of indicating the nameless, the unknown: *In the beginning was the Word.*

Jews, who preceded Jesus, of whom Jesus was the very culmination.... The Judaic spirit came to a fulfillment in Jesus. Of course they denied Jesus; that is another story. Sometimes it happens that somebody amongst you attains to the fulfillment of the whole race, but the fulfillment is so vast and so great and you are so low that you cannot believe it, you have to deny it.

Christ rose high. Jews had been waiting for centuries for this man – look at the irony! They had been waiting for centuries for this man to happen. All their hope was with this man who would transform their lives and who would bring the kingdom of God on earth...and then this man happened and they themselves who had been waiting for him could not believe, could not trust. What happened? They became too addicted to waiting itself. Now if this is the man, then what will they do? Then the waiting will have to stop, will have to be stopped. And they had waited so long – in fact, waiting itself had become their whole activity, their whole religious activity – waiting for the son of God to come. And now suddenly this man is there and says, "I am here." But now they would rather cling to their waiting than look at this man – because to look at this man will be the end; now there is nothing else to wait for. Future disappears, hope disappears, desire disappears. This man will kill all hopes, all desires, all future – that is too much! The old mind has become addicted to its own waiting, the old mind has become addicted to its own misery, frustration – now it is too much.

It happens: if you have been ill a very long time, by and by you start having a certain investment in the illness. You become afraid – if you become healthy again, fear arises because you will have to go to the office again, to the marketplace. For these few years you have been resting, there has been no anxiety, you could relax. Now again the responsibility. And not only that, for these few years that you have been ill everybody has been sympathetic to you, almost everybody tried to love you. You have become the center of your family, friends, acquaintances; everybody has been kind. To move again in the harsh and cruel world, the mind recoils; it doesn't seem worth it.

If a race has been waiting for too long...and Jews have always been waiting. They are still waiting – and the man has happened and gone. But they have invested too much in waiting. Their waiting has become their prayer – their synagogues are nothing but waiting rooms for the messiah to come. And he has been here! And I tell you, if he comes again – though I don't think he will commit the same mistake again – if he comes again, Jews still will not accept him, because then what will happen to their waiting? They have lived too much in it; their imprisonment has become their home and they have decorated it. And now to move in the harsh, open sky where sometimes the sun is burning too much, and sometimes it is raining, and sometimes it is cold or it is hot – it is dangerous. They are sheltered.

In the beginning was the Word. Jews have been insistently emphasizing that God's name should not be asserted because it is something to keep deep down in the heart. To assert it is to make it profane, to say it is to make it part of the ordinary world and language. To say it again and again is to make it lose its meaning and significance. If you love somebody and the whole day you say, "I love you, I love you" many times – and you enjoy saying it – in the beginning the other person may be happy, but sooner or later the thing is going to be too much. "I love you, I love you" – you are making a beautiful word useless. Don't use it too much then it is significant, then it carries some meaning. In fact those who are really in love may not use it at all. If the love is not shown by itself, it cannot be said – there is no need to say it. And if it is shown by itself, then what is the need to say it? There should be a few key words which you use rarely, very rarely. They should be kept for rare occasions when you touch a peak.

The Jews have always insisted that the name of God should not be taken. It was the custom in the old days, before Christ, that only the high priest of the Temple of Solomon was allowed to use it – and once a year only. Nobody else was allowed. So 'the word' is the code, the code for God's name. Something has to be used to indicate it and this is a beautiful code, 'the word'. They don't use any name, they simply say 'the word'. The same has been done in India also. If you ask Sikhs, the followers of Nanak, they will say *Nam*, 'the name'. They don't say any name, they simply say 'the name'. It means the same as 'the word'.

Only the high priest was allowed, and the high priest had to purify himself. The whole year he would purify himself and fast and pray and get ready. Then one day in the year the whole community would gather. Then too the high priest would not utter the word before the crowd. He would move into the innermost shrine of the temple; the doors would be closed. Deep in silence where nobody could hear – the crowd would be waiting outside and there was no possibility for them to hear – he would assert the name in such sanctity, deep love, intimacy. He was asserting the name for the whole community.

It was a blissful day when the name was asserted. Then for the whole year the name was not to be brought to the lips. You have to carry it in the heart; it has to become like a seed. If you bring the seed out of the soil again and again it will never sprout. Keep it deep down. Water it, protect it, but keep it deep in darkness so that it sprouts, dies and is reborn.

The name of God has to be kept deep in the heart. You should not even hear it. It should be so deep in your being, in your subliminal depths, that it never even reaches to your own mind – that is the meaning of why the high priest goes into the innermost shrine. Nobody hears, the doors are closed, and he asserts the name once. The meaning is this: go into the deepest shrine of your temple of the heart, purify yourself.... And once in a while, when you feel that you are pure, when you feel the fragrance of your being – when you are at the peak of your energy, when you are really alive and not an iota of sadness lingers around you; you are happy, tremendously happy, ecstatically happy and tranquil and silent, and you are in a state where you can thank, where you can feel grateful – then go into the innermost shrine. Your mind will be left out – that is the crowd. You move deeper into the heart and there you assert so silently that even your mind will not be able to hear it. There 'the word' has to be carried.

In the beginning was the Word, and the Word was with God, and the Word was God. There is no difference between God and his name. He has no name, he himself is his name. His 'is-ness' is his name, his existence is his name. A child is born. What name does he have? – no name. But he is. That 'is-ness' is his name. Then for utilitarian purposes we give a name to him, and by and by he will forget his 'is-ness' and he will become identified with the name. If somebody insults the name he will be angry, if somebody praises the name he will be very happy – and the name never belonged to him!

God is the child, always the child, always the innocence of the world. He has no name. That is the meaning of this saying *...and the Word was with God.* 'Is-ness', existence, being: *...and the Word was God.* His name is his being. Don't repeat his name, move into his being – that is the only way to attain him. In fact, forget about him. Move into your own being and 'is-ness', and you will attain to him.

> All things were made by him
> and without him was not any thing made
> that was made.

God is creativity. To say that "God is the creator" is already to falsify him, but to say "God is creativity" will not be understandable. Then people will think, "Then why use 'God'? Just 'creativity' will do." We say, "God is the creator," but because of this expression much nonsense arises. Then when did he create the world? Then why didn't he create it before? Why couldn't he create it before? Why did he create it at the time he created it? Why has he created it the way it is? Why can't he improve it?

So much misery, so much suffering in the world, and he is the creator? Then God becomes the culprit. Then we feel angry: "If he is the creator then he is responsible for all. Why can't he change it?" Then all sorts of problems arise, and theologians go on answering these questions.

In the first place, they need not arise if you look at the thing directly. God is not the creator, he is creativity. Creativity is his being. And he has always been creating; he cannot be on a holiday from his creativity. That is not possible; you cannot go on a holiday from your innermost nature – no. Whatsoever you can leave is not your nature; that which you *cannot* leave is your nature.

God's nature is creativity. He has always been creating. And there is no other way: the only way the world can exist is how it exists. It is the only way. Whatsoever you think or condemn or appreciate is meaningless. It is like going to a rose and asking, "Why do you only have so many petals? A few more could be there. What was wrong?"

But if a few more were there, the same question would have again been relevant.

Whatsoever the world, the mind will always create questions. So those who know drop the mind and accept the world. And there are two ways: either accept the mind and be against the world or accept the world and drop the mind. This is the only way things are and can be. And there is nobody you can complain to, and there is nobody who can listen to your complaints and improve things. God is creativity, not a creator.

All things were made by him – all things really are made *of* him, not *by* him – *and without him was not any thing made that was made.* And not only in the past – even now, whenever a thing is created he is the creator, you are only the instrument.

You paint a picture or you write a song. What do you think – you are the creator? In the moment of deep creativity you disappear, God again starts functioning. So it is not a question of the past. Wherever and whenever creativity happens, it is always through him. Ask all the great poets. They will say that whenever great poems have descended on them they were, at the most, passive receivers. It happened; they were not the creators.

The idea that you can create is simply your illusion. All creativity belongs to him. Even through you, whatsoever is created, he is the creator. To understand this is a great illumination. To understand this the ego disappears; to understand this is to allow him to take total possession of you. You become an instrument – in small things, great things become possible. Then he moves through you. If you dance, he dances. You are at the most the field where he dances. When you sing, he sings. You are at the most the flute, an empty flute, which just becomes a passage to it. At the most you can allow – it is always he who is doing things.

This is what I mean when I say, float, when I say, flow with the river. Allow his creativity to flow through you. Don't impose any pattern on him; don't impose your will. If you can allow yourself to be totally possessed, there is no misery and you are no more a human being. The Jesus within you has become Christ the very moment you allow total possession. Then the Jesus disappears and the Christ appears. Christ is the principle, Jesus is the son of the carpenter Joseph. Jesus disappeared at a certain moment and Christ entered. 'Christ' simply means that now the man is no longer man, the man is God-possessed. Just as when somebody goes mad and you say, "The man is maddened," you can say, "The man is goddened." Now the man is no more there.

> In him was life;
> and life was the light of men.

God is the only existence, the only being: the only life there is, the only dance there is, the only movement, the only energy there is. In the ocean and in the waves, in the illusory world and in the truth, in the dreams and the dreamer, the only energy there is, is God. All is he, he is all. *In him was life; and life was the light of men.* And whenever you come to understand this – this, that he is the only life – your life becomes enlightened, then you are full of light. *God is life!* If you understand this your whole life becomes full of light, his life becomes light in your understanding. When his life is reflected within you, it becomes light.

> And the light shineth in darkness;
> and the darkness comprehended it not.

And the light is shining all around you. Life is all around you

– in the bird, in the tree, in the river. Life is all around you, there is nothing else. You are living in the ocean of life – out and in, within and without, only life is bubbling – a great stream of life, and you are just like a fish in it.

And the light shineth in darkness; and the darkness comprehended it not. But you don't comprehend it. You are still identified with darkness, your eyes are still closed. You are blind. This is a beautiful thing to understand:

There was a man sent from God...

This should be so. These are parables, but I say they should be so, because how will a man who has lived in darkness be able to come to light by himself, alone? A master will be needed.

If you are fast asleep, how will you awaken yourself? – it seems impossible. Somebody who is already awake will be needed to shake you out of your sleep, to give you a jerk, so your needle of unconsciousness jumps out of the groove and takes a new route. For a single moment you open your eyes and you look.

There was a man sent from God, whose name was John.

Unless God himself is going to do it, it seems almost impossible that you will be able to realize what is what. So all the religions of the world.... Hindus say *avatara*. They say, "Man himself is so helpless that God has to descend." 'Avatara' means descendence of God. He has to come himself to awaken you.

This simply shows how deeply you are in sleep, nothing else – not that you have to make it a fanatic belief that God comes down. It simply shows that you are so fast asleep that unless

God comes down, there seems to be no possibility for you. And if sometimes you awaken, it simply shows that God must have come down to awaken you.

> There was a man sent from God,
> whose name was John.
>
> The same came for a witness,
> to bear witness of the Light,
> that all men through him might believe.

I am here. If you can look into me, you will come to trust in things that you have not been able to realize yourself. Through me, you can have a little glimpse of that which is still unseen. And God is the unseen. Somebody is needed who can be a witness, who can bear witness, who can say, "Yes, I know him," who can resound in your depths, who can give you a taste by his touch that "Yes, God exists." God can never be just a belief, because a belief will be impotent. It will be intellectual, heady, but it won't transform you. You can carry the belief for your whole life – it will be a part of your junkyard – it won't change you.

Trust, faith, is different. Belief is intellectual; trust is existential. But how can you come to trust unless you come close to a man who can bear witness, who can say from his very depths of being that "Yes, God is"? If you allow yourself to become vulnerable to him and his being stirs something within you, then a trust is born.

The same came for a witness – John became a witness – *to bear witness of the Light....* He has known the light, he is coming from the light. And remember, whosoever knows the light also knows that he is coming from the light, because there is no other way of being here.

You may not be knowing it, but you also come from the light.

That is the very source – the seed and the source of all life. You may be unaware, you may have forgotten, you may have become completely oblivious of the fact of where you come from – the source is so far away that you don't remember at all – but whosoever within you will become aware of the light will immediately become aware that "I am coming from him." In fact, he will immediately become aware that "I am him, I am he, my father and I are one." As above, so below. He will claim, just as the seers of the Upanishads have claimed: "*Aham brahmasmi*...I am that." Or he will say, like Mansoor: "*Ana'l haq*...I am the truth." Or like Jesus: "I and my father are one." Jesus says, "If you trust me, you have trusted him who has sent me; if you love me, you have loved the one that you know not."

The same came for a witness, to bear witness of the Light, that all men through him might believe. John is a door, a window, from whom you can have a glimpse of the faraway Himalayan peaks.

> He was not that Light,
> but was sent to bear witness of that Light.

This has to be understood, this is one of the really significant things. Whenever a man like Jesus comes, he is always preceded by someone who prepares the ground. It has to be so because a ready ground is needed. Life is a deep continuity; everything is related, it is one whole. John came to prepare the ground because there were many weeds. Grass was growing, a thousand and one types of trees trespassed the whole land. They had to be cut, weeds removed, the soil changed. Only then could the gardener come and sow the new seeds.

Whenever there lives a man like Jesus, he is always preceded.

So the gospel says: *He was not that Light, but was sent to bear witness of that Light* – he had come to prepare the ground.

> He came unto his own,
> and his own received him not.

He has come to help; he has come to fulfill the aspiration of ages. He has come unto his own, but...*his own received him not*. This is something very ironical, but it has always happened. John was born a Jew: Jews would not accept him. Buddha was born a Hindu: Hindus would not accept him. This is how it has always been. Why? Because whenever a man like Jesus or Buddha is born, he is such a rebellion that all that is established is shaken.

An ordinary man lives in the past – for the ordinary man the past is more important because the past is already established, grounded. He has much at stake in the past, much investment in the past. For example, if I suddenly come to you and tell you that the way you have been praying is wrong, and you have prayed that way for fifty years – now there is much at stake. To believe me will be to believe that your fifty years have been useless. To believe me will be to disbelieve fifty years of your own life. To believe me will be to believe that you have been a fool for fifty years. This is too much! You will fight, you will defend.

And when it is a question of a race...thousands of years the race has been doing certain things, and then a Jesus comes and he throws things upside down. Everything is again a chaos. He melts all that is established, uproots all that was thought to be very significant, creates confusion. He has to, because he has now brought you the right thing. But you have been believing that something else was right for so many centuries. What to choose – Jesus or your own long past? What to choose – Jesus or the tradition?

Do you know where the word 'tradition' comes from? It comes from the same root as the word 'trade'. It also comes from the same root as the word 'traitor'. Tradition is a trade, it is a business – and tradition is also a betrayal. Tradition believes in certain things which are not true, tradition is a traitor to truth, so whenever truth comes there is conflict. You can see this here: I am born a Jaina, but Jainas won't accept me. Here you can find Christians, Jews, Mohammedans, Hindus, Buddhists, but very few Jainas...impossible for them to accept me. *He came unto his own, and his own received him not.*

Jainas are too much against me. Hindus are not so much against me but they are also, a little. But Christians – no. Jews – not at all. The further away you go, the less is the antagonism. I am born a Jaina – Jainas are a small community, surrounded everywhere by Hindus; Jainas are almost Hindus. So Jainas will be very antagonistic, Hindus a little less, and Mohammedans, Christians and Jews not so much. The further away you go, the less will be the antagonism. Hence you can understand why so many people from so many countries are here and not so many Indians. With Indians there is a problem: their tradition is at stake. If they believe me, then their tradition...they will have to lose it.

That's why you will see more young people near me and less old people, because young people do not have much investment in their past. In fact, a young man is looking for the future, an old man looking after the past. A young man has a future; an old man has only a past. The future means death; his whole life is past. So whenever a man of seventy comes to me it is very difficult to change him because seventy years will be fighting me. When a small boy of seven comes, a little Siddhartha, there is nothing to fight. He can surrender absolutely, there is nothing...he has no past, just the future. He can be adventurous, he can take the risk;

he has nothing to lose. But an old man...he has much to lose. That's why if a *pundit* comes – one who knows too much without knowing it – he will have much fight, he will have all sorts of arguments, he will defend himself. He has much to lose. But when an innocent man comes who says, "I don't know much," he is easy, he is ready to let go.

> He came unto his own,
> and his own received him not.
>
> But as many as received him,
> to them gave he power
> to become the sons of God,
> even to them that believe on his name.
>
> And the Word was made flesh...

Very few people came to him. John lived near the River Jordan in the wilderness, outside the cities and towns. People who really wanted to be transformed, they would seek him and come to him. Very few came, but those who came ...*to them gave he power to become the sons of God, even to them that believe on his name.* Those who could trust were transformed. And he prepared the ground – these were the first prepared people to whom Jesus was to appear.

> And the Word was made flesh,
> and dwelt among us,
> (and we beheld his glory, the glory
> as of the only begotten of the Father),
> full of grace and truth.

And the Word was made flesh – one of the most beautiful sentences in the gospel – *and dwelt among us.* Jesus is as if 'the word' has become flesh; God has become man. The secret has become open, the hidden has become unhidden, the mystery has become an open truth. All the doors of the temple are open. *And the Word was made flesh, and dwelt among us....* John created the situation, because 'the word' can become flesh only when the listener is ready.

If you are ready, then I can tell you what I carry within my heart. If you are not ready, it is impossible to utter it; it will be absolutely useless. In fact, it cannot be brought out unless you are ready. When your heart is ready, that very readiness will bring the truth that I carry within my heart. Then the heart can talk to the heart, depth can respond to depth.

John created a group, a small group of chosen people who would be able to trust, who would be able to see with the eyes of trust. Only then is Jesus possible. Remember this: if the listener is ready, only then can the truth be uttered.

I was traveling in this country for many years, all year round, just to find people who would be able to transform themselves so that whatsoever I carry within me can become flesh, it can be uttered. Now people ask me why I don't go anywhere. That work is done. Now those who are ready will come to me. Now this is the only way.

That's why I don't want masses and crowds to come here – because if they come, then I will not to able to utter that which I carry…and I would like to share it before I leave. If you are ready, then and only then can something of the beyond descend on you.

And the Word was made flesh, and dwelt among us, (and we beheld his glory, the glory as of the only begotten of the Father).... And this is really something to be understood, because Christians have been misinterpreting it continuously. They go on saying Christ is the only begotten son of God. Yes, it is true in a way – but not true in the way Christians say it.

Buddha is also the only begotten son of God, and Krishna is also the only begotten son of God. Remember, I emphasize: the only begotten son of God. And I am also the only begotten son of God, and you are also the only begotten son of God. Then why say 'only begotten'? If all are his sons, then why say it?

It has some significance, some meaning – it has to be said. It is just like this: you fall in love with a woman and you say, "You are the only woman, the only beautiful woman in the world." Not that this is true, but still in a certain moment of love it is true. It is not an ordinary fact, it is a truth. When you say to a woman, "You are the only beautiful woman in the world who has ever existed or will ever exist," that doesn't mean that you know all the women who have existed in the world before or that you know that all the women who are going to exist will not be more beautiful than this. How can you know, how can you compare? This is not a logical fact; this is a poetic realization.

In that moment of love it is not a question of statistics. Some logician can raise the argument, "Wait! Do you know all the women that exist right now in the world? Have you looked, searched, and have you found that this is the most beautiful woman in the world? What are you saying? You are using comparative language." But you will say, "I'm not worried about other women, and this is not comparative. I am not comparing, I am simply asserting a truth about my *feeling*. It is not a fact of the outside world, it is a truth of my inner feeling. This is how I feel: that this is the most beautiful woman in the world. I am not saying anything about the woman. I am saying something about my heart. I don't know all the women …there is no need." It is not comparison. It is a simple feeling. You are so possessed by the feeling that *not* to say this will be wrong.

When you love Jesus, he is the only begotten son of God.

So this sentence is good, it says: ...*the glory as of the only begotten of the Father.* 'As' – *as if* he is the only begotten son of God. Those who fall in love with Jesus, for them he is the only begotten son of God. They are not saying anything about Buddha or against Buddha. They are not comparing.

That's what I mean when I say Buddha is also the only begotten son, you are also. Everybody in this world is unique. Once you attain to your inner realization you are the only begotten son of God – as if the whole existence exists for you and only for you. The trees flower for you and the birds sing for you and the rivers flow for you and clouds gather together for you. You become the sole center of existence when you attain.

Or if you fall in love with a Buddha, a Jesus or anybody.... These assertions of lovers should not be taken as statements of fact. They are poetic realizations. You cannot argue with them; they are not arguments at all. They assert something of the heart.

And the Word was made flesh, and dwelt among us...full of grace and truth. Wherever truth is, there is grace. And wherever there is grace, there is truth. Try to understand this. You can be graceful only when you are true. If you have a certain lie within you that lie will disturb your grace, that lie will be poisonous to your heart, because that lie has to be hidden, suppressed. Nobody is to be allowed to know it. You cannot be open; you will be shut by the lie.

If you deceive, you cannot be free and flowing. You will be stuck with your deception. So I don't say that lies are bad because they are harmful to others – no. They are bad because you will miss your own grace. Deceptions are not bad because you deceive others, deceptions are bad because they will disturb your flow and you will not be flowing – you will start freezing. In many places you will be stuck, dead. You will have blocks in your being.

Look at a child. Every child has grace. Then where does it disappear to? When every child brings grace into the world, where does it disappear? By and by it is lost, and then everybody becomes graceless, ugly. It is rare that somebody is capable of being as graceful as he was when he was a child. What happens? Why is a child graceful?

Have you seen a child who you can say is ugly? No, that never exists. A child, and ugly, is impossible. All children are beautiful, unconditionally beautiful. They are flowing and they are true. When they want to cry, they cry; when they want to laugh, they laugh. When they are angry, they are angry and when they are loving, they are loving. They are true to the moment, they are never deceiving. But soon they learn the politics. Soon they will learn that "Mother likes it if I smile. It is easier to persuade her, it is easier to manipulate her if I smile." A small child is becoming a politician! He waits. He may be angry inside, but when the mother comes he smiles because that is the only way to get the ice cream. Now the smile is false, and a false smile is ugly because the whole being is not in it, it is something painted from without. Then more and more things will be painted, more and more personalities will gather around and the essence will be lost. Then you become ugly. Truth and grace are always together. Truth is grace, and grace is truth.

The gospel catches the exact point of Jesus' being: truth and grace. He was true, profoundly true to the very core – utmost, utterly true. That's how he got into trouble. To live with a society which is absolutely untrue, to live with it with utter truthfulness, is to get into trouble.

And the grace…. He was not a politician and he was not a priest. He simply loved life and lived it. He was not here to preach anything, he had no dogma to inculcate, he had no ideas to force on people. In fact, he lived a pure, graceful, flowing life, and he was infectious. With whomsoever he moved, whomsoever came into contact with him was magnetized, hypnotized. This man was a child, an innocent child. People were attracted. People left their houses, their jobs — they simply started following him.

He was not a preacher, and he was not giving any political revolution to the world, and he was not giving any reformation to the world. He was just giving you a way to live flowingly. And that was the trouble — because Jews are one of the most suppressed races in the world. Very suppressive, moralistic, puritans. That became the troublesome thing. They live by principles. They live by the law, and the law has to be followed. Of course, they are very successful people in the world. If you live by the law you will be very successful. If you live by love, you are bound to be a failure. It is miserable, unfortunate, but it is so. In the world, law succeeds, love fails. In God, love succeeds, law fails — but who bothers about God?

Jews are very lawful, very good citizens, and wherever they move they are always successful because they always move by the law. They live by arithmetic. That is why they get most of the Nobel prizes in the world. Nobody can compete with them — very talented. In business, they are successful. In politics, whatsoever they do, they do exactly the right thing. But they are very formalistic puritans, in a deep bondage with the mind. A deep hangover in the mind continues.

And Jesus started talking about law. The gospel says:

> And of his fullness have all we received,
> and grace for grace.

> For the law was given by Moses,
> but grace and truth came by Jesus Christ.

...*The law was given by Moses.* Moses is the foundation of Judaism. Of course it was needed because unless law is established, love will not be possible. Law is a must, it is a necessity, but it is not enough.

Moses gave the law to the world. The people were primitive, uncultured; they had no sense of society. Moses created a society, and one of the most enduring societies – the Jews. And, in fact, Moses must have been a great genius because he provided the law, and Jews have survived all sorts of catastrophes. He must have given them a very permanent base. But he was a lawgiver, just as Manu was the lawgiver to Hindus. Moses is the Manu of Jews, he gave the law.
Let me tell you a small story....

It happened that Moses was passing by and he came across a man who was praying. But he was doing such an absurd prayer, not only absurd, but insulting to God, that Moses stopped. It was absolutely unlawful. It is better not to pray than to pray in such a way, because the man was saying things which are impossible to believe. The man was saying, "Let me come close to you my God, my Lord, and I promise that I will clean your body when it is dirty. Even if lice are there, I will take them away. And I am a good shoemaker, I will make you perfect shoes. You are walking in such ancient shoes, dirty, gone completely dirty.... And nobody looks after you, my Lord. I will look after you. When you are ill, I will serve and give you medicine. And I am a good cook also!"

He was doing this type of prayer! So Moses said, "Stop! Stop your nonsense! What are you saying? To whom are you talking – to God? And he has lice on his body? And his clothes are dirty and you will clean them? And nobody is there to look after him, and you will be his cook? Who have you learned this prayer from?"

The man said, "I have not learned it from anywhere. I am a very poor and uneducated man and I don't know how to pray. I have made it up myself and these are the things that I know. Lice trouble me very much, so he must be in trouble. And sometimes the food is not good – my wife is not a good cook – and my stomach aches. He must be also suffering. This is just my own experience that has become my prayer. But if you know the right prayer, you teach me."

So Moses taught him the right prayer. The man bowed down to Moses, thanked him, tears of deep gratitude flowing, and he went away. Moses was very happy. He thought that he had done a good deed. He looked at the sky to see what God thought about it and God was very angry!

He said, "I have sent you there to bring people closer to me, but you have thrown away one of my greatest lovers. Now he will be doing the right prayer, but it won't be a prayer at all – because prayer has nothing to do with the law. It is *love*. Love is a law unto itself; it needs no other law."

But Moses is the lawgiver. He founded the society, he brought the Ten Commandments. Those Ten Commandments have remained the foundation of the whole Western world: Judaic, Christian, Mohammedan – all three religions depend on the law of Moses.

So the whole world has known only two lawgivers: the East knows Manu and the West knows Moses. Hindus, Jainas, Buddhists have been supplied the law by Manu, the law has been given by Manu; and Moses has given to Mohammedans, Christians, Jews. These two lawgivers have created the whole world. And there must be something – both are 'M': Manu and Moses. Then comes Marx who is the third 'M'. China, Russia – he has given the law to them. These are the three great 'M's – lawgivers.

For the law was given by Moses.... Law is for the society, love is for the individual. Law is how you behave with others, love is how you behave with yourself. Love is an inner flowering, law is an outward performance. Because you live with people you have to be lawful, but that is not enough – good, but not enough. If a person is simply lawful, he will be dead. He will be a good citizen, but he will be dead. Law can be the foundation of the society, but it cannot be the very building. You can live *on* the law, but you cannot live *in* it. It has no space for that. For that, love is needed.

Jesus was the fulfillment of Moses. What Moses started, Jesus was completing, but Jews denied him. What Manu started, Buddha was completing, but Hindus denied him. Marx still needs a Buddha or a Jesus in the world. Someday he will come, but communists will deny him.

Because people have become law-oriented, love looks against law. In fact, law is needed only so that love can become possible. Law is needed so that people can live peacefully and love. Law is not, in itself, the end, it is the means. Love is the end. But when people become too law-abiding, then love itself seems to be unlawful. They become afraid of love, because who knows? – you are moving on a dangerous path.

Love is mad; law is calculation. Law is dependable – the society can decide on it. But love is not reliable, who will decide? Love knows no rules. It is not arithmetic, it is poetry. It is dangerous! Love is always wild, and law is social.

Remember this, be lawful, but don't end there otherwise you lived in vain – in fact, you lived not. Be lawful because if you are not lawful you will be in trouble. You have to be in the society, you have to follow certain rules, but they are only rules – there is nothing ultimate about them, there is nothing from God about them.

Let me tell you this: the Ten Commandments were created by Moses, they were not from God, they cannot be. Those Ten Commandments are human rules of the game. "Don't steal!" – because property is individual. But if the game changes and the property becomes social property, then "Don't steal!" will not be much of a law. Or if someday the world becomes really affluent then there will be so much that nobody steals, because stealing is possible only if poverty is there. People are hungry and poor – they steal. But if the society is affluent, as it is going to be someday, and there are too many things – whatsoever you need, more is available – who will be a thief? Then the commandment will disappear; there will be no need for it. The Ten Commandments are social.

Moses brings the law; Jesus brings truth, grace, love. Love is from God; law is from the mind. Love is of God; law is of man. And with love grace happens, and with love – truth. Remember this, because to understand Jesus is to understand the phenomenon of love. To understand Jesus is to understand the intricacies of grace. To understand Jesus is to understand truth. Remember, if you can understand truth, truth liberates. And there is no other liberation.

Enough for today.

Chapter 2

My Way Is
Via Positiva

THE FIRST QUESTION:

> Beloved Osho,
> Who prepared the way for you?

Nobody has prepared the way for me, and neither am I preparing the way for anybody. This has to be understood.

There are four possibilities. One, the oldest and the most used, is what happened in Jesus' case. John the Baptist prepared the way; the disciple preceded the master. It has its own benefits, but it has its own limitations and defects also – bound to be so. When the disciple precedes the master he will create limitations which belong to him and the master will have to function within those limitations. It has its benefits because when the master comes he will not be worried about preparing the ground – the ground will be ready, he can immediately start sowing the seeds. But the ground will be ready according to the disciple. It cannot be according to the master, so he will have to function under limitations. That's what created the whole trouble in Jesus' story.

John the Baptist is a different type of man from Jesus, a very fiery man, almost in flames – and always in flames. He uses a language which fits him, but which can never fit Jesus. Jesus is very silent, very peaceful. John the Baptist is not that type of man. He is a prophet, Jesus is a messiah, and the difference between a prophet and a messiah is great.

A prophet is a religious man, deeply religious, but functioning like a politician: using the language of revolution, using a very violent language – arousing the hearts and beings of men, stirring them. A prophet is like an earthquake. A messiah is very soothing, silent like a Himalayan valley – lazy, sleepy. You can rest in a messiah. With a prophet, you will always be on the go.

Because of this, John the Baptist used the terminology of politics: revolution, the kingdom of God. And even that 'kingdom' has to be taken by force. It has to be, in fact, attacked. He was misunderstood because whenever you use the language of the outside world for the inner world, you are bound to be misunderstood. The politicians became afraid: What kingdom is this man talking about? About what revolution? What does he mean by saying that the kingdom has to be taken by force? John the Baptist was very impatient. He wanted immediate change; he could not wait. He created the atmosphere in which Jesus had to function. John the Baptist died in imprisonment; he was beheaded by the rulers. He was absolutely misunderstood – but nobody was at fault, he himself was.

But because of him.... And Jesus was to follow him, Jesus was a disciple of his own disciple. He was initiated by John the Baptist because John the Baptist preceded him. He became linked and then he had to use the same terminology. It was almost certain that he would be misunderstood. John the Baptist died in prison – beheaded. Jesus died on the cross – killed, murdered. He was also talking about the 'kingdom' of God. Of course he was not so aggressive, but the very terminology appeared political. He was a very innocent man; nothing to do with politics.

But John the Baptist helped in a way. Jesus could work because all the disciples of John the Baptist were ready to receive him, he was not a stranger. John the Baptist had created a small opening, a small clearance in the wilderness of humanity. When he came he was received, there was a home ready for him – a few people receptive to him. That would not have been possible if he had come alone without a predecessor. But the home was made by John the Baptist, and the disciples whom he attracted were attracted by *him* – that created the trouble.

This is the oldest format: the master is preceded by a disciple who functions as a predecessor and prepares the ground. Because of its defects and limitations, there has been another, the opposite.

Ramakrishna was succeeded by Vivekananda; he was not preceded by anybody. The master comes first, then follows the disciple. This has its own benefits because the master creates the whole climate, the master creates the whole possibility of growth – how the thing is to go. He gives language, pattern, direction, dimension.

But there are defects because the master is infinite and when the disciple comes he is very finite. Then the disciple has to choose, because he cannot move in all directions. The master may be showing all the directions, he may be leading you towards infinity, but when the disciple comes he has to choose, he has to select, and then he forces *his* pattern.

Ramakrishna was succeeded by Vivekananda. Ramakrishna was one of the greatest flowerings that had ever happened; Vivekananda was the prophet. Ramakrishna was the messiah, but Vivekananda set the whole trend. Vivekananda's own inclinations were extrovert, not introvert. His own inclinations were more towards social reformation, political change. He was more interested in bringing riches to the people, destroying poverty and hunger and starvation. He turned the whole trend around.

The Ramakrishna Mission is not true to Ramakrishna; it is true to Vivekananda. Now the Ramakrishna Mission functions as a social service. Whenever there is famine, they are there to serve people. Whenever there is an earthquake, they are there to serve people. Whenever there is flood — and there is no lack of these things in India — they are there. They are good servants, but Ramakrishna's inward revolution has completely disappeared into the desert land of Vivekananda.

Ramakrishna functioned more freely than Jesus because there was no pattern for him. He lived more spontaneously than Jesus. There was no confinement anywhere; all the directions were open to him. He could fly just like a bird in the sky, no limitations existed. But then comes the disciple. He organizes it. He organizes, of course, in his own way.

Both ways have their benefits, both have their defects. Then there is a third possibility which has never been used before. Krishnamurti is the first in the world to have used a third possibility. The third possibility is to deny both: the predecessors and the successors both. It is negative.

Krishnamurti's method is *via negativa*. So first he denied those who prepared the ground for him. That was the only way to get out of the limitations. He denied the whole Theosophical movement — Annie Besant, Leadbetter. They were the people who prepared the whole ground and worked hard for Krishnamurti. They were the John the Baptists for him. They created a vast opportunity in the whole world for him. But then he looked when he was ready and he saw the defects and the limitations, that the same would be the case as happened with Jesus. He simply denied. He denied that they created a ground or that there was any need to create the ground.

While denying them he was aware that he had to deny his messiahship also — because if he said that he is the messiah then he could deny the predecessors, but the successors would follow. Then the same trouble would be there as it had been with Ramakrishna. So he denied: "There is nobody who has preceded me and there is nobody who is going to succeed me." He denied Leadbetter, Annie Besant and the Theosophical movement, and for his whole life he has been denying that anybody is going to become his heir or successor.

This has its own beauty, but its problems also. You may be free, very free, absolutely free – because there is no limitation on either side, before or after – but your freedom is in negativity. You don't create. Your freedom comes to no fulfillment, it is futile – you don't help. It is as if somebody is so conscious about not falling ill – he continuously works and remains aware not to fall ill – that he forgets that sometimes you have to enjoy the health also. Otherwise you may not fall ill, but the very awareness that "One should not fall ill and should remain aware" becomes an illness of a sort.

Krishnamurti is so alert about it – that no bondage should be created anywhere, no fetters should be created anywhere – that he worked hard, but couldn't help anybody. It is beautiful for himself, but it has not been beneficial for humanity. He is a free man, but his freedom is his alone. That freedom could not become a taste in thousands and thousands of throats; it could not create an urge. He has remained a pinnacle of freedom, but no bridge exists. You can look at him – he is like a beautiful painting or beautiful poetry – but nothing can be done about it, it doesn't change you. He has broken all the bridges. This is the third possibility – never tried before. He is the first to try it.

I have tried the fourth. That also has never been tried. The fourth is that half of my life I have worked myself as John the Baptist, and now half of my life I will function as a christ. That is the fourth possibility: to prepare the ground and to sow it also, to sow the seeds.

There are problems about it also; it is impossible to find a way which has no problems. It has its own benefits, it has its own defects. The benefit is that I am both, so I am, in a way, totally free. Whatsoever I have done in my first step, I have done knowing perfectly well what the second step is going to be. John the Baptist in me was perfectly aware of the Christ who was going to follow, they were in a deep harmony. They are one person; there is no problem about it. So John the Baptist in me could not create any limitations for the Jesus to follow — a total freedom.

And no Vivekananda is going to follow me. I am my own Vivekananda and I am my own John the Baptist, so nobody can put a limitation on me when I am gone. And I am positive: if Krishnamurti is via negativa, I am *via positiva*. I have accepted both the roles and I have a certain freedom even Krishnamurti cannot have. He has to always deny, and denial in itself becomes a worry, a deep anxiety. I have nothing to deny, I just have to say yes to the total.

But there are problems, and the greatest problem is that I will always be contradictory. Whatsoever John the Baptist has said, the Christ in me has to contradict it. I will always be contradictory.

For many years I was moving around, reaching to every person whomsoever had *any* capacity to grow. Nobody ever thought that someday the wanderer in me would simply sit in his closed room and would not even come out of the room — contradictory! For years I was talking in terms of revolution. Of course, the John the Baptist has to talk that way. Then suddenly I stopped talking about revolution, the society, the welfare of humanity; I forgot all about it. Now only the individual exists — contradictory. If you look you can find two currents parallel, and the first current has been continually contradicted by the other current. For those many years the *Acharya*, the John the Baptist, was doing one thing. Now the Osho is doing totally something else, a very contradictory thing.

It will be impossible later on to decide whether this man was one or two. And I suspect that somebody is going to suspect someday that this man was two, because the contradictions are so naked and there is no way to resolve them. This is the trouble with me – but somebody had to try the fourth and I am happy that I tried it. On this earth everything has its own problem, so you cannot escape from the problem. From somewhere or other the problem will enter, so it is only a question of choice – whatsoever fits you.

This fits me perfectly. To be free to contradict is a great phenomenon because then I am not worried at all about what I say. I don't keep any accounts, I need not be worried about what I said yesterday. I can contradict – this is a great freedom.

And if you love me, I know that you will find somewhere deep within me that the contradictions are already resolved. But that will happen only to those who trust, that will happen only to those who come closer and closer to me. All the contradictions are on the surface, deep down within me they are already resolved because I am one.

I have functioned as John the Baptist; now I will function as Christ. So nobody has preceded me, nobody is going to succeed me. I am a perfect circle.

The second question:

> Beloved Osho,
> Why do I feel hesitation in enjoying anything?

Joy is not allowed; you are preconditioned against joy. From the very childhood you have been taught that if you are happy then something is wrong – unhappy, everything is good. If you are miserable nobody is worried about it, but if you are too happy everybody is worried about you. You must have done something wrong.

Whenever a child is happy the parents start looking for the cause: he must have done some mischief or something. Why is he so happy? The parents are not happy. They have a deep jealousy towards the child because he is happy. They may not be aware of it, but they are jealous. It is easy to tolerate somebody else's misery, but it is almost impossible to tolerate anybody else's happiness.

I was reading an anecdote....

A very religious father was bringing up his son as perfectly as possible. One day when they were going to church he gave the boy two coins: one, a one *rupee* coin; another, a one *paise* coin. He also gave him the choice that whatsoever he thought was right he could put in the donation plate in the church. He could choose the rupee or the paise.

Of course the father believed and hoped that he would put the rupee in the church plate. He had been brought up in such a way – he could be expected to, relied upon.

The father waited. After church he was very curious to know what happened. He asked the boy, "What did you do?"

The boy admitted that he had donated the one paise coin and kept the rupee for himself.

The father couldn't believe it. He said, "Why did you do this? We have always been inculcating great principles in you."

The boy said, "You ask why: I will tell you the reason. The priest in church spoke rightly. In his sermon he said, 'God loveth a cheerful donator.' I could donate the one paise coin cheerfully – not the one rupee!"

God loveth the cheerful giver. I am absolutely in agreement with the boy. What you do is not the question, you are religious if you can do it cheerfully. It may be a one paise coin, it doesn't matter. It is immaterial because the real coin that you are giving is your cheerfulness.

But from the very beginning every child is taught not to be so cheerful. To be cheerful is to be childish. To be cheerful is to be natural, but not civilized; to be cheerful is somehow primitive, not cultured. So you have been brought up not to be cheerful and whatsoever you have ever enjoyed was condemned again and again. If you enjoyed just running and shouting around the house, somebody was bound to be there saying, "Stop that nonsense! I am reading the newspaper!" – as if the newspaper is something very valuable.

A child shouting and running is a more beautiful sight than any newspaper. And the child cannot understand: "Why? Why do I have to stop? Why can't you stop your newspaper reading?" The child cannot understand: "What is wrong in my being happy and running?"

"Stop!" – the whole cheerfulness is suppressed, the child becomes serious. Now he sits in a corner unhappy. The energy needs movement, and a child is energy, he delights in energy. He wants to move and dance and jump and scream and shout. He is so full of energy he wants to overflow, but whatsoever he does is wrong. Either the mother is saying, "Keep quiet," or the father or the servant or the brothers or the neighbors. Everybody seems to be against his flowing energy.

One day it happened:

Mulla Nasruddin's wife was very angry. Her small boy was making too much of a nuisance, creating too much nuisance. Finally she was exhausted and she ran after him

– she wanted to thrash him well – but he escaped, escaped upstairs, and hid himself under a bed. She tried hard, but she couldn't get him out. She was a very fat woman, she couldn't get underneath, so she said, "Wait, let your father come."

When Mulla Nasruddin came, she told the whole story. He said, "Don't be worried, leave it to me. I will go and put him right."

So he went upstairs, walked very quietly, looked under the bed and was surprised – surprised by the way the boy greeted him. The boy said, "Hello, Dad – is she after you also?!"

Everybody is after him. The overflowing energy is looked at as a nuisance. And that is *delight* for the child. He doesn't ask much; he simply asks a little freedom to be happy and to be himself. But that is not allowed.

"It is time to go to sleep!" When he doesn't feel like going to sleep, it is time. He has to force himself. And how can you force sleep – have you ever thought about it? Sleep is nothing voluntary, how can you force it? He turns in his bed – unhappy, miserable – and cannot think how to bring on sleep. But it is time; it has to be brought or it is against the rules.

And then in the morning when he wants to sleep a little longer, then he has to get up. When he wants to eat something, it is not allowed; when he does not want to eat something, it is forced. This goes on and on. By and by the child comes to understand one thing: that whatsoever is cheerful for him has something wrong about it. Whatsoever makes him happy is wrong, and whatsoever makes him sad and serious is right and good and accepted.

That's the problem. You ask, "Why do I feel hesitation in enjoying anything?" Because your parents, your society, are still after you.

If you are really with me, drop all that nonsense that has been forced on you. There is only one religion in the world and that religion is to be happy. Everything else is immaterial and irrelevant. If you are happy you are right, if you are unhappy you are wrong.

It happens every day, people come to me – the wife comes or the husband comes – and the wife says she is very unhappy because the husband is doing something wrong. I always tell such people that if the husband is doing something wrong, let him be unhappy. "Why are you unhappy? The wrong itself will lead him towards unhappiness – why are you worried?"

But the wife says, "But he is not unhappy. He goes to the pub and he enjoys. He is not unhappy at all."

Then I say, "Something is wrong with you, not with him. Unhappiness is the indicator. You change yourself; forget about him. If he is happy, he is right."

I tell you, if you can go happily to a pub, that is better than going unhappily to a temple – because finally one comes to discover that happiness is the temple. So what you do is not the question – what quality do you bring to it while doing it? Be happy and you are virtuous; be unhappy and you are committing what religious people have called sin. You must have heard them say that the sinner will suffer some day in the future, in some future life, and the saint will be happy somewhere in the future, in a future life. I say that is absolutely wrong. The saint is happy here and now, and the sinner is unhappy. Life does not wait for so long; it is immediate.

So if you feel yourself unhappy, you must have been doing something wrong with yourself. If you cannot enjoy – if some hesitation comes in, if you feel afraid, guilty – it means somewhere by the corner the shadows of your parents are still lurking. You may be enjoying, or trying to enjoy ice cream, but deep in the unconscious the shadow of the mother or the father is lurking. "This is wrong. Don't eat too much, this is going to harm you." So you are eating, but the hesitation is there. The hesitation means the contradiction is there.

Try to understand your hesitation and drop it. And this is one of the most unbelievable phenomena: that if you drop the hesitation it may come to pass that you stop eating too much ice cream automatically – because that eating too much may be part of it. Because they have *denied* it, they have created a certain attraction in it. Every denial brings attraction. They have said, "Don't eat it," and that has created a hypnotic, a magnetic, attraction to eat it.

If you stop having any hesitations, you drop all the parental voices, all the upbringing that you have been forced to go through. You may suddenly see the ice cream as just an ordinary thing. Sometimes one can enjoy it, but it is not a food. It has no nutritious value – it may even be harmful. But then you understand. If it is harmful you understand it, you don't eat it. And you can always eat it sometimes. Sometimes, even harmful things are not so harmful. Once in a while you can enjoy it, but there is no obsession to eat it too much. That obsession is part of the repression.

Drop hesitations. People come to me and they say they want to love, but they hesitate; they want to meditate, but they hesitate; they would like to dance, but they hesitate. If this hesitation is there and you go on feeding it, you will miss your whole life. It is time – drop it – and nothing else is to be done. Just become alert that this is just the way you have been brought up, that's all.

Consciously, it can be dropped. It is not your being, it is just in your brain. It's just an idea which has been forced upon you. It has become a long habit – and a very dangerous habit – because if you can't enjoy, then what is this life for?

And these people who cannot enjoy anything…love, life, food, a beautiful scene, a sunset, a morning, beautiful clothes, a good bath; small things, ordinary things…if they cannot enjoy these things – and there are people who cannot enjoy anything – they become interested in God. They are the most impossible people; they can never reach to God. God enjoys these trees, otherwise why does he go on creating them? He is not fed up at all, not at all. For millennia he has been working on trees and flowers and birds. And he goes on listening and he goes on replacing: new beings, new earths, new planets. He is really very, very colorful! Look at life, watch it, and you will see the heart of God – how it is.

People who are very uptight, unable to enjoy anything, unable to relax, incapable even of enjoying a good sleep, they are the very people who become interested in God. And they become interested for wrong reasons. They think that because life is useless, futile, they have to seek and search God. Their 'God' is something against life, remember.

Gurdjieff used to say that "I have searched into every religion, into every church, mosque and temple, and I have found that the 'God' of the religious people is against life." And how can God be against life? If he is against, then there is no reason why life should exist or should be allowed to exist. So if your God is against life, in fact, deep down, you are against the real God – godliness. You are following a Godot, not a God.

God, godliness, is the very fulfillment of life, godliness is the very fragrance of life, godliness is the total organic unity of life. God is not something that exists like a dead rock; God is not static, God is a dynamic phenomenon. God does not exist, it happens; when you are ready it happens. Don't think that God exists somewhere and you will find a way to reach him. No, there is nowhere and there is no God existing somewhere waiting for you. Godliness is something that happens to you when you are ready. When you are ready – when the sadness has disappeared and you can dance, when the heaviness has disappeared and you can sing, when the heavy weight of conditioning is no more on your heart and you can flow – godliness happens. God is not a thing that exists; it is something that happens. It is a dynamic, organic unity.

And when godliness happens, everything happens: the trees, the stars, the rivers. And to me, to be capable of enjoying is the door. Serious people have never been known to reach him. Seriousness is the barrier – the wrong attitude. Anything that makes you serious is irreligious. Don't go to a church that makes you serious.

It happened once:

A woman purchased a parrot, but by the time she reached home she was very much puzzled, worried. She had paid a good price for it; the parrot was beautiful. Everything was good, only one thing was very dangerous – once in a while the parrot would say loudly, "I am a very wicked woman." This was something!

The woman lived alone. And she was a very religious woman – otherwise why live alone? She was a very serious woman, and this parrot would say again and again – and even passers-by would hear and listen – and the parrot would say, "I am a very, very wicked woman."

She went to the vicar because he was the only source of her wisdom and knowledge and information. She said, "This is very bad, and I am puzzled about what to do. The parrot is beautiful and everything is good...only this."

The vicar said, "Don't be worried. I have two very religious parrots. Look!" – one was in his cage tolling the bell and another was praying in his cage. Very religious people. "You bring your parrot. Good company always helps. Leave your parrot for a few days here with these religious people, and later on you can take your parrot back."

The woman liked the idea. She agreed, brought the parrot, and the vicar introduced the parrot to his parrots. But before he could say anything, the parrot said, "I am a very, very wicked woman."

The vicar was also nonplussed – what to do? In that moment the parrot who was praying stopped praying and said to the other parrot, "You fool! Stop tolling the bell, our prayers are fulfilled."

They were praying for a woman! "Stop tolling the bell; the prayer is answered!" In fact, whenever you see somebody praying, suspect something has gone wrong. They are praying for a woman, praying for money, praying for something, praying for happiness. A really happy person does not pray. Happiness is his prayer. And there cannot be a higher or a greater prayer than just to be happy.

A happy person does not know anything about God, does not know anything about prayer. His happiness is his God, his happiness is his prayer, he is fulfilled. Be happy and you will be religious; happiness is the goal.

I am a hedonist, and as far as I see it, all those who have known have always been hedonists, whatsoever they say. A Buddha, a Jesus, a Krishna – all hedonists. God is the ultimate in hedonism: that is the peakest peak of being happy.

Drop all the conditioning that you carry with you. And don't try to condemn your parents because that won't help. You are a victim of *their* conditioning, but what could they have done? They where victims of the conditionings of *their* parents, so it is a long succession. Nobody is responsible, so don't feel angry that your parents destroyed you. They couldn't help it. If you understand, you will feel pity for them. They were destroyed by their parents, and their parents were destroyed by somebody else, and it has always been going on. It is a succession, a chain. You simply get out of it.

There is no point in condemning anybody and there is no point in being angry – an angry young man and this and that. There is no point. That is again a foolishness. Once you are sad, then you become angry. That is as bad as sadness. Just look at the whole thing and get out of it. Simply slip out of it without making any noise. That's what I call rebellion.

The revolutionary gets angry. He says the education has to be changed, he says the society has to be changed, he says a new type of parent is needed in the world. Then only will everybody be happy. But who will do this? The doers are always in the same mess, so who will be the help? "Create a new education" – but who will create it? The teachers have to be taught first. And the revolutionaries are just as much a part of this nonsense as the reactionaries, so who will bring the revolution? The hope is futile.

There is only one hope: you can bring light to your being. And it is available immediately, there is nothing to it. Have you ever seen a snake slipping out of his old skin? – it is just like that. You simply slip out of it, forgive and forget. Don't be angry against your parents, they themselves were victims. Feel pity for them. Don't be angry against the society, it could not have been otherwise. But one thing is possible, you can slip out right now. Start being happy from this very moment. Everything is available – only a deep attitudinal change that from now on you will look at happiness as the good and misery as the sin.

The third question:

> Beloved Osho,
> Will I be able to take all that I feel here
> with you when I leave, or will all that has
> happened just be a memory?

When you leave, if you don't leave yourself here, if you take your 'I' with you, then whatsoever has happened will become a memory. Then whatsoever has happened will be left behind. If you want to carry it with you, then you cannot carry yourself within. The choice is open: either leave yourself here, then whatsoever has happened will be carried within you; or take yourself back home, then whatsoever has happened will be left here. The choice is yours.

If you can drop the ego, then whatsoever is happening is real. But if you cannot drop the ego then it is going to become a memory, and it will create more trouble for you because the memory will become a haunting. You have had a glimpse and now it is lost. You will be more miserable than ever. You know that it exists, but now you have lost the track. You know it is somewhere. Now you cannot simply say that it doesn't exist; that argument won't help. Now you cannot easily become an atheist and say there is no God and there is no meditation and there is no inner core to human beings – you cannot say that. You have tasted it. Now the taste will surround you, haunt you, will call you.

The choice is yours. You can drop your 'I' with me, and the vision that has happened will become part of your reality. It will be integrated in your organic unity, it will be crystallized. But you cannot have both, you can have only one, so before you leave, please make certain that you are leaving your 'I' with me. Make certain that your surrender is

real and total, make certain that you are really surrendered. Then wherever you are, you are close to me.
It is because of your surrender that you are close to me, it is not a question of physical space. Surrendered – you may be on another planet – you are close to me. Not surrendered – you may be just sitting close to me – you are far away.

The fourth question:

> Beloved Osho,
> Yesterday you mentioned that law is anti-love, but yet without it love cannot exist and grow. Please explain in which way law is needed for love to grow.

For every growth the opposite is needed because the opposite creates the tension. Without the opposite, things relax into death. This is one of the most fundamental things in life.
Love cannot exist without the law; the law is the opposite. The law is the nonspontaneous, the mechanical; love is the spontaneous, the nonmechanical. Love is uncaused, law is within cause and effect. Love is individual, law is social. Can you exist without the society? Without the society you will not be born. You need a mother, a father, you need a family to grow in, you need a society to thrive in. Without a society you cannot exist.
But remember, if you just become a part of society, you have already moved into nonexistence again. Without the society you cannot exist and you cannot exist just as a member of the society either. Jesus says, "Man cannot live by bread alone." Do you think it means you can live without bread? Man cannot live by bread alone – absolutely true – but can man live without bread? No, that too is

not possible. Man needs bread. It is necessary, but not enough. It simply gives you a base, but it doesn't give you a jump, a flight. It is a jumping board. Don't get stuck at that. Jesus says, "The Sabbath is created for man, not man for the Sabbath." The law is needed because the society is needed. The law is the bread. But if there is only law – if you exist as a member of the society, a law-abiding member of the society, and nothing else exists in you which is beyond law – then you exist in vain, then you exist "just by bread alone." Then you eat well, you sleep well, and nothing else happens. It is good to eat well, but not enough, something of the unknown is needed. Something from the invisible is needed to penetrate you; the romance of the unknown is needed. Without it you will be a syllogism of logic, but you will not be a poetry. Without it you may be quite right, but just 'quite right' – no romance, no poetry, no dance.

Love is the mysterious, the law is the nonmysterious. The law helps you to be in the world, love gives you the reason to be. The law gives you the *cause* to be and love gives you the *reason* to be. The law gives you the base; love becomes the home, the house. And remember one thing: that the base can exist without the house, but the house cannot exist without the base. The lower can exist without the higher, the higher cannot exist without the lower. A man can exist with just bread – he will not have anything worth having, he will not have any reason to exist, but he can exist – he can just vegetate. But even a great lover cannot exist without bread. Even Jesus or Buddha cannot exist without bread. They have found the celestial home of love, but they cannot exist without bread.

The lower is, in a way, independent of the higher. The higher is dependent, in a way, on the lower. But this is so. And it seems simple, it is easy. You make a temple.... What we call in India the *kalash*, the golden cap of the temple, cannot exist without the whole temple there. If you remove the temple, the kalash, the golden cap, will fall down. It cannot exist without the temple. Of course, the temple can exist without the cap; there is no problem about it.

Just think: a man is hungry – can he dance? Dance is impossible. The man is starving, he cannot even think. He cannot imagine what dance means. He may have known it in the past, but he will not even be able to believe that he has known it. It seems impossible, it seems almost nonexistential – it cannot exist in a starved body. How can you think of a dance descending? But think of another man who is well fed and without any dance. There is no trouble – you can vegetate. The higher is not a must, it is a freedom. If you want, you grow in it; if you don't want, there is nobody forcing you to grow in it. The lower is a need, it is not your choice. It has to be fulfilled.

Law is anti-love. If you are too lawful, you will not be able to love anybody – because the very quality of love is spontaneity. It comes from the blue, it can disappear into the blue. It has no reason, no cause here. It happens like a miracle; it is magical. Why it happens, how it happens, nobody knows. It cannot be manipulated – it is anti-law, it is anti-gravitation, it is anti-science, it is anti-logic. It is against all logic and against all law.

Love cannot be proved in any lab and love cannot be proved by any logic. If you try to prove it by logic you will come to know that there is nothing like love – that love is impossible, it cannot exist – but it exists! Even great scientists fall in love. They cannot prove it in their labs, they cannot argue for it, but they also fall in love. Even an Einstein falls in love.

Love makes everybody humble. Even Einstein – so proud of his logic, argument, science – suddenly falls in love one day. An ordinary woman – Frau Einstein. Suddenly his whole science disappears and he starts believing in the impossible. Even in his later life he used to shrug his shoulders, "It happens, but if you ask me as a scientist I cannot vouch for it. But it happens if you ask me as a man." In his last days he said, "If love exists, then God must also exist, because if one impossible is possible, then why not the other?" He died as a deeply humble and religious man.

Somebody asked him, "If you are born again, what would you like to be?"

He said, "Not a scientist again. I would rather be a plumber."

What is he saying? He is saying that he has seen the falsity of all logic and he has seen the futility of all scientific argument. What he is saying is that he has seen through and through that cause and effect may be the base, but they are not the pinnacles. The real temple, the real mystery of life, moves through love, prayer, happiness – all impossibles. If you think of them you cannot believe, but if you allow them to happen then a great trust and a great grace arises in you.

Moses is the law. The society cannot exist without Moses, he is a must. The society cannot afford to lose him. The society would be a chaos without a Moses. He is absolutely needed, he is the very foundation. But Jesus is love. Moses is needed, is necessary, but not enough. If Moses alone rules the world, the world will not be worth living.

Jesus…a breeze from the unknown…nobody knows from where it comes, nobody knows where it goes: a penetration of eternity into time…the entry of the mysterious into the known.

Jesus cannot come without Moses, remember. Moses will be needed. He is the bread, Jesus is the wine. You can live by bread, but the bread has nothing of romance in it. The wine – that is the romance, the poetry, the dance, the celebration, the joy, the ecstasy. Yes, Moses can exist without Jesus. Jesus cannot exist without Moses. That's why Jesus says again and again, "I have come to fulfill, not to destroy." Moses was just a foundation; Jesus raises the temple of God on it.

Moses is the 'absolutely right' citizen, the good man. Jesus is not so good. Sometimes one suspects whether he is good or bad; he confuses. He moves with drunkards, he stays with a prostitute. No, never – you cannot conceive of Moses doing that. Moses is an absolutely right man, but that's where he misses something: the beauty, the freedom. He always moves on the right track, he is a railway line. Jesus is like a river, he changes – sometimes left, sometimes right – sometimes he changes the path completely.

Moses is absolutely believable, Jesus not so. Sometimes one suspects whether this man is right or wrong. That was the problem for the Jews. They had lived on the bread of Moses, they had followed Moses and his Ten Commandments, and now this man comes and says, "I am the fulfillment of all that has preceded me," and "I have come not to destroy, but to fulfill." But what type of fulfillment is this? He does not look like Moses at all. He has no condemnation of the bad. He says, "Judge ye not!" Moses is a great judge, and Jesus says, "Judge ye not, so that ye may not be judged." Moses says, "Don't do evil," and Jesus says, "Resist not the evil" – very confusing. He must have created great chaos. Wherever he moved he must have brought confusion and conflict to people's minds, he must have created anxiety. That's why they took revenge and killed him; it is absolutely logical.

Buddha was not killed in India, Mahavira was not killed – sometimes a few stones were thrown or things like that, but they were not killed, crucified. They never confused the mind so much as Jesus. They had something of the Moses in them, and Jesus has nothing of the Moses in him.

Mahavira has much of the Moses in him; he has something of the law and something of love, both.

Jesus is pure love. That's why he was crucified. He had to be crucified – such pure love cannot be tolerated, such pure grace is impossible to bear – the very presence is intolerable because it hurts. The very presence of Jesus throws you into confusion, and the only way to protect yourself and defend yourself is to kill this man, destroy this man. By destroying Jesus, the people tried to live with Moses and law alone, and not be bothered by love. The day Jesus was crucified, it was nothing but an indication that the ordinary mind would like to live without love. Love was crucified, not Jesus. He is just symbolic.

There are many complications. Jews have always been puzzled about why this man Jesus influenced the whole world so much and he could not influence the Jews at all. Jews are great scholars, their rabbis are great *pundits*, and they have been trying to prove that Jesus did not say a single new word, that all that he said is written in Jewish scriptures. Then why has this man become the very axis of humanity? What happened? – it seems unbelievable.

They are right in a way: Jesus has not said a single word that cannot be found in the sayings of old rabbis. No, he has not said a single new word. But that is not where he is unique. He is unique in the way he has said it – not the word, but the way he has asserted it. In the Old Testament you come again and again across the expression "The lord hath said...." But that is not characteristic of Jesus. Whenever he says this, he says, "I say unto you..." not "The lord...." He *is* the lord. The Old Testament says, "The lord says this." Jesus says, "I say unto you." The old rabbis stammer, Jesus speaks; the old rabbis have a *borrowed* glory, Jesus has his own. The old rabbis speak *from* authority; Jesus, *with* authority – and that is a great difference.

It is said that once the enemies of Jesus had sent a man to catch hold of him and bring him to the temple. He was teaching near the temple and a crowd had gathered. The man went there to catch hold of him, to imprison him, but the crowd was big and he had to enter the crowd to reach the man – it took time. While he was penetrating the crowd, he had to hear what this man was saying. Then he stopped, he forgot why he had come. Then it became impossible to imprison this man. He came back.

The enemies asked, "Why have you come back? Why have you not caught hold of him?"

He said, "I was going to, but his words fell in my ear. And I tell you, no man has ever spoken like this man! The very quality, the authority, the power that he speaks with overpowered me. I was hypnotized. It became impossible to catch hold of this man."

Jesus is love. Love has authority of its own, it is not borrowed. The old rabbis and the Old Testament people are like the moon – the borrowed light. Jesus is the sun, he has his own light. Love has its own authority; law never has its own authority. The authority is from Moses, Manu, Marx; the authority is from the scripture, the tradition, the convention. The authority is always of the old, it is never fresh and new.

Love is anti-law. But if you have love you can be lawful also, there is no problem in it. But then you are more than the law; you have something of love within you.

You live in the society, you have to follow the rules. They are just like: keep to the left, or keep to the right – nothing ultimate about them; just rules to keep the traffic in control, otherwise it will be almost impossible to move. Good as far as it goes, but don't think of yourself that because you always keep to the left, you have attained something.

Of course it is good as far as it goes, but nothing much — what have you attained? The traffic will be convenient, that's all — but what have you attained?

All morality, all law, is good as far as it goes, but it doesn't go far enough. Love is needed. Love is a sort of madness, illogical, irrational.

The fifth question:

> Beloved Osho,
> Witnessing, awareness, meditation, suddenly seem distant and sterile adult ideas in the face of the flood of wild and childish adoration which fills me while I am listening to you talk about Jesus. My adult self says, "Beware; don't indulge in sloppy, sleepy sentimentality — this is just the mind, childhood Christian conditioning." But the impulsive, yearning seven-year-old feels like sticking out her tongue at the twenty-eight-year-old seriously spiritual seeker. Which is the real me?

Neither — but the one who is watching both, the one who has asked the question. You are neither a seven-year-old nor a seventy-year-old. Oldness is irrelevant to you, age does not belong to you. You are eternal — neither the child, nor the young man, nor the old man. Always fall back to the witness, go deeper and deeper into witnessing. Never allow any other identification to settle: of the child or the adult — no. All identifications are bondages.

Total freedom is not of identification; total freedom is non-identification with each and every thing. Someday, when all identifications are broken and they fall down — like clothes drop – and you are absolutely nude in your freedom, then you will know who you are.

You are gods in exile. Only by witnessing will you remember who you are. Then all misery disappears, all poverty disappears. You are the very kingdom of God.

The last question:

> Beloved Osho,
> Why do you give sannyas to
> so many creeps?

It is from Anand Bodhisattva. If not, then, Bodhisattva, how could you be a sannyasin?

I love creeps. They are good people. Everybody is accepted. I make no conditions, because I don't look at how you look. I am not bothered by your appearance. I look at you, and you are gods in exile, maybe sometimes with dirty clothes, sometimes with an unwashed face, but still a god.

Sometimes you look like a creep, but you are not. Because I can see you deep within your reality, I accept you totally. Whatsoever you pretend to be, you cannot deceive me. These are all pretensions. You may be deceived by your own pretension; I am not deceived. I look direct and immediate; I look into you. And I always find the fresh, the eternal, the beautiful: truth and grace – divinity. You are sovereigns....

Enough for today.

Chapter 3

And Lo,
The Heavens Opened

And Lo, the Heavens Opened

Matthew 3

1   In those days came John the Baptist, preaching in the wilderness of Judaea,

2   And saying, "Repent ye: for the kingdom of heaven is at hand."

11 "I indeed baptize you with water unto repentance: but he that cometh after me is mightier than I, whose shoes I am not worthy to bear: he shall baptize you with the Holy Ghost, and with fire."

13 Then cometh Jesus from Galilee to Jordan unto John, to be baptized of him.

14 But John forbade him, saying,
"I have need to be baptized of thee,
and comest thou to me?"

15 And Jesus answering said unto him,
"Suffer it to be so now: for thus
it becometh us to fulfill all righteousness."
Then he suffered him.

16 And Jesus, when he was baptized,
went up straightway out of the water:
and lo, the heavens were opened
unto him, and he saw the Spirit of God
descending like a dove,
and lighting upon him.

17 And lo, a voice from heaven,
saying, "This is my beloved Son,
in whom I am well pleased."

I HAVE HEARD A STORY – IT HAPPENED IN THE DAYS OF knights and castles. A young Englishman was searching for his fortune, wandering all over the land. Tired, he paused under a tree near a castle to rest. The duke of the castle was passing by. He stopped and inquired why the young man was waiting there, what he was looking for. The young man said, "I am an architect and I am in search of employment."

The duke was very pleased because he needed an architect. He said, "You come with me. You be my architect, and whatsoever your needs are, they will be fulfilled from my castle and from the land. You can live like a really rich man. But be faithful, and remember one thing: if you leave, you will have to leave as empty-handed as you are coming in."

The young man agreed. Weeks passed and then months and he worked faithfully, and the duke was very pleased with him. All his needs were fulfilled, he was looked after – he really lived like a rich man in the castle. But by and by he started feeling uneasy. In the beginning it was not clear what the cause of it was, because in fact there was no cause to be uneasy, every need was taken care of. It was like a cloud surrounding him, a heaviness, the feeling of something being missed. But not knowing exactly what it was he was confused. Then one day it flashed like lightning before him – he understood the cause. He went to the duke and said that he was leaving.

The duke could not believe it. He said, "Why are you leaving? If there is any difficulty you simply tell me and it will be done. I have been very much pleased with your work and I would like you to be here for your whole life."

The young man said, "No, I am leaving. Please allow me to leave."

The duke asked, "But why?"

The young man said, "Because nothing belongs to me here. Empty-handed I have come, empty-handed I will have to leave. This is a dream: nothing belongs to me here."

This is the point where a person starts becoming religious. If something belongs to you in this world, then you are not yet ready to be religious. Empty-handed you come, empty-handed you go. Once you realize this, like a flash of lightning everything becomes clear. This world cannot be your home — at the most an overnight stay...and in the morning we go.

Once you have the feeling that you are here only momentarily — you cannot possess anything, you cannot have anything here — it becomes a dream, what Hindus call *maya*. It becomes illusory. That is the definition of 'maya' — something which appears to be yours and is not, something which appears to be real and is not, something which seems to be eternal and is only momentary, something which is made of the stuff dreams are made of.

Unless one understands it, one goes on doing things which are eventually found to be meaningless. The day death comes your whole life proves to be meaningless. Confronting death, you will see that your hands are empty — and you worked hard! You were in so much anguish and anxiety for things which cannot be possessed.

It is not in the nature of things that they can be possessed. Possession is impossible because you are here only for a few moments. Things were here before you, things will be here after you. You come and go, the world remains.

Be a guest, and don't start feeling and believing that you are the owner here. Then your life changes immediately; then your life takes on a new hue, a new color, a new dimension. That dimension is religion.

Once you understand it, you need initiation – initiation into the other world. That is available just by the corner. Once this world is understood to be just a dream, the other becomes available.

This was the whole message of John the Baptist:

> "Repent ye: for the kingdom of heaven is at hand."

It has been tremendously, terribly misunderstood by Christians. From the very beginning the message was misunderstood. People thought that the world was going to end and John the Baptist was forecasting, was predicting, the end of the world. *"For the Kingdom of heaven is at hand."* People thought that this world was going to end – this was the misunderstanding – so they waited. John the Baptist died, and there was no sign of the kingdom coming. This kingdom continued and that kingdom never came. Then Jesus was again saying the same thing: "Repent ye: for the kingdom of heaven is at hand." Then they waited…then he was crucified…and the kingdom never came. And Christians have been waiting for twenty centuries since then.

Now much doubt has arisen in the mind. Even the priest in the pulpit goes on repeating these words, but they are no longer meaningful. He knows himself they are not meaningful. He goes on saying, "Repent ye: for the kingdom of God is at hand," but he knows that for twenty centuries it has not happened and the world has continued.

But this is not the meaning at all. The world is not going to end; *you* are going to end. When John the Baptist said, "Repent ye: for the kingdom of heaven is at hand," he never meant that this world is going to end. He simply meant that you are going to end, and before you die, make contact with the other world. Repent for all that you have done to possess this world, repent the way you have lived in this dream as if it was reality, repent for all that you have been and have been doing and thinking, because all of that is baseless.

Unless you repent, you will not be able to see that the kingdom of God is just by the corner. Your eyes will remain filled with this world; you will not be able to see the other. Before the other can be seen your eyes have to be completely cleaned of this world – the world of things, the world of matter, the world of lust, possession, the world of greed and anger, the world of jealousy, envy, the world of hatred – the world of the ego. Your eyes have to be completely cleaned, washed, before you can see the kingdom of God. In fact, the moment your eyes attain to clarity this world disappears…just as in the morning when you become awake the world of dreams disappears…another world opens its door. The kingdom of God is the reality and *this* world is only a projection of your mind.

John the Baptist and, later on, Christ, were saying you are going to end, but that is difficult for the mind to understand. The mind always thinks, can think and believe, that everything else is going to end, but "Not me." The mind goes on saving itself, defending itself.

Somebody dies. You see the dead body, but it never occurs to you that you are going to die. You sympathize with the family of the dead man. You say, "Poor man. He could have lived a little longer. He was not yet old enough. His family was so dependent on him – now what will happen?"

The wife is crying and weeping, and the children are mad. What will happen? You think about the dead man, you think about the dead man's family, you think about the future of the children – orphaned. You think of the wife – widowed. But you never think that this death is your death also. You always hide yourself, you always go on defending yourself. And deep down everybody thinks that he is not going to die. Death always happens to others.

The mind interprets in such ways that it misses the whole point. The world is to continue: it has always been there and will always be there. Only you will not be there; death will take you away. As empty-handed as you had entered, you will have to leave. If that understanding penetrates your being, then repentance becomes possible. And repentance is nothing but attaining to the clarity of vision. This word 'repentance' is very, very significant. There is no other word more significant in Jesus' terminology because repentance will open the door of the divine. What is this repentance?

You have been angry and you repent. You feel sorry: you have behaved badly with someone and you repent and you ask to be pardoned. Is Jesus' and John the Baptist's repentance the same? Then it cannot go very far, because you have repented many times and you have not changed. How many times have you repented? How many times have you been angry, greedy, violent, aggressive, and you have repented? But your repentance has not transformed you, it has not brought you near the kingdom of God. It has not opened any new doors, new dimensions; you remain the same. Your repentance and Jesus' repentance are not the same. In fact, they are almost diametrically opposite.

So whatsoever you have been understanding about repentance is absolutely false. Try to understand. When you repent, in fact you don't repent. When you repent, in fact you try to repair the image. It is not repentance, it is repairing the broken image that you had of yourself.

For example, you have been angry and you have said things. Later on, when the rage is gone, the madness gone, you cool down and you look back. Now there is trouble. The trouble is that you have always been thinking that you are a very peaceful, peace-loving man; you have always been imagining that you never become angry. Now that image is broken. Your ego is shattered: now you know that whatsoever you have been believing has proved wrong. You have been angry, you have been very angry, and you have said and done things which are against your ego. You have shattered your own self-image. Now you have to repair it.

The only way to repair it is to repent. You go and repent, you say good things. You say, "It happened in spite of me. I never wanted it to be so. I was mad, I was not in my senses. The anger possessed me so much that I was almost unconscious, so whatsoever I have said, forgive me, I never meant it. I may have uttered it, but I never meant it."

What are you doing – repenting? You are simply repairing. The other man relaxes because when somebody asks to be forgiven, he has to repair his image also. If he cannot forgive, then he is not a good man. He was also angry – about your anger – and he was planning to take revenge, but now you have come to be forgiven. If he does not forgive, then he will not be able to forgive himself, then his image will be broken.

And that is the trick you are playing. Now if he does not forgive you, you are the good guy and he is the bad guy. Now the whole thing has been thrown upon him. This is a trick, a very cunning trick. If he does not forgive you, he is a bad man. Now you are at ease, your image repaired.

You have thrown the whole guilt on him. Now he will feel guilty that he cannot forgive, and a good man has to forgive. If he forgives, it is good; if he does not forgive, then it is good for you. Now it is a question for him to decide.

This is not repentance. When John the Baptist and Jesus say, "Repent!" they mean totally, absolutely, a different thing. What do they mean? They mean: try to see, try to understand what you have been doing. Look through and through. Go to the very roots of your existence, being, behavior, and see what you have been doing, what you have been *being*. It is not a question of any particular act that you have to repent for, it is your whole quality of being – not any anger, not any greed, not any hatred – no. Not any enmity – nothing. It is nothing about any particular act. It is something about your very being: the way, the style, of your existence. It has no concern with any particular fragmentary act.

When you repent, you repent about a certain act. Your repentance is always in reference to certain acts, but Jesus' repentance is not about certain acts – it is about your being. The way you have been has been absolutely wrong. You may not have been angry – still you have been wrong. You may not have been full of hatred – still you have been wrong. You may not have possessed much wealth – still you have been wrong. It is not a question of what you have done, it is a question of how you have been. You have been asleep, you have been unconscious; you have not lived with an inner light, you have lived in darkness.

When they say, "Repent!" they mean repent for the whole way you have lived up to now, the way you are. It is not a question of asking forgiveness from somebody – no, not at all. It is just a returning. The word 'repent' originally meant return. In Aramaic, which Jesus and John used as their language, 'repent' means return – return to your source, come back to your original being.

What Zen masters say: "Search for your original face," is the meaning of "Repent ye." – drop all the masks. It is not a question between you and others, it is a question between you and your God. "Repent ye" means drop all the masks and stand before God in your original face – the way he has made you. Let that be your only face – the way he wanted you to be. Let that be your only being. Return to the original source, come back to your deepest core of being. Repentance is returning back; it is one of the greatest spiritual turnings.

This is what Jesus means by conversion. A Hindu can become a Mohammedan, a Mohammedan can become a Christian, a Christian can become a Hindu – that is not conversion. That is again changing masks. When a Christian becomes religious, a Hindu becomes religious, when a Mohammedan becomes religious, *then* it is conversion. It is not moving between one religion and another, because there are not two religions in the world. There cannot be two: religion is one.

Religiousness is a quality; it has nothing to do with sects and doctrines and dogmas, churches and temples and mosques. If you are in a mosque and you become religious, you will no longer be a Mohammedan…you will simply become a pure being who has no adjective attached to him. If you are praying in a temple and the temple disappears, you are no longer a Hindu…you have become religious. This is conversion.

I was reading the life of a very famous bishop. He went to St. Mary's Church in Cambridge to deliver a university sermon. Thirty, forty years before, when he was a young man, he was an undergraduate there. And he was full of reminiscences, memories of his young age. He looked around – could he recognize anybody who was there when he was an undergraduate? He recognized an old verger. After the sermon he went to him and said, "Do you recognize me? I was a student here forty years before. Everybody else has gone, I can only recognize your face. Thank God you have good health. You served him well."

The verger said, "Yes, I thank God, I thank him very much, because after listening – and I have been listening to each and every sermon that has been delivered in this church for fifty years! – thank God after listening to all sorts of nonsense for fifty years, I am still a Christian."

It is difficult to be a Christian if you listen to all sorts of nonsense that has been preached in the name of Christianity. It is difficult to be a Hindu if you know all the nonsense that has been written in the name of Hinduism. It is difficult to be a Mohammedan if you know what it means to be a Mohammedan. Because you don't know, it is easy. You remain a Hindu because you don't know what it means. You don't know the hatred implied in it, you don't know the politics intrinsic to it.

It is easy to be a Christian, not knowing what Christianity has done in the past. It has been murderous. Christianity killed more people than communism. But it is easy if you don't know. The more you know, the more it will become difficult to be a Christian, to be a Mohammedan, to be a Hindu. In fact, you will understand that these are the ways of *not* being religious, these are the ways which prevent you from being religious, these are the ways which are the barriers. They deceive you that you are religious, they give you a false coin; they are fakers, counterfeits. To be religious is not to be a Mohammedan, not to be a Christian, not to be a Hindu. To be religious is just to be religious, nothing else is needed. That is conversion. If you repent, conversion happens. Conversion is the by-product of repentance. One does not have to repent for his acts, because that is not real repentance. One has to repent for his whole being. Only then transformation is possible.

Now, listen to these words of the gospel:

> In those days came John the Baptist,
> preaching in the wilderness of Judaea...

John's name has become 'John the Baptist'. Nobody else's name in the whole history of the world has become so connected with baptism. He initiated hundreds of seekers, and his way of initiation was something unique. He initiated them in the River Jordan. First they would meditate with him for a few days, a few months, or sometimes for a few years. When they would be ready, then he would take them into the river. They would stand in the river and he would pour water on their heads – and something would transpire, something would happen in their hidden-most being and they would no longer be the same people as they were before. It was a secret rite, a secret ceremony. Something was being transferred from the master to the disciple. The water was used as a medium.

There have been two types of initiation in the world. In one type of initiation water has always been used, and in the other type of initiation fire has been used. In India, fire has been used as a medium of initiation for centuries. Zarathustra used fire as a medium of initiation. John the Baptist used water. Both can be used, and both have to be understood.

Water and fire have different qualities and yet they are very deeply joined together. They are opposites, but complementary. If you put water on a fire, the water will disappear, evaporate. If you pour water on a fire, the fire will disappear. They are opposite, but in a deep unity. Water flows downwards, fire flows upwards. Naturally, water will never go upward; naturally, fire will never go downward. They move in different dimensions, different directions. If something has to go downwards in you, water has to be used as a medium, as a vehicle. If something has to go upwards in you, fire has to be used as a medium and vehicle.

John the Baptist would pour water, and with the falling water – after a long preparation and meditation – your whole being would concentrate on the falling water and the coolness of it which would cool you within also. And through the water the magnetism of this man, John the Baptist, would flow in you. Water is a very, very vulnerable vehicle. If a man who has healing power in his hands just touches the water, the water becomes a healing medicine. And water is deeply related to your body: sixty percent or even more of your body is nothing but water. Just watch it: sixty percent of your body is water.

And have you watched what your breathing is doing to you? The breathing brings fire, it is oxidation. Your body is water, your breathing is fire; with these two, you exist. When the breathing stops, the fire disappears; then the body loses warmth, then it is dead. If water is gone from the body, the body becomes too hot, feverish, and you will die soon. A deep communion between water and fire, a deep balance, is continuously needed.

You eat food: through food, fire from the sun reaches your body. You breathe: through breathing, oxygen reaches into the body. You drink water: continuously water is being replaced in the body. Between fire and water you exist.

John the Baptist used water to bring something from the above within you. That is one way of initiation. There is a higher way – to bring something within you upwards.

Then it becomes initiation by fire.

> In those days came John the Baptist,
> preaching in the wilderness of Judaea,
>
> And saying,
> "Repent ye: for the kingdom of heaven
> is at hand."

Every moment the kingdom of heaven is at hand. This very moment the kingdom of heaven is at hand, it is absolutely urgent to repent. That was his meaning. Don't waste a single moment – because if you waste it, it can never be recaptured, regained. All time gone is gone. It could have been a deep celebration in God, you wasted it – for nothings, for dreams. *"Repent ye: for the kingdom of heaven is at hand."*

> "I indeed baptize you with water
> unto repentance: but he that cometh
> after me is mightier than I,
> whose shoes I am not worthy to bear:
> he shall baptize you with the Holy Ghost,
> and with fire."

John the Baptist prepared people so that God could descend into them, then Jesus prepared people so that they could ascend into God. Both are the possibilities: either you ascend into God or God descends into you. Descendence is easier because you simply wait – receptive, like a womb. You must have observed: Lao Tzu never talks about fire, he always talks about water. His method of initiation was just like John the Baptist's. That's why he talks about the feminine mind – one has to become feminine to receive. Just as water descends from the clouds, God descends.

"Jesus," John the Baptist says, "will baptize you with fire. He will take you to God, he will help you to go upwards." That is difficult – an uphill task – and before anybody can go uphill, he has to learn how to go downhill. Before one is ready to be baptized by fire, one has to be ready and baptized by water, because if you cannot go downwards, you cannot go upwards. To go downwards is very easy, to just wait and receive is easy, but if even that is difficult, what to say about going uphill? It is going to be very difficult.

So first let God descend into you. The moment God descends into you, you will become very powerful because you will no longer be yourself. Then going uphill becomes very easy – then you can fly, then you can become fire.

John the Baptist prepared people, prepared the ground for the seed to descend. Look – when you throw a seed in the soil, it descends into the soil. When it breaks, it starts rising upwards. The first act is baptism by water: you throw the seed into the soil, it descends deep and rests there. The seed has nothing to do, it just has to rest and everything happens. Then an upward energy – the seed starts moving, sprouts; becomes a big tree, goes to the sky.

The tree needs to be watered every day so that the roots can go deeper and deeper into the earth, and the tree needs also sun, the fire, so that the branches can go higher and higher. In deep forests of Africa, trees go very high because the forests are so dense that if they don't go high they will not reach the fire. They have to rise higher and higher so that they can open their being to the sun and the fire can be received. If you give only water to the tree, the tree will die; if you give only fire to the tree, the tree will die. The tree cannot exist with water only, it cannot exist in a desert with fire only. It needs a deep combination.

So a baptism of water is needed in the beginning, that is the first initiation. Then a baptism of fire is needed, that is the second initiation. And between the two — when the balance is achieved — is transcendence. Between the two, when the balance is totally achieved and neither is too much and neither is too little — just the right proportion — suddenly the transcendence. In balance is transcendence.

> "I indeed baptize you with water
> unto repentance: but he that cometh
> after me is mightier than I,
> whose shoes I am not worthy to bear:
> he shall baptize you with the Holy Ghost,
> and with fire."

'Holy ghost' is just symbolic of balance. In Christianity the concept of three exists as the Trinity. God the father, Christ the son — but these are two poles, father and son. Something has to balance these two and that is the holy ghost. It is just pure spirit, neither son nor father, which is just in between the two — the balance. Between fire and water, the holy ghost happens.

These are symbolic terms: the holy ghost is not a being somewhere. The holy ghost is the music, the harmony between duality. The holy ghost is the river between two banks. The holy ghost is where.... If you go on looking for him somewhere, you will not find him. The holy ghost is there where any duality ceases within you. Love/hate ceases within you — a sudden balance. You cannot say whether it is love, you cannot say whether it is hate — it is neither. It is something absolutely unknown, you have never known it before...the holy ghost has happened.

> Then cometh Jesus from Galilee
> to Jordan unto John,
> to be baptized of him.

This must have been one of the rarest moments in the history of human consciousness: the master was to be initiated by the disciple.

> But John forbade him, saying,
> "I have need to be baptized of thee,
> and comest thou to me?"

A few things before we can understand it.

Up to now Jesus had lived a very ordinary life. He was just the son of the carpenter Joseph – helping his father in the workshop, doing ordinary things which were needed. Nobody knew anything about him, not even his family was aware of what he was. A shroud surrounded him, a cloud which had to be broken.

He was waiting for the right moment. When John's work was ready, the ground prepared, he could go to him. Then he would break down the shroud and the cloud would disappear. He needed to be related to John because that was the only way to be related to John's disciples; otherwise there would be no link.

John recognized him immediately: "This is the man for whom I have been waiting, this is the man for whom I have been working. He has come." *John forbade him, saying, "I have need to be baptized of thee, and comest thou to me?"* And you have come to be baptized by me? That seems absurd.

Jesus is on a higher plane, the plane of fire; John is on a lower plane, the plane of water. John is not yet an absolutely realized soul. He has attained to his first *satori*, otherwise he would not have been able to work for Jesus; he has attained the first glimpse, otherwise he would not have been able to recognize Jesus – but he has not attained to absolute buddhahood, he is not yet a christ.

"I have need to be baptized of thee, and comest thou to me?" No, he forbade it: "Don't ask for this."

> And Jesus answering said unto him,
> "Suffer it to be so now: for thus
> it becometh us to fulfill all righteousness."
> Then he suffered him.

Jesus said, "Let it be so, because it is written in the scriptures that it will be so." Jesus lived a Jew and died a Jew – he was never a Christian – and he tried hard to become part of the Jewish milieu. These were the ways he tried.

It was written in the old scriptures that the messiah who is to come will be baptized by a man named John who will be baptizing people near the River Jordan. It was a long-standing prophecy. Jesus said, "Let it be so – as it is written in the scriptures." He tried in every way to become part of the tradition so that the innermost revolution that he was trying to bring did not become lost in the desert of politics. But still it happened, still it became lost in the desert of politics, because to bring that inner revolution is to ask almost the impossible from the human mind.

The human mind clings to the old. That's why Jesus is saying, "Let it be so. Please baptize me so I don't look like an intruder and a stranger, so I become part of the tradition and from within I can work outwardly, from within I can create a great revolution. I would like to work from within."

But that was not going to be so. Jesus tried, it was impossible; Buddha tried, it was impossible. Buddha remained a Hindu all his life – he just wanted to create a revolution in the Hindu mind from within – but the moment he started saying his things the old mind became alert.

I have heard a story:

There was a very old church – very ancient, very beautiful, hallowed by tradition – but it was almost in ruins and there was danger that it may fall any day. The worshippers had stopped coming in; any moment it may fall. Even the trustees of the church wouldn't have a meeting in the church, they would meet somewhere else to decide things about the church. But they were reluctant to destroy it.

They asked great architects, but they all suggested that the building was too dangerous, it was beyond repair, it had to be destroyed and a new church had to be built. Reluctantly.... They never wanted it to be destroyed; it was very ancient, it had a long tradition, it had become part of their being – to destroy it looked as if they were going to destroy themselves. Reluctantly they called a meeting of the trustees and they passed three resolutions. They are beautiful.

The first resolution: that the church, the old church, had to be destroyed and a new church had to be built – passed unanimously. The second resolution: that until the new church was ready they would continue to worship in the old church – passed unanimously. And the third resolution: that the new church had to be built on exactly the same spot where the old church stood...and with the stones of the old church! – passed unanimously.

This is how the traditional mind goes. It goes on clinging and clinging – even if it becomes contradictory, it goes on clinging. It avoids seeing the contradiction. It avoids seeing the death that has already entered. It avoids seeing that the body is no longer alive – a corpse, stinking, deteriorating.

Jesus tried to relate himself to the old mind. He says to John: You baptize me. Let it be so. *"Suffer it to be so now: for thus*

it becometh us to fulfill all righteousness." Then he suffered him.
John understood his point: otherwise Jesus would have been a foreigner from the very beginning and things would become almost impossible.

Still things were impossible – but nobody can say that Jesus had not tried; nobody can say that Buddha had not tried. On their part they did everything that could be done to become a continuous flow with the ancient, with the old, with the traditional. They wanted revolution not against tradition but *in* it. But it never happened; the old mind is really very, very obstinate, stubborn.

> And Jesus, when he was baptized,
> went up straightway out of the water:
> and lo, the heavens were opened
> unto him, and he saw the Spirit of God
> descending like a dove,
> and lighting upon him.

The initiation by water, the baptism by water. Jesus saw God descending:

> ...and lo, the heavens were opened
> unto him, and he saw the Spirit of God
> descending like a dove,
> and lighting upon him.

> And lo, a voice from heaven,
> saying, "This is my beloved Son,
> in whom I am well pleased."

Immediately after the baptism by John, Jesus went out of the river and on the riverbank this vision happened. This vision was not a dream because John was also a witness to it – and not only John, a few other disciples who were present on the bank. It was an objective reality. Everybody saw something descending like a dove...very peaceful, pure...a white bird of heaven descending and lighting on Jesus as if heaven opened. It happens that way. When you become open to heaven, heaven becomes open to you. In fact, heaven has always been open to you, only you were not open.

Up to now Jesus had lived a closed life. It was good; he needed it, otherwise he would have been in danger from the very beginning. Christians have no story about what happened in Jesus' youth. He must have lived absolutely unknown. Nobody knew about him; he was just an ordinary young man like any other. His ministry lasted for only three years – when John baptized him he was thirty and when he was crucified he was thirty-three. The ancient, the old, the traditional mind could not tolerate him for more than three years; within three years he was crucified. That's the reason he lived absolutely unknown – an ordinary man amongst other ordinary mortals – not revealing his identity.

Immediately as he was baptized he revealed who he was for the first time. John was a witness, a few other disciples on the bank were witnesses. But the quality of John's being and of Jesus' being was very different. John was a fiery prophet and Jesus was a messenger of peace. Soon afterwards John was arrested and thrown into jail and Jesus started preaching.

News started coming to John which he could not believe, because this man was saying something else – something he had never meant to say. By and by the differences became so great that even John, who had initiated Jesus and who had seen with his own eyes the opening of heaven and the descending of the dove, even he became suspicious.

In the last days of his life, before he was beheaded, he sent a note to Jesus, just a small note asking, "Are you really the one for whom we were waiting?" He became suspicious because this man was saying something else, absolutely something else. "Be humble," this man was saying, "Blessed are the humble because they shall inherit the earth." John was not a humble man, he was really very proud – a very strong man, believing that he could bring revolution to the whole world, almost mad with his strength – and Jesus was saying, "Blessed are the poor...." "What nonsense this man is talking," John must have thought.

Jesus was saying, "If somebody slaps you on one side of the face, give him the other side also" – absolutely unlike John. And Jesus was saying, "If somebody snatches your coat, give him your shirt also." How is this man going to bring revolution? These are not revolutionary teachings.

These are the *only* revolutionary teachings. But John could not understand them; he had his own idea of a revolution. He could have understood Lenin, he could have understood Trotsky, he could have understood Marx, but he could not understand Jesus, his own disciple. The problem was of a totally different kind of revolution. One revolution – which is brought by violence, aggression – is social, in a way forced. Another revolution – which is not brought by force, not even by discipline; which comes by spontaneity, by understanding – is of the heart.

Jesus was bringing a totally new kind of revolution to the world. Nobody had talked about that revolution before. That's why I say Jesus is the turning point in the history of human consciousness – even more than Buddha, because there had been many others like Buddha, talking on the same lines; he was not new. He may have been the end of a long procession of buddhas, but he was not the first.

Jesus brought something totally new to the earth; he was the beginning of a new line, of a new search, of a new inquiry. John could not understand. Lao Tzu, if he had been there, would have understood – but not John. John was a totally different type of man. In his last days he was very worried that something had gone wrong: Has this disciple betrayed me or what? He sent a note, "Are you the one we were waiting for or has something gone wrong?" When you have a certain idea of a certain thing, that becomes a barrier to understanding. What to say of others? – even John could not understand Jesus perfectly.

I have heard one story:

There was a very great, rich merchant who used to go all around the world to collect silk, spices, perfume. In these three things he was one of the most perfect merchants: he knew where to get them at a low price, from what markets of the world, and where to sell them and profit much. And he had profited much. That was his only interest, to find out more and more about perfumes and spices.

One day, passing through a town, somebody told him, "Here lives a very wise man. Whatsoever your inquiry, he is always helpful."

The merchant thought, "Maybe he knows something about silk, spices, perfume. Maybe he can be helpful in showing me some market where I can get even more low-priced commodities."

He went to the wise man. Before he had even asked, the wise man said, "Yes, I know. You go to the north, in the Himalayas," and he gave him a particular peak to go to. "Go to that peak and sit on that peak for three days. In those three days you will see something which you have never seen before. Then come back."

The man rushed. He had the fastest horse in the country. He rushed to the mountains, he found the peak. Fasting, praying, he sat there for three days looking around and dreaming about silk, perfume, spices. He was waiting there – some unknown door was going to open and he would become the master of all the silk that is in the world, all the spices, all the perfumes.

The key was going to be handed to him within these three days. He waited and waited, and he fantasized and he dreamed. He could not even see the beautiful valley that was around or the beautiful, silent river that passed by not making even a slight noise. He could not hear the birds singing in the morning, he could not see the beautiful sunset. He could see nothing because he was so full of dreams and he was so tense, waiting for something.

Three days passed and nothing happened. He was very annoyed and angry. He rushed back to the wise man and he said, "Nothing happened. I could not see anything that I had not seen before. What went wrong?"

The wise man laughed and said, "Your idea of riches." Then he said, "Now don't go to that valley again, you will never find it, but all around on the bank of the river there were diamonds. Those were not stones, they were diamonds. But you missed."

Then the man remembered, as if through his dream he *had* seen something – dim, vague, cloudy – but he had seen something. Yes, in the morning with the sun rays many times he had a glimpse of many stones that were shining. But he had his own idea of riches, and that was too much.

Even John had his own idea of revolution, of what religion is. He became suspicious. But that day, when Jesus was baptized, he was a witness. He had seen the opening of heaven.

> And Jesus, when he was baptized,
> went up straightway out of the water:
> and lo, the heavens were opened
> unto him, and he saw the Spirit of God
> descending like a dove,
> and lighting upon him.

The dove is one of the oldest symbols of silence, of peace, of purity, of harmony. Have you seen a dove descending? Watch a dove descending...in the very coming down you will feel a silence surrounding the dove. That's why it has become a symbol. And Jesus is peace, silence. He is not war, he is not revolution in the ordinary sense of the word, he is not violence. He is the humblest man and the purest who has ever lived on the earth.

Baptism by water always brings descendence of the purest spirit, which is surrounding you always...just the moment you are ready it descends in you. It is raining all the time, only your pot is upside down. You cannot gather it because your pot is upside down. Once your pot is right-side up, immediately you are fulfilled. In deep initiation the master tries to put your pot right-side up.

In the West the science of initiation is completely lost. In the East it is also, almost, lost. In the West it is lost because it never existed there in its totality, only fragments from the East traveled and reached the West. In the East it is lost because it has almost become a dead thing: everybody knows about it...and nobody knows about it. It has become a businesslike thing: you go and you can be initiated by anybody.

Initiation is not so easy. You can be initiated only by one who has attained at least the first satori, the first *samadhi*.

There are three satoris. The first satori means that you have had a glimpse from far away: you have seen the Himalayas away, far away, shining in the sun. That is the first satori. The second satori is one when you have reached the peak. You have arrived. And the third satori is one when you and the peak have become one. That is the last, the ultimate samadhi.

One who initiates you must have attained to at least the first. If he has not attained to the first, initiation is just bogus. This is on the part of the master: that he should have attained to the first satori.

And much is needed on the part of the disciple, because unless the disciple is ready – through deep meditation and purification, through deep catharsis and cleansing – even if the master is there, you will not allow him to put your pot right-side up. You will resist, you will not surrender, you will not be in a let-go. The disciple needs to be in deep trust, only then can the master do something in the innermost being of the disciple. It is a great turning, a conversion, so much is needed on the part of the disciple. Only then is initiation possible.

I was just reading a story about a seeker who went to see Bayazid, a great master. The seeker asked, "Please allow me to be a part of your family."

Bayazid said, "But there are requirements to be fulfilled. If you really want to be a disciple, there are many duties you will have to do."

The seeker asked, "What are the duties?"

The master said, "First, the winter is coming. You will have to go to the forest and chop wood for the winter and collect wood. Then you start working in the kitchen. And after that, I will show you what to do."

The seeker said, "But I am in search of truth. How is it going to help to work in the forest and chop wood? What connection is there between chopping wood and attaining to truth? And working in the kitchen? What do you mean? I am a seeker."

The master said, "Then you seek somewhere else, because you will have to listen to me. And howsoever absurd the demand you will have to fulfill it. That's how you will become ready for let-go. I know chopping wood has nothing to do with truth, but to be ready to chop it because the master has said it, has something to do with truth. I know working in the kitchen has nothing to do with truth: so many people are working, every housewife is working – if that was the way to attain, then everybody would attain. It has nothing to do with truth, but when *I* say that you have to do it, you have to do it in deep love and trust. That will prepare you, that has something to do with truth. But I cannot reveal that to you right now; you will have to wait."

Reluctantly the seeker said, "Okay, but I would also like to know what are the duties of a master?"

The master said, "The duty of the master is to sit around and order."

The disciple said, "Then please help me to become a master, train me to become a master. I am ready."

The ego is always seeking its own enhancement. And the ego is the barrier, because of the ego, your pot is upside down. The rain goes on falling and you remain empty.

On the part of the disciple, initiation means allowing the master to do *whatsoever* – unconditionally. And on the part of the master, it is possible only when he has attained to at least the first satori, otherwise you can be initiated by a thousand and one masters and you will not attain to anything. When these two requirements are fulfilled, then a communion happens between the master and the disciple. This communion happened that day. Jesus was 'opened', as they say in Subud. Jesus was opened by John the Baptist and the spirit of God descended on him like a dove:

> And lo, a voice from heaven,
> saying, "This is my beloved Son,
> in whom I am well pleased."

This always happens. Whenever someone opens to heaven, it is always heard deep down in the heart, it resounds: *"This is my beloved Son, in whom I am well pleased."* This has been taken wrongly in Christianity. They think Jesus is the only son of God – foolish. The whole existence comes from God, the whole existence is related to God as son to father.

A few things to be understood.... It would have been better if we had thought of God as mother because the son is more deeply related to the mother. He lives in the womb, he is part of the mother – blood and bones and flesh and everything. But there is also a very significant meaning in thinking of God as father. It is not baseless.

Father is indirect, mother is direct. You know who your mother is; you simply believe who your father is. A mother knows exactly that you are her son, but the father believes. Father is indirect, mother is very direct. And God is not so direct, God is very indirect. He fathered you, that means you are related to him, but the relationship is of a trust, a belief, a deep faith. You will come to know your father only when you trust.

Mother is more of a scientific fact, empirical; father is more a poetical fact, not so empirical. Mother is very close, in fact too close; father is very far away, somewhere up in the sky. To feel for the mother is instinctive; to feel for the father, one has to learn it. Mother is already there. God has to be discovered. So the symbol of father is also very meaningful, it carries some hidden meanings in it.

But whenever it happens to anybody that the heart opens up and the dove descends, this is always heard: *"This is my beloved Son, in whom I am well pleased."* Why is God well-pleased? You have come back home. You went astray, you did all sorts of things irrelevant to your being. You have repented, you have come back home.

The whole existence is pleased — the whole existence is pleased whenever somebody becomes a christ or a buddha, the whole existence celebrates, because even if *one* person becomes a buddha or a christ the whole existence becomes, in a way, more aware and alert.

Certainly the world was different before Jesus than after Jesus. The trees are more alert after Jesus and the rocks are more alive after Jesus because his consciousness, the attainment of his consciousness, has spread all over the existence. It has to be so. Flowers flower more. They may not be aware, but the very quality of the whole has changed. Even if one drop of consciousness attains to God, the whole ocean cannot be the same. That one drop has raised the being of the whole, the quality is different.

You cannot conceive of yourself if there was no Buddha and no Christ, no Krishna. Just remove twelve names from history and the whole of history will disappear. Then humanity will not be there. In fact, the existence that you know around you will not be there. You will be far more asleep and unconscious, you will have gone far more astray. You will be far more violent, aggressive: the glimmer of love that beats in your heart will not be there, the grace that sometimes appears in your eyes will not be there. Your eyes will be more like animals' — ferocious, violent.

But when a Jesus has happened, his eyes become part of your eyes — a very minute part, but still sometimes it happens that that part spreads all over your eyes and you look at existence in a totally different way. The world remains the same but your eyes change, and with your eyes the whole changes. In your heart a very minute part has become Buddha with Buddha, Christ with Christ, Krishna with Krishna. I know it is a very minute part, but the possibility to grow exists with it.

Look deep down within yourself to the part that has been contributed by Christ or Buddha. Protect it, help it to grow, sacrifice all that you have for it to grow, and you will be on the right track. Let that part win, let that part be victorious, let the Galilean within you win, and immediately – whenever that part is victorious – you are also going to hear: *And lo a voice from heaven, saying, "This is my beloved Son, in whom I am well pleased."*

Enough for today.

CHAPTER 4

I'm Simply
Mirroring Jesus

THE FIRST QUESTION:

> Beloved Osho,
> A single session of your Dynamic Meditation has left within me a greater bliss and sense of being than twenty years of having had to listen to the stories of The New Testament and to pray to an almighty and distant God who stayed an unexperienceable Godot to me. Is it possible that the teachings of Jesus just might not be helpful to all seekers – yes, might even be poisonous to them, or to some?

Christianity and Christ should never be confused. Christ is totally different from Christianity, so whenever you want to understand Christ, go directly and immediately – not via Rome, then you will never understand Christ. Christ or Krishna or Buddha cannot be organized: they are so vast that no organization can do justice to them. Only small things can be organized. Politics can be organized – not religion. Nazism can be organized, communism can be organized – not Christ, not Krishna. The sheer vastness is such that the moment you try to force them into a pattern they are already dead. It is as if you are trying to grasp the sky in your small hands – with closed fists. With an open hand the sky may be touching, may be a little bit on your hand, but with a closed fist it has already escaped out of it.

Whatsoever you have been hearing about Jesus is not about Jesus, the real man; it is about the Jesus that Christians have invented, decorated to be sold in the market. The Christian Jesus is a commodity to be sold; Christ himself is a revolution. You will have to be transformed through him; he is the baptism of fire. You can be a Christian conveniently. You can never be a *real* Christian conveniently.

If you are *really* following Jesus, there is bound to be trouble. He himself ended on the cross, you cannot end on the throne. But if you follow Christianity there is no trouble, it is a very convenient way to adjust Christ to yourself rather than adjusting yourself to Christ. If you adjust yourself to Christ there will be a transformation; if you adjust Christ to yourself there can be none. Then Christ himself becomes part of the decoration of your imprisonment, part of your furniture – your car, your house – a convenience at the most, but you are not related to him. That's why twenty years look like they have been wasted.

The same will happen with me. You are fortunate that you are doing meditation with me. Once I am gone, the meditation is going to be organized – it is impossible to prevent it; it is the way things move. Then you will do it for twenty years – or two hundred years – and nothing will happen. It does not happen through the technique; technique is just dead. It happens through the love that you feel for me, that I have for you. The technique is just an excuse, it is not the most important thing. The most important thing is your love, your trust. In that trust the technique works and functions, becomes alive, gets roots into your heart.

Sooner or later everything becomes organized – prayer, meditation, everything. Then the glory is lost. Then you can go on doing it – you may become absolutely perfect, skilled; it may also give some sort of consolation – but the mutation will be missing. You will remain the same, a continuity. It will not be a baptism: you will not die in it and you will not be reborn. That's why my insistence is on searching for an alive master.

Scriptures are there. At one time those rivers were flowing, but now they are frozen, they are lost in the desert land of churches, temples and organizations. The poetry no longer throbs in them, they are dead dogmas, arguments; the love has disappeared. Remember this always: if you can find a living master, forget all about scriptures. The living master is the only scripture which is alive. Read his heart and allow your heart to be read by him. Be in a communion – that is the only way.

Jesus worked the same way as you feel with me, but twenty centuries have passed. The first disciples who came around him staked their lives, they left all that they had, they moved with this man, they risked everything. It was worth it. This man was a treasure of the world, unknown. Nothing was too much. Whatsoever was asked they did. And they had the opportunity to walk with a god on this earth, to be in close affinity with divinity. Others were saying, "This man is wrong," but those who were close to him knew that only this man was right – and if this man was not right, then *nothing* could be right, then 'right' cannot exist. They crucified this man, but those who were close knew that you cannot crucify him. This man had already entered immortality, this man had already become part of their immortal souls. You can kill the body, but not the spirit.

They had lived, walked, breathed, in the being of this man; they were transformed. It is not a question of technique. They prayed with this man, but the real thing was not prayer, the real thing was just to be in the presence of this man. This man had a presence.

Have you observed? – very few people have what you call presence. Rarely do you come across a person who has a presence – something indefinable around him, something that you suddenly feel but cannot indicate, something that fills you but is ineffable, something very mysterious and unknown. You cannot deny it, you cannot prove it. It is not the body because everybody has a body; it is not the mind because everybody has a mind. Sometimes a very beautiful body may be there, tremendously beautiful, but the presence is not there. Sometimes a genius mind is there, but the presence is not there; and sometimes you pass a beggar and you are filled, touched, stirred – a presence.

Those who were in the presence of Jesus, those who were in his *satsang* – those who lived close, those who lived in his milieu – breathed him. If you allow me to say it, those who drank him and ate him, who allowed him to enter into their innermost shrine.... *That* transformed, not the prayer; prayer was just an excuse to be with him. Even without prayer it would have happened, but without prayer they might not have found an excuse to be with him.

You are here with me. I go on inventing meditations for you. They are just excuses so that you can be here a little longer, a little while more, so that you can linger around me – because nobody knows when my presence will touch you. Nothing can be said about it; it cannot be manipulated. It happens when it happens; nothing can be done directly for it. Just be here. Even without meditations the thing will happen, but without meditations you won't have any excuse to be here.

I go on talking to you. Even without talk it can happen, it *will* happen, but if I don't talk, by and by you will disappear because you won't have an excuse. What are you doing here? I have to give you something to do so that you can be. I have to engage you and occupy you so that you don't feel restless. The thing is going to happen from some other dimension, but when you are occupied that dimension remains open. If you are not occupied, you become too restless. All meditations and all prayers and all methods are toys invented for children to play with, but that is useful, very significant. Once you are occupied your innermost shrine is open to me — you are not restless, you are doing meditation — and then I can do *my* work. It is not good to say that I do my work, *then* it starts happening.

You are right, twenty years of Christian teaching, listening to The New Testament stories, may have been futile — not because those stories are futile, they are superb as far as stories go. The poetry of The New Testament, the poetry of the whole Bible, is something not of this world. There are great poets — Shakespeare and Milton and Dante — but nobody can surpass the Bible. The poetry is tremendously simple, but it has some quality which ordinary poetry cannot have. It has awe; that is the religious quality.

Have you watched sometimes? You see a beautiful flower. You may appreciate it, it has an aesthetic quality. You appreciate it and you move ahead. You may see a beautiful face, even the face of a Cleopatra — the lines, the proportion, the marble-like body — but that too is aesthetic. And sometimes you come across a few things or a few beings that inspire not only aesthetic appreciation, but awe. What is awe?

Facing some thing or some being, thinking stops. Your mind cannot cope with it. You can cope with a Cleopatra, you can even cope with an Einstein — howsoever abstruse, abstract, difficult, you can cope with it, just a little more training of the mind may be needed — but when you come across a Jesus or a Buddha the mind falls flat, it bogs down. *Something* is too much for it. You cannot think about anything, you are as if in a deep shock — and yet the shock is blissful. That is awe.

The Bible has awe in it – the quality of putting your mind completely at a stop – but that you will have to reach directly. The missionary, the priest, the bishop destroy it because they start interpreting. They put their minds in it and their minds are mediocre. It is as if you are looking at a tremendously beautiful thing from the mind of a very stupid man. Or you are looking into a mirror that is broken, completely broken – it has gathered rust, nothing can be mirrored perfectly – and you look in the mirror and see the moon, distorted. That's how it has been happening.

The Bible is one of the greatest events in the world – very pure, purer than the Bhagavadgita because the Bhagavadgita is very refined. The people who created it were very cultured and educated, and of course whenever a thing becomes very refined it becomes ethereal, unearthly. The Bible is rooted in the earth. All the prophets of the Bible are people of the earth. Even Jesus moves on the earth; he is the son of a carpenter, uneducated, not knowing anything about aesthetics, poetics – nothing. If he speaks poetry, it is because he *is*, not knowing it at all, a poet. His poetry is raw and wild. Jesus has something of the peasant in him: wisdom but not knowledge. He is not a man of knowledge; no university would be willing to confer an honorary degree on him, no. He wouldn't fit at Oxford or Cambridge; he would look very foolish in the gowns and clown-like caps. He would look very foolish, he wouldn't fit. He belongs to the earth, to the village, to ordinary, plain people.

Just the other night I was reading a small story, an Arabian story.

A man died. He had seventeen camels and three sons and he left a will in which, when it was opened and read, it was said that one-half of the camels should go to the first son, one-third to the second and one-ninth to the third.

The sons were nonplussed – what to do? Seventeen camels: one-half is to go to the first son – is one to cut one camel in two? And that too won't solve much because then one-third has to go to the second. That too won't solve much: one-ninth has to go to the third. Almost all the camels would be killed.

Of course they went to the man of the town who was most knowledgeable: the Mulla – the *pundit*, the scholar, the mathematician. He thought hard, he tried hard, but he couldn't find any solution because mathematics is mathematics. He said, "I have never divided camels in my life, this whole thing seems to be foolish. But you will have to cut them. If the will is to be followed exactly then the camels have to be cut, they have to be divided." The sons were not ready to cut the camels. So what to do? Then somebody suggested, "It is better that you go to someone who knows something about camels, not about mathematics."

So they went to the sheikh of the town who was an old man, uneducated, but wise through experience. They told him their problem. The old man laughed. He said, "Don't be worried. It is simple." He loaned one of his own camels to them – now there were eighteen camels – and then he divided. Nine camels were given to the first and he was satisfied, perfectly satisfied. Six camels were given to the second – one-third; he was also perfectly satisfied. And two camels were given to the third – one-ninth; he was also satisfied. One camel was left. That was loaned. He took his camel back and said, "You can go."

Wisdom is practical, knowledge impractical. Knowledge is abstract, wisdom is earthly; knowledge is just words, wisdom is experience.

The Bible is very simple. Don't be deceived by its simplicity. In its simplicity it has the wisdom of the ages. It is very poetic; I have never come across anything more poetic than the Bible. One can simply go on relishing it, one can go on repeating the words of Jesus. They come from the heart and they go to the heart. But don't go through a mediator. Those mediators are mediocres, they destroy the whole thing. I have looked through many commentaries on the Bible, but I have never come across a single intelligent commentary. They all destroy. I have never seen any single commentary from any theologian who has added anything to the Bible, who has in any way made its glory more manifest. They *dim* it. And that is bound to be so. Only a man of the quality of Jesus can reveal the truth of it, only a man of the quality of Jesus can enhance its beauty. People who live in the dark valleys and people who live on the sunny peaks of the Himalayas don't understand each other's language. When the man from the peak speaks and the man from the valley interprets, everything goes wrong.

Yes, it is right – your twenty years may have been wasted. But it will be a total misunderstanding if you think that Jesus is not for you. Jesus is for all, that is not the question. But go direct: become more meditative, become more prayerful, and go direct. And forget all that has been told to you about the Bible; the Bible is enough.

And in a sense if you want to understand the Upanishads, it may be difficult to understand them directly because they are very refined. The people who were talking in the Upanishads were great philosophers; they need commentaries. But Jesus is plain, his truth is plain. He is a very ordinary villager; no commentary is needed. He is his own light. And if you cannot understand Jesus, then who will you be able to understand? Throw all the foolish commentaries away. Go direct. Jesus is so simple, you can have a direct contact.

I am not commenting on Jesus, I am simply responding. I am not a commentator. To be a commentator is to do a very ugly job. Why should I comment on Jesus? He is plain, he is absolutely simple. Just like two plus two make four; he is that simple. Just like in the morning the sun rises and everybody knows it is morning. He is so simple. I am not commenting on him, I am responding. I read his words: something echoes in me. That is not a commentary. My heart throbs with him, something parallel echoes in me, and I tell you what it is.

So don't take my words as commentaries. I am not trying to explain Jesus to you, there is no need. I am simply mirroring – I am telling you *my* heart. I am telling you what happens to me when I am listening to Jesus.

The second question:

> Beloved Osho,
> Often during the lecture I find a part of me waiting for your glance. When you finally look at me, something in me runs away. The feeling is like being in a desert, waiting for ages for some water to come, and when it finally rains, the mouth snaps shut. Why is this?

This is from Krishna Radha. No need to think that there is some great secret in it: just the woman, just the woman within you. That is the way of the woman. She waits for something, she attracts something, she asks, invites something, and when it comes she becomes afraid and escapes. It is the way of all women. And unless you understand it and drop it, your whole life will become miserable.

First you attract, and when the thing that you have invited comes to you, you become afraid and you escape. This hide-and-seek goes on. This has been my observation: that the feminine mind asks for something, but when it rains, it is never there to receive it. So the feminine mind becomes a long, endless waiting. Every moment the fulfillment was possible, but whenever it comes close, the woman becomes afraid. The woman asks for love and is afraid of love, because when love comes it brings death with it. Love has to bring death because only then can you be reborn. There is no other way.

I will read the question again: "Often during the lecture I find a part of me waiting for your glance. When you finally look at me, something in me runs away."

You wait for my glance. A deep love arises in you, a waiting. But when my glance comes to you, it brings death. Then you become afraid, you escape, because you were waiting for love and the glance brings death also. It brings love also, but love and death are two aspects of the same glance. If I really love you, I have to be a death to you. There is no other way, the love cannot happen in any other way. And when the glance penetrates you something shrinks, escapes; something runs away, becomes afraid. Then my glance moves. Then you are again at ease waiting for me.

There is no other secret in it: just the woman. And when I say 'the woman' you should not misunderstand me. Many men behave just like a woman. In love everybody behaves like a woman. You would like to take a jump into the unknown and you don't want to renounce the known. You want to move on two boats together and they are moving in different dimensions, diametrically opposite. You want to be yourself, and you would like to have a new life also. You ask the impossible. You want to cling to whatsoever you have and you would like to grow also – and that very clinging is preventing you from growth. No, both are not possible together.

When you wait for my glance you wait as you are, but when I come and knock at your door I have come to destroy you as you are, because I know that only then will the hidden within you be released. Then you become afraid.

People like freedom, but they are fearful also. When the freedom is not there they think about it, they dream about it, they fantasize, but when freedom comes they become afraid because freedom brings with it many more things than they ever thought about. Freedom brings insecurity. Freedom brings adventure, but insecurity also. Freedom brings a bigger sky, it gives you wings, but then the bigger sky can be dangerous also. Freedom is very dangerous. To live in freedom is to live dangerously. You come to me, you seek freedom, but deep down I see you are also saying, "Don't make us free, please don't push us into freedom. Let us cling to you, let us depend on you." And you go on asking and praying, "Give us freedom." With one hand you ask, with another hand you deny; one part of you says yes, another part of you goes on saying no.

Have you watched your mind? You say yes/no together. Maybe one is a little louder and the other is not so loud, maybe you are very cunning and you don't listen to the other when you say the one, but just be a little watchful. Whenever you say yes, just by the side lingers the no. Then you are in a constant conflict. You would like for me to come to your door – but then you will close the door because I will come as I am, not as you expect me. I will come as I am, not according to your dreams.

Always remember to find the small causes for the things that happen in you and around you. Sometimes you start asking for very deep and great reasons which are not there – and particularly in the West for everything –

because of the two hundred years of psychology, and the training in psychology and psychiatry. The knowledge of psychology has become common knowledge, everybody knows about it. People go on digging deep into small things which have nothing much in them, simple facts, and they go on bringing things up which are not at all connected.

Just this morning I was reading an anecdote.

A psychoanalyst and a friend were standing, looking at the sky through the window and discussing something. The psychoanalyst said, "Remarkable! Look!" Some work was going on. A building was to be demolished and a few laborers were working with barrows. He said, "Look, twelve persons are working with barrows – eleven are pushing them in front of them and one is pulling it. Eleven pushing, one pulling: there must be an explanation for it. There must be some deep-rooted inhibition in that man. Or something happened in childhood with his parents, something to do with a primal. There must be some deep-rooted problem involved. We must go and ask." So they went down.

They stopped the laborer who was pulling the barrow behind him and the psychoanalyst said, "Please, just help us to discover something very deep-rooted in you. Eleven persons are pushing their barrows in front of themselves; only you are pulling your barrow. There must be some explanation for it. Something tremendously traumatic must have happened in your childhood, a deep repression, obsession, compulsion – some complex. Please tell us something about it. What do you feel?"

The laborer looked at them and said, "Blimey, guv'nor, I just hates the sight of the thing, that's all. That's why I'm carrying it behind." Just *hates* the sight of the thing!

Krishna Radha, there is nothing to it, you are just a woman. Go beyond it. Man has to go beyond his manhood and woman has to go beyond her womanhood. And when you are neither man nor woman, then you will be able to allow my glance to reach to the deepest core of your being. Then you will be able to open your doors. Then my knock will not go unanswered.

The third question:

> Beloved Osho,
> Surely that which happens in the
> instant of death by drowning is the true
> explanation of Jesus' baptism at the
> hands of John. Was not the skill and
> strength of the baptist that of taking a
> man to that point, and the preparation
> you talk of beforehand employed
> so that a man be transformed by the
> experience rather than terrified by it?

Yes, exactly so. The baptism is possible only when you are ready to die. That is the symbolic meaning: that John the Baptist used to take his disciples to the river when they were ready to die, when they were ready to let go, when they were ready to flow with the river. When the resistance was broken, when they were no longer fighting, when the whole struggle to survive had disappeared, only then would he take them to the river. They were ready to be drowned by him, to be murdered by him.

There is a story I would like to tell you about a Sufi mystic, Sheik Farid.

He was going towards the river one day to take his morning bath. A seeker followed him and asked him, "Please, just wait for one minute. You look so filled with the divine, but I don't even feel a desire for it. You look so mad and just watching you I have come to feel that there must be something in it. You are so happy and blissful and I am so miserable, but even the desire to seek the divine is not there. So what to do? How to create the desire?"

Farid looked at the man and said, "You come with me. I am going to take my morning bath. You also take a bath with me in the river and maybe, right while you are taking a bath, the answer can be given. Otherwise we will see after the bath. You come with me."

The man became a little puzzled. This Sheik Farid looked a little mad: how was he going to answer while taking a bath? But nobody knows the ways of the mystics, so the man followed. They both went into the river and when the man was taking a dip, Farid jumped on him and pressed him down in the river. The man started feeling restless. What type of answer was this? At first he thought Farid was joking, but then it became dangerous, he was not going to leave him! He struggled hard.

Farid was a very heavy, strong man and the seeker was very thin — as seekers are. But when your life is at stake.... Even that thin-looking man threw Farid off, jumped on him and said, "Are you a murderer? What are you doing? I am a poor man. I have just come to ask you how the desire can arise in one's heart to seek the divine and you were going to kill me!"

Farid said, "Wait. A few questions first. When I was pressing you down in the river and you were suffocating, how many thoughts were in your mind?"

The man said, "How many? Only one thought — how to get back to the air to take a breath."

Farid asked, "How long did that one thought stay?"

The man said, "That too did not stay long because my life was at stake. You can afford thinking when nothing is at stake. Life was in danger – even that thought disappeared. Then to come out of the river was not a thought, it was my whole being."

Farid said, "You have understood. This is the answer. If you are feeling suffocated in this world, pressed from all sides, and if you feel nothing is going to happen in this world except death, then the desire to seek truth or God or whatsoever you name it, will arise. And that too will not last long. By and by that desire is no more a desire, it becomes your being. The very thirst becomes your being. I have shown you the path," said Farid. "Now you can go."

Just try to understand the whole situation in the world: if it is already destroying you, jump out of it. The real question is not how to seek God, the real question is how to understand that where you are thinking life is, there is no life but only death.

John the Baptist, or anybody who has ever baptized anybody else, who has ever initiated anybody else, who has ever brought anybody to the world of truth out of the world of dreams, has to prepare you for death. Yes, that is the meaning. By baptism he was saying, "Your old self has gone down the river; you are no more the same. A new identity has arisen; now you have a new nucleus. Function through it and don't function through the past."

The same has been done through initiation by fire. In India, initiation by fire, not by water, has traditionally been used. There have been a few side-currents that have been using water baptism also, but the main current in India has been using fire. So in every master's house – what they used to call a *gurukul*, the family of the master – there was a fire constantly burning in the middle of the house, a constantly burning fire, twenty-four hours a day. All the teachings were delivered near the fire. By and by, the fire symbol became deep-rooted in the disciples.

There is a beautiful story in the old Upanishads about when a disciple, a very famous disciple, Svetketu, was with his master....

The master waited for twelve years and wouldn't initiate him into the mysteries. The disciple served and served, tending the fire in the house – for twenty-four hours the fire had to be kept alive. It is said that the fire itself became very much worried about this Svetketu. For twelve years he had been serving the fire, tending it, bringing wood from the forest. The story is beautiful. It says that the fire became worried. Even the fire started feeling that the master was a little too hard, a little unjust. The fire started feeling compassion for Svetketu.

The fire talked to the master's wife when the master was out and said, "This is going too far. This Svetketu has been serving so silently for twelve years. He has earned it already; the secret has to be revealed to him. You persuade your husband."

"But," the wife said, "he won't listen. If I say anything, he may even become harder. He is not a man who can be persuaded. One has to wait. He knows how to work and how not to work, what to do and what not to do, and I cannot say anything."

It is said that the fire became so much concerned, that the fire itself revealed the secret to Svetketu. And when the secret was revealed, the master danced. He said, "Svetketu, I was waiting. Because when the fire reveals itself, that's something. I was forcing the fire itself to reveal the secret because compassion *will* arise, existence is compassionate.

I could have given you the secret any day, but that would not have been so vital, it would have been from me. But now the doors of existence have been opened for you by existence itself. Now you are in communion with fire itself – you have been initiated by fire."

What secret can the fire give to you? – the secret of death. In India we have been burning dead bodies to make it deeply associated with death, so that fire becomes associated with death. Even those who are not seekers also know that fire is the symbol of death – one dies in it. But those who know and seek on the path also know that one is resurrected through it: dies and is reborn. But in both the cases, whether through water or fire, death is the point. One has to die to attain to life abundant, one has to carry one's cross. Nobody else can initiate you, only death. Death is the master. Or, the master is death.

If you are ready to die, then nobody can prevent you from being reborn. But this death should not be suicidal. Many people commit suicide. They are not resurrected. A suicidal death is not a death through understanding; a suicidal death is a death through misunderstanding. You die confused, in agony. You die obsessed with the world, you die attached to the world. You die as a complaint.

Watch people who think of committing suicide. They are not against life. In fact, on the contrary, they are so attached to life that life cannot fulfill them. They take revenge, they complain. They murder, they kill themselves, just to lodge a complaint against the whole existence – that it was not a fulfillment. They are grumbling; they are saying, "Life is not worth it." But why is life not worth living? They expected too much; that's why it is not worth it. They asked too much; they never earned it. They asked too much and it was not delivered. They are

frustrated. One who is ready to die *without* frustration....
Seeing the truth of life, seeing the truth that life is just a
dream...it cannot fulfill anything, it cannot frustrate also.
Fulfillment, frustration, both are parts of the illusion that
life is real. One who sees that life is unreal, just like a
dream, becomes detached. A renunciation comes.

In the Upanishads there is one very vital saying: *"Ten tykten
bhunjithah*...those who have indulged in life have always
renounced." It is very revolutionary; the implication is
tremendous. It says: those who have indulged in life are
bound to renounce because they have seen the truth
– that life is false. They have looked into it and found
nothing. Not that they are frustrated, because if you are
frustrated that only shows that you were still expecting
something. Frustration shows deep expectation. One who
has become aware that life can only promise but can
never deliver – it is a dream! – is neither frustrated nor
fulfilled in life. Then comes renunciation. Renunciation is
not leaving life; renunciation is seeing life as it is. Then
one is ready to die because there is nothing in life.

That readiness for death is the point John the Baptist was
driving people towards. When they were ready he would
bring them to the River Jordan and do the ritual, the final
touch. With the water flowing over the head and down
the river, the ego, the old personality, is gone. Pure essence
– bathed in a new sense of being, with a new mystery of
being alive, with a new sense of existence – is born.

Of course, death can either be a very terrifying experience
or tremendously beautiful. It depends on the attitude. If
you feel terrified in death then you will die, but you will
not be resurrected. If death becomes a beautiful experience, then you are dying and at the same time resurrecting.
Ordinarily death is terror; that's why you are so afraid to
die. In life nothing beautiful happens until you die, but

you are terrified. A master has to persuade you, by and by, about the beauty of death. He has to sing the glories of death. He has, by and by, to convince you and create a trust in death so that you can let go. Once you let go nothing dies, only the ego. You remain for ever and ever.

You are eternity, you cannot die – the fear is absolutely futile and unbased – but the ego has to die. The ego is a created phenomenon. It was not there when you were born, society created it. Society has given you the ego, and that ego can be taken by the society...and that ego is absolutely going to be taken by death. You will go as you had come: empty-handed you come, empty-handed you go. The ego is just an illusion in between. That ego is afraid of death. Once you understand that you are not going to die – only the ego, only the disease – you are ready. You are ready for baptism.

The fourth question:

> Beloved Osho,
> You say that seriousness is a disease.
> Whenever I remember myself
> I feel serious, so what should I do?

Don't get serious about it. Let it be so, and laugh. If you can laugh at yourself, everything is okay. People laugh at others, but never laugh at themselves. It has to be learned. If you can laugh at yourself, seriousness is already gone. It cannot make its abode within you if you are capable of laughing at yourself.

In Zen monasteries every monk has to laugh. The first thing to do in the morning is to laugh, the *very* first thing. The moment the monk becomes aware that he is no longer asleep he has to jump out of bed, stand in a posture like a buffoon, like a circus joker, and start laughing, laughing at himself. There cannot be any better beginning of the day. Laughing at oneself kills the ego, and you are more transparent, more light when you move in the world. And if you have laughed at yourself, then others' laughter toward you won't disturb you. In fact, they are simply cooperating, they are doing the same thing that you were doing. You will feel happy.

To laugh at others is egoistic; to laugh at oneself is very humble. Learn to laugh at yourself – about your seriousness and things like that. But you can get serious about seriousness. Then instead of one, you have created two diseases. Then you can get serious about that also, and you can go on and on. There is no end to it; it can go on *ad nauseam*. So take hold of it from the very beginning. The moment you feel you are serious, laugh about it and look for where the seriousness is. Laugh, give a good laugh, close the eyes and look for where it is. You will not find it. It exists only in a being who cannot laugh. A more unfortunate situation cannot be conceived, a poorer being cannot be conceived of, than the man who cannot laugh at himself. So start the morning by laughing at yourself, and whenever you can find a moment in the day when you have nothing to do, have a good laugh for no particular reason – just because the whole world is so absurd, just because the way you are is so absurd. There is no need to find any particular reason. The whole thing is such that one has to laugh.

Let the laughter be a belly laughter, not a heady thing. One can laugh from the head – then it is dead. From the head everything is dead; the head is absolutely mechanical. You can laugh from the head, then your head will create the laughter, but it will not go deep in the belly to the *hara*.

It will not go to your toes, it will not go to your whole body. A real laughter has to be just like a small child laughs. Watch his belly shaking, his whole body throbbing with it. He wants to roll on the floor – hm? because it is a question of totality. He laughs so much that he starts crying; he laughs so deeply that the laughter becomes tears, tears come out of him. A laughter should be deep and total. This is the medicine that I prescribe for seriousness.

You would like me to give you some serious medicine. That won't help. You have to be a little foolish. In fact, the highest pinnacle of wisdom always carries foolishness in it, the greatest wise men of the world were also the greatest fools. It will be hard to understand. You cannot think of how they can be fools because your mind always divides: a wise man can never be a fool, and a fool can never be a wise man. Both attitudes are wrong. There have been great fools who were very wise.

In the old days, in every king's court there was a great fool – the court fool. He was a balancing force because too much wisdom can be foolish, too much of anything can be foolish. Somebody was needed who could bring things back to earth. A fool was needed in the kings' courts who would help them to laugh, otherwise wise people tend to become serious, and seriousness is an illness. Out of seriousness you lose proportion, you lose perspective. So every king's court had a fool, a great fool, who would say things and do things and bring things back to the earth.

I have heard that one emperor had a fool. One day the emperor was looking in the mirror. The fool came, jumped, and hit him with his feet in the back. The emperor fell against the mirror. He was, of course, very angry and he said, "Unless you can give some reason for your foolish act which is more criminal than the act itself, you will be sentenced to death."

The fool said, "My Lord, I never thought that you were here. I thought the queen was standing here."

He had to be pardoned because he had given a reason that was even more foolish. But to find such a reason, the fool must have been very wise.

Every great wise man — Lao Tzu, Jesus — they have a certain quality of sublime foolishness. This has to be so because otherwise a wise man will be a man without salt, he will taste awful. He has to be a little foolish also. Then things are balanced. Look at Jesus — riding on a donkey and saying to people, "I am the son of God." Look at it! He must have been both. People must have laughed, "What are you saying? Saying such things and behaving in such a way...."

But I know that's how perfect wisdom appears. Lao Tzu says, "Everybody is wise, except me. I seem to be foolish. Everybody's mind is clear; only my mind seems to be murky and muddled. Everybody knows what to do and what not to do; only I am confused." What does he mean? He is saying that "In me, wisdom and foolishness meet together." And when wisdom and foolishness meet together there is a transcendence.

So don't be serious about seriousness. Laugh about it, be a little foolish. Don't condemn foolishness; it has its own beauties. If you can be both you will have a quality of transcendence within you.

The world has become more and more serious. Hence so much cancer, so much heart disease, so much high blood pressure, so much madness. The world has been moved, forced towards one extreme too much. Be a little foolish also. Laugh a little, be like a child. Enjoy a little, don't carry a serious face everywhere and suddenly you will find a deeper health arising in you – deeper sources of your health become available.

Have you ever heard about any fool who went mad? It has never happened. I have always been searching for a report of any foolish man who went mad. I have not come across one. Of course a fool cannot go mad because to be mad you need to be very serious.

I have also been searching to see if fools are in any way prone to be more healthy than the so-called wise. And it is so: fools are more healthy than the so-called wise. They live in the moment and they know that they are fools, so they are not worried about what others think about them. That worry becomes a cancerous phenomenon in the mind and body. They live long and they have the last laughter.

Remember that life should be a deep balancing, a very deep balancing. Then, just in the middle, you escape. The energy surges high, you start moving upwards. And this should be so about all opposites. Don't be a man and don't be a woman: be both, so that you can be neither. Don't be wise, don't be a fool: be both, so you can go beyond.

The fifth question:

> Beloved Osho,
> Please explain why we don't feel the divine which is here/now, within/without, which is you/me and all.

This is from Swami Yoga Chinmaya.

Because you are too much, and too heavy on yourself. Because you cannot laugh, the divine is hidden. Because you are too tense, you are closed. And these things that you think

– that the divine is here/now, within/without, you/me – are only head things, they are not your feelings. They are thoughts, not realizations. And if you go on thinking on these lines they will never become experiences. You can convince yourself by a thousand and one arguments that this is so, but they will never become your experience. You will go on missing. It is not a question of argument, philosophy, thinking, contemplation – no. It is a question of drowning yourself deep in the feeling of the phenomenon. One has to feel it, not to think about it. And to feel it, one has to disappear.

You are trying an absolutely impossible thing: by thinking, you are trying to realize God. It will remain a philosophy, it will never become your experience. And unless it is an experience it is not liberating. It will become a bondage; you will die in that bondage of words.

You are too much – Yoga Chinmaya's head has to be cut off, beheaded, completely – too much in the head, and too much of yourself. God is not more important; you are more important. *You* want to know God: God is not the emphasis, *you* are the emphasis. *You* want to achieve God: not that God is important, *you* are important – and how can you live without achieving God? God has to be possessed, but the emphasis is on *you*. That's why you go on missing.

Drop the 'you'. Then there is no need to worry about God – he comes by himself. Once you are not, he comes. Once you are absent, his presence is felt. Once you are empty, he is rushing towards you. Drop all the philosophies and all that you have learned, and all that you have borrowed, and all that has become heavy on the head.

Drop it! Be clean of it; it is all rot. Once you are clean, in that cleanliness you start feeling something arising. In that innocence is virginity. God is always available.

The last question:

> Beloved Osho,
> How is it possible that the mind
> can go on producing thoughts constantly,
> and how can we stop that which we
> have not started?

You cannot stop that which you have not started. Don't try it, otherwise you will simply be wasting time, energy, life. You cannot stop the mind because you have not started it. You can simply watch, and in watching it stops. Not that you stop it, in watching it stops. The stopping is a function of watching, it is a consequence of watching. Not that you stop it; there is no way to stop the mind. If you try to stop it, it will go faster; if you try to stop it, it will fight with you and create a thousand and one troubles for you. Never try to stop it. This is exactly the truth: you have not started it, so who are you to stop it? It has come through your unawareness; it will go through your awareness. You have nothing to do to stop it. Become more and more alert.

Even the idea that one has to stop it will be the barrier because you can say, "Okay, now I will try to be aware so that I can stop it." Then you miss the point. Then even your awareness won't be of much help because again the same idea is there – how to stop it. Then after a few days of futile effort – futile because it will not happen because the idea is there – you will come to me and you will say, "I have been trying to be aware, but the mind doesn't stop."

It cannot be stopped; no method exists to stop it. But it stops! Not that you stop it; it stops by itself. You simply watch. In watching, you withdraw the energy that helps it to run. In watching, the energy becomes the watcher and the thinking automatically becomes feebler and feebler and feebler. Thoughts are there, but they become impotent because the energy is not available. They will move around you, half dead, but by and by more energy will be coming to the awareness. One day suddenly the energy is no longer moving into thoughts. They have disappeared. They cannot exist without your energy. So please forget about stopping them. That is none of your business.

And the second thing, you ask: "How is it possible that the mind can go on producing thoughts constantly?" It is just a natural process. Just like your heart goes on beating constantly, your mind goes on thinking constantly; just like your body goes on breathing constantly, your mind goes on thinking constantly; just like your blood goes on circulating constantly and your stomach goes on digesting continuously, the mind goes on thinking constantly. There is no problem in it, it is simple. But you are not identified with the blood circulation, you don't think that *you* are circulating. In fact you are not even conscious that the blood circulates; it goes on circulating, you have nothing to do with it. The heart goes on beating; you don't think that *you* are beating. With the mind, the problem has arisen because you think that *you* are thinking; the mind has become a focus of identity. The identity just has to be broken. It is not that when the mind has stopped, then it will not think forever, no. It will think only when it is needed; it will not think when it is not needed. Thinking will be there, but now it will be natural: a response, a spontaneous activity, not an obsession.

For example, you eat when you are hungry. But you can get obsessed and can go on eating the whole day. Then you will go mad; then you will commit suicide. You walk when you want to walk. When you want to go somewhere, then you move your legs. But if you go on moving your legs when you are sitting on the chair, people will think you are mad and that something has to be done to stop you. If you ask how to stop these legs which are moving and if somebody says, "Stop them by holding them with your hands. Force them!" then you will be in even more trouble because the legs are moving and now the hands are also engaged, and your whole effort is how to stop them. Now your energy is fighting with yourself. You have become identified with the mind, that's all. That too is natural because the mind is so close to you and you have to use the mind so much. One is constantly sitting there.

It is as if a driver has been driving a car for years and has never been out of the car. He has forgotten that he can go out, that he is a driver. He has forgotten completely; he thinks that he himself is the car. He cannot go out because who is there to go out? He has forgotten how to open the door, or the door is completely blocked by not having been used for years, it has gathered rust, it cannot open easily. The driver has been in the car so much that he has become the car, that's all. A misunderstanding has arisen. Now he cannot stop the car, because how is he to stop it? Who is going to stop it?

In the mind you are just the driver. It is a mechanism around you, your consciousness goes on using it. But you have never been out of your head. That's why I insist: drop a little out of the head, go to the heart. From the heart you will have a better perspective that the car is separate from you. Or try to go out of the body. That too is possible. Out of the body you will be absolutely out of the car. You will be able to see that neither the body nor the heart nor the mind is you; you are separate.

Right now, continue to remember only one thing: that you are separate. From everything that surrounds you, you are separate. The knower is not the known. Go on feeling it more and more so that it becomes a substantial crystallization in you that the knower is not the known. You *know* the thought, you *see* the thought – how can you *be* the thought? You *know* the mind – how can you *be* the mind? Just drop away; a little distance is needed. One day, when you are really distant, thinking stops. When the driver is out the car stops, because there is nobody to drive it now. Then you will have a good laugh, seeing that it has just been a misunderstanding. Now, whenever you need it, think.

You ask a question to me: I respond. The mind functions. I have to talk to you through the mind; there is no other way to talk. But when I am alone, the mind doesn't function. The mind has not lost the capacity to function. In fact, it has gained more capacity to function and to function rightly; because it is *not* constantly functioning it gathers energy, it becomes more clear. So 'when the mind stops' does not mean that you will not be able to think again. In fact, only after that will you be able to think for the first time. Just to be engaged in relevant, irrelevant, thoughts is not thinking. It is a mad sort of thing. To be clear, clean, innocent, is to be on the right path for thinking. Then when a problem arises you are not confused; you don't look at the problem through prejudices. You look directly at it, and in that direct look the problem starts melting. If the problem is a problem, it will melt and disappear. If the problem is not a problem but a mystery, it will melt and deepen. And then you will be able to see what a problem is. A problem is that which can be solved by the mind.

A mystery is that which cannot be solved by the mind. A mystery has to be lived; a problem has to be solved. When you are in the thoughts too much, you cannot know what is a mystery and what is a problem. Sometimes you take a mystery as a problem. Then your whole life you struggle and it is never solved. And sometimes you think of a problem as a mystery and you foolishly wait – it could have been solved.

A clarity, a perspective, is needed. When thinking – this constant inner chattering and inner talk – stops, and you have become alert and aware, you are capable of seeing things as they are, you are capable of finding solutions and you are also capable of knowing what a mystery is. And when you come to feel a mystery, you feel reverence, you feel awe. That is the religious quality of being. To feel reverence is to be religious; to feel awe is to be religious. To be so deeply in wonder that you have again become a child is to enter into the kingdom of God.

Enough for today.

Chapter 5

The Kingdom Of God Is At Hand

The Kingdom Of God Is At Hand

Matthew 4

17 From that time Jesus began to preach,
and to say,
"Repent: for the kingdom of heaven
is at hand."

18 And Jesus, walking by the Sea of Galilee,
saw two brethren, Simon called Peter,
and Andrew his brother,
casting a net into the sea:
for they were fishers.

19 And he saith unto them,
"Follow me, and I will make you
fishers of men."

20 And they straightway left their nets,
and followed him.

23 And Jesus went about all Galilee,
    teaching in their synagogues,
    and preaching the gospel of the kingdom,
    and healing all manner of sickness
    and all manner of disease
    among the people.

24 And his fame went throughout all Syria:
    and they brought unto him
    all sick people that were taken
    with divers diseases and torments,
    and those which were possessed with devils
    and those which were lunatic,
    and those that had the palsy;
    and he healed them.

25 And there followed him great multitudes of
    people from Galilee, and from Decapolis,
    and from Jerusalem, and from Judaea,
    and from beyond Jordan.

Once a rabbi was asked to tell the whole Bible message in brief. He replied that the whole Bible message is very simple and short. It is God shouting to man: "Enthrone me!"

This is what happened that morning in the River Jordan. Jesus disappeared, God was enthroned. Jesus vacated the house, God entered. Either you can be, or God can be; both cannot exist together. If you insist on existing, then drop the search for God; it is not going to be fulfilled. Then it is impossible, absolutely impossible. If you are there, then God cannot be: your very being, your very presence, is the hindrance. You disappear, and God is. He has always been there.

Man can live as a part, separated from the whole. Man can create around him ideas, dreams, ego, personality, and think of himself as an island, unconnected with the whole, unrelated with the whole. Have you ever seen any relationship between you and the trees? Have you seen any relationship between you and the rocks? Have you seen any relationship between you and the sea? If you don't see the relationship, then you can never come to know what God is. God, godliness, is nothing but the whole, the total, the one. If you exist as a separate part, you unnecessarily exist as a beggar. You could have been the whole. And even while you think that you are separate, you are not separate – that is just a thought in the mind. The thought is not befooling God, it is only befooling you. The thought is just a barrier for your eyes to open.

That morning in the River Jordan when John the Baptist initiated Jesus, he killed Jesus utterly. Jesus disappeared. And in that moment of nothingness, a buddha – what Buddha calls *shunyata*, emptiness.... The heavens opened and the spirit of God like a dove descended on Jesus, lighted on him.

This is just symbolic: Jesus died, God was enthroned. This is what in Zen they call a special transmission, outside the scriptures. No knowledge was given by John the Baptist to Jesus, no scripture was conveyed – not even a single word was uttered. No dependence on words or letters, just a direct pointing to the soul of man: seeing into one's nature – an attainment of buddhahood. This is what happened that day.

Christians have missed the point: it was not knowledge that was transferred from John the Baptist to Jesus, it was a vision. It was not verbal, it was existential. It was more like knowing than knowledge. Eyes were transferred: a new way of seeing the world and being in the world was transferred, a special transmission outside the scriptures. That's why Jesus immediately felt one with God, but cut off from Jews. Jews are 'the people of the book'. The 'Bible' doesn't mean anything else; it simply means 'the book'. Jews are the people of the book – the people who have believed in the scriptures tremendously, who have loved and relied on the scriptures for centuries.

Jesus became one with God, but immediately was cut off from his own tradition. Then he tried in a thousand and one ways to remain part of the community, but it was impossible. He could not be part of the scriptures, could not be part of the tradition. Something of the beyond entered in him and when God enters, all scriptures become useless. When you yourself have come to know, all knowledge is rubbish.

That was the struggle between Jesus and the rabbis. They had knowledge, Jesus had knowing – and they never meet. The man of knowing is rebellious: the man of knowing has his own eyes; he says whatsoever he sees. The man of knowledge is blind: he carries the scripture, he never looks around; he just goes on repeating the scripture. The man of knowledge is mechanical, he has no personal contact with reality.

Just a few days before I was reading about a very high-powered New York psychiatrist. He was talking to one of his new patients and he told the patient, "I am very busy, in fact too busy. It will be good if you can help me. The first interview is always one-sided: you will be telling me all that you want to tell me. If I can get it down and look at it, and study it later on at my own convenience, it will be a great help. So here is the tape recorder. I will leave the tape recorder – put the machine on and talk to the tape recorder. Whatsoever you have to say.... Say all that you would like to say to me and then later on I will listen to it." The psychiatrist asked, "Are you willing?"

The man said, "Of course. It is perfectly alright."

The tape recorder was put on and the psychiatrist left, but after just two minutes he saw the man leaving the office. He ran after him, stopped him and said, "So soon? You could not have talked much to the tape recorder."

The man said, "Listen, I am also a very busy man. In fact, more busy than you. And you are not the first psychiatrist I have consulted. Go back to the consulting room and you will see sitting just by the side of your tape recorder my small dictaphone – talking to the tape recorder."

Knowledge is just like this. Nobody is present: dictaphones talking to tape recorders. Your mind is just a tape recorder and scriptures are old dictaphones – an old medium, but still the same. Somebody has said something, it is recorded there. Then you read it and it becomes recorded in your own tape recorder – but there is no personal touch.

Knowing is personal, knowledge mechanical. Through a mechanical approach you can never come to discover the reality, the truth. It is going to be a dead affair. You will attain much information, but you will never attain to transformation. You may come to know many things, but you will never know the thing which needs to be known: the being that you are and the being that surrounds you – and that which surrounds you is the same as that which is within you. A deep personal contact is needed. That morning in the River Jordan, Jesus came in personal contact with the divine. John the Baptist initiated him to be a nothing.

When you come to me, you are not coming to a man who knows much, you are coming to a man who has a lot of nothingness in him. I can share that nothingness with you. The day you are ready to share my nothingness, you are initiated.

You can be here in two ways. You can be a student. Then you will be related to me in a mechanical way, you will collect information from me – which was never meant to be done. You will start knowing many more things from me. That is an addiction. The ego may feel stronger, but the soul will become more and more impoverished. Or you can be a disciple here and not a student. Then you share in my nothingness. Then by and by you disappear completely. Then there is nobody inside you who knows – and that nobodiness is the only way to know. In that nothingness your heart is open, in that nothingness the island disappears and you become the continent. In that nothingness the separation disappears: you become the whole. Then the whole exists through you.

The rabbi was right who said, "God shouting to man: 'Enthrone Me!'" Jesus, Krishna, Christ, Mohammed, Lao Tzu, all are shouts of God to man: "Enthrone Me!"

Immediately, Jesus started to preach:

> From that time Jesus began to preach...

Immediately: knowledge needs time, knowing is immediate. If I want to share my knowledge with you it will take time, but if I want to share my nothingness with you, time is not needed. Immediately, right here now, it is possible. Only your readiness is needed. Time is not a requirement at all, it can happen in a split second.

Whenever I read this gospel the thing that strikes me immediately is: the moment Jesus was baptized and the heavens opened and the spirit of God descended like a dove, he moved out of the river, went to the bank – a crowd was gathering – and he started to preach. Before that he had never uttered a single word, before that he had not taught anything to anybody.

That's how it should be. A teacher can go on teaching without knowing, but not a master. Teachers are many, masters few. A master is one who teaches through his knowing and a teacher is one who teaches through his knowledge. A teacher prepares himself for years, then he can teach. But a master in a single moment of courage, in a single moment of daring, in a single moment of death, in a single moment of jumping into the unknown, becomes capable of teaching. Once you know, that very knowing wants to be shared; once you are blissful, that very blissfulness starts flowing, it starts seeking the heart. Once you are, you are already on the way to be shared by many.

Jesus moved out of the river:

> From that time Jesus began to preach, and to say, "Repent: for the kingdom of heaven is at hand."

John the Baptist was saying the same thing. Jesus could have said the same thing just by hearing John the Baptist — he was a well-known preacher, great multitudes used to visit him, great crowds used to wait and listen to him. Everybody knew that his message was this: "Repent ye for the kingdom of heaven is at hand." Jesus must have known about it, but he had never uttered those words before.

To utter such great words without knowing is sacrilegious, it is a betrayal. Never utter such great words unless you know yourself, because you can destroy others' minds. You can fill their minds with your rot. If you don't know, and you go on saying things to people, as it has happened all over the world....

Go and look at the priests in the churches and the temples and the mosques — they go on teaching and they go on preaching, not knowing anything, whatsoever they are saying. They are not aware of what they are doing at all — dictaphones! They have learned, but they have not known. They have studied, but they don't have their own eyes; their own hearts are as dead as those to whom they are preaching. Their minds may be more cultivated, but their hearts are as ill as anybody else's.

Jesus had never uttered these words before. Nobody had known about this man Jesus before this. He remained in his father's workshop; he worked, he helped his father. Suddenly a new quality of man, a new man, altogether fresh, was born. Baptism is a birth.

From that very moment he ...*began to preach, and to say, "Repent..."* — because now he can utter those words with authority. Now they are no longer John the Baptist's words he is repeating, now they are his own. He has repented and he has come to know what they mean. Now they are not futile, parrot-like words; they are pregnant, alive. He has touched the reality of those words, he has come to see the mystery of them.

The actual word in Hebrew is *teshuvah*: repent. Teshuvah means 'return' and teshuvah also means 'answer'. Both meanings are beautiful. To return to God is an answer to him. This is one of the most beautiful things in Judaism, one of the greatest contributions of Judaism to the world. It has to be understood, because without it you will never be able to understand Jesus.

Judaism is the only religion in the world which says that not only is man seeking God, but God is also seeking man. Nobody else in the world believes that. There are Hindus, Mohammedans and other religions, they all believe man is seeking God. Judaism believes God is also seeking man. And this should be so if he is a father. This should be so. He is the whole, and if a part has gone astray, the whole – out of his compassion – must seek the part.

Judaism has a beauty of its own. Man seeking God is just like stumbling in darkness. Unless God is also seeking you, there seems to be no possibility of any meeting. How will you seek him who is unknown? Where will you seek him? You don't know the address – where will you address your prayers? Where will you move, where will you go, what will you do? You can only stumble, cry and weep; tears can be your only prayer. A deep desire – but how to fulfill it? You can burn with it, but how to arrive? Judaism says: man can seek, but man cannot find unless God wills it.

God is within reach, but not within grasp. You can spread your hands – he is within reach, but not within grasp. He comes within grasp because he is also seeking you. He can seek you immediately and directly, he knows exactly where you are. But he cannot seek you unless you are on the search. He can seek you only when you are searching, when you are doing everything that can be done, when you are not withholding anything, when your search is total. When your search is total, immediately heaven opens and the spirit of God descends in you. He is waiting, waiting with a deep urge to meet you.

This should be so, because existence is a love affair. It is a hide-and-seek play, it is a game. The mother is playing with the child and hiding. The mother is waiting, and if the child does not come the mother will start seeking him. But God gives you total freedom. If you don't want to seek, he will not interfere, he will not be an intruder; if you want to seek only then does he knock at your door. If you have invited, only then does the guest come. The guest may be just waiting to knock on the door; only your invitation is needed. Otherwise he can wait for eternity, there is no hurry. God is not in any haste.

"Repent: for the kingdom of heaven is at hand." It would have been absolutely different if the word was not translated as 'repent', if it was left to the original 'return'. That is what Patanjali says in his Yoga Sutras: that *pratyahar* is 'returning to oneself'. That is what Mahavira means when he says to move withinwards: *pratikraman*, 'to go in'.

The word 'teshuvah' has a totally different meaning from 'repent'. The moment you say 'repent' it seems that man is a sinner: a deep condemnation comes in. But if you say 'return', there is no question of sin, no condemnation enters. It simply says that you have gone far away, you have played too long – please come back. The child has been playing outside and the evening is descending. The sun is setting and the mother calls, "Please return." A totally different quality, a totally different connotation.

There is no condemnation in it, just a deep love call: "Return!"

Just listen to the sentence if I say: "Return ye: for the kingdom of heaven is at hand." All condemnation, all sin, and the whole nonsense that has created guilt in man disappears just by a single word translated rightly. A single word can be significant, but the whole of Christianity will disappear if you translate repent as 'return'. All churches – the Vatican – everything will disappear because they depend on repentance.

If it is a question of return – and you are not condemned and you have not committed any sin – then guilt disappears. And without guilt there cannot be churches, without guilt the priest cannot live. He exploits the guilt, he makes you feel guilty – that is his trade secret. Once you are made to feel guilty you have to seek his help because he will ask for forgiveness for you, he will pray for you; he knows the way to pray. He is in a deeper relationship with God. He will defend you, he will persuade God for you and he will show you the way not to be a sinner again, how to be virtuous. He will give you the commandments: do this and don't do that.

All the churches of the world are founded on the word 'repentance'. If it is only a question of return, the priest is not needed; you can return home. It is not a question of condemnation: nobody is needed to purify you; you have never been wrong. You *had* gone a little farther away, but nothing is wrong in it. In fact, it could not have been so if God were not willing for you to go so far. There must be something in it: that going far must be a way of coming back. Because when you have gone too far and then you come back home, for the first time you realize what home is.

It is said that travelers in foreign countries realize for the first time – as you must be realizing in Pune – how beautiful home is. It is difficult to realize when you are at home, everything is taken for granted. But when you go away, now everything is difficult. It is no longer a home, you cannot take anything for granted. There are a thousand and one inconveniences, discomforts – and nobody is there to look after you, you have to look after yourself. Nobody cares; you move in an alien world, a stranger.

In contrast, suddenly for the first time the home, the meaning of the home, arises. First it was just a house to live in, now it is a home. Now you know that houses are different from homes. A house is just a house; a home is not just a house, it is something plus – plus love. Maybe it is needed that man should go a little astray – off the track, into the wilderness – so that, in contrast, coming back to home becomes significant, meaningful.

I say 'return', I don't say 'repent'. Jesus never said 'repent'. He would laugh at the word, because the whole thing is corrupted by the word. Now churches know well that the word is a wrong translation, but they still insist on it because it has become their foundation. 'To return' is so simple: it depends on you and your God; no mediator is needed, no agent is needed.

From that time Jesus began to preach, and to say, "Return: for the kingdom of heaven is at hand." Another meaning of the Hebrew word teshuvah is 'answer'. Your return is your answer. Answer to what? Answer to the shout, "Enthrone me!" The answer to the question God has been asking you, "Come back home?"

This is again a very beautiful contribution of Judaism. Every religion has contributed something original. Judaism says: "God asks the question, man answers." Ordinarily other religions say that man asks the question and God answers. Judaism says, "No, God asks the question, man answers."

The moment you answer, that is the return. The moment

the child says, "Yes, I am coming," he is already on the way. Have you heard the question? If you have not heard it yet, how will you be able to answer?

People come to me and they say, "Where is God?"

I say, "Forget about God – have you heard the question?

They say, "What question?"

"The question that God asks!"

If you have not heard the question, you cannot know where God is. The moment you hear the question the direction is clear – the moment you hear the question that arises deepest in your being, at the deepest core, and becomes a constant haunting in the heart: Who are you? why are you here? why do you go on existing? for what?

If the question has arisen in the heart you will know God is, because who is asking this question? *You* cannot ask it. You are unconsciousness, a deep sleep – you cannot ask. Somewhere deeper within you God is asking the question, "Who are you?" If you have heard the question, you know the direction. And the answer can only be: "Return back. Follow that direction, move back."

But your questions are false. You have not heard them; somebody else has taught them to you. Your questions are false and then your answer becomes false. You learn the question from others, you learn the answer from others, and you remain phony.

The word 'phony' comes from 'telephone'. Have you ever observed that listening to a man directly – listening to your wife or husband or friend directly, face-to-face – is a reality because a personal contact is there, but listening to him on the phone everything becomes phony? One never knows who is there – whether the person really is there or a tape recorder, a dictaphone. Nobody knows. And the sound seems to be coming not from the heart, but from the mechanism. Have you sometimes watched people...?

I have watched a few people, I know a few people who will put their specs on whenever they phone. I was worried: What is the matter? The person is not there, so who are you trying to see? Just a deep urge to see the person. A deep urge – otherwise the thing seems to be phony. But this is how the mind has become corrupted.

I went with a friend once to visit the Taj Mahal. He is a good photographer...and he had no time to see the Taj Mahal, he was seeing it through the camera lens. I told him, "We have come here to see the Taj Mahal."
He said, "Forget about it. It is so beautiful that I will take pictures and see them at home!"

But those pictures are available everywhere – what is the need to come to the Taj Mahal? The direct vision is lost.

Mulla Nasruddin's first child was born. I went to see him. The Mulla was sitting with the boy, a small boy – beautiful. I said, "How beautiful!"
He said, "This is nothing – you must see the photographs!"

Phony...everything becomes more and more indirect. Then it loses the touch of reality, the concreteness, the clarity. Then it goes far away, far away.

The answer can be true only if the question has been really heard. Every day I come across somebody or other who says, "I want to meditate, I want to search, but nothing happens." He is complaining as if existence has not been just to him – "Nothing happens." But I look into his eyes: his desire is phony. In the first place he never wanted to meditate, he has come as part of a crowd. Somebody else was coming, a friend was coming, and he followed. Or he had a holiday and he thought, "Let us go and see." Nothing is happening. Nothing can happen because meditation and prayer and God are not questions of technique. You can learn the technique, but nothing will happen unless the question has been heard first, unless it has become a deep desire in you for which you can stake your life, unless it has become a question of life and death, unless it penetrates to the very center of your being – unless it becomes a thorn in the heart, unless it becomes a deep anguish and pain. If the question is heard, then the answer....

We can translate this sentence in two ways: *From that time Jesus began to preach, and to say, "Repent: for the kingdom of heaven is at hand."* Either we can translate it, "Return: *for the kingdom of heaven is at hand."* Or "Answer: *for the kingdom of heaven is at hand."*

And the kingdom of heaven is always at hand, it is its nature. It has nothing to do with Jesus' time: right now it is true, exactly as it was then. It was true before Jesus and it will always be true. The kingdom of God is *always* at hand – just grope. His hand has always been seeking you, but your hand is not groping. You answer, you return, and he is available. All that you need is available, only you are not ready to move towards it. You are afraid to lose something which you don't have, and because of that fear you cannot attain to that which has always been yours to take.

> And Jesus, walking by the Sea of Galilee,
> saw two brethren, Simon called Peter,
> and Andrew his brother,
> casting a net into the sea:
> for they were fishers.
>
> And he saith unto them,
> "Follow me, and I will make you
> fishers of men."

> And they straightway left their nets,
> and followed him.

This will come many times in Jesus' life. You will be surprised at the quality of people in whom and with whom he was moving: simple people — farmers, villagers, fishermen, carpenters — but real people, not phony. People who live with nature are real, because with nature you have to be real otherwise nature won't yield to you. With nature you have to be alive, otherwise you will not be able to cope with it. The more surrounded you are with unnatural things, the more unnatural you become. If you live just surrounded by mechanisms, you will become a mechanism yourself.

It is said that a man is known by his company. I say to you: a man is *made* by his company. If you live surrounded by mechanical gadgets, as modern man is living, by and by you become unreal. If you live with nature — with trees and rocks and the sea and the stars and the clouds and the sun — you cannot be unreal, you cannot be phony. You *have* to be real because when you are encountering nature, nature creates something in you which is natural. Responding to nature continuously, you become natural.

A man who lives with nature is always trusting. A farmer who goes on sowing seeds has to trust. If he doubts, he will never sow the seeds — because there are a thousand and one doubts possible: whether this year the earth is going to do the same as it did last year or not. And who knows, the earth may have changed its mind. Who knows if the rains are going to rain or not? Who knows about the sun — whether it will rise tomorrow morning or not? Sitting in your easy chair surrounded by your books you can doubt, there is nothing at stake. But if a farmer working in the field with the earth doubts, he is lost; if a fisherman doubts, he is lost.

Living with nature, trust arises. Trust is natural to man just like health is natural; doubt is unnatural just like disease is unnatural. A child is born trusting. I'm not talking about the modern child – maybe a modern child is not born trusting because he is born in a climate of skepticism.
I was reading a story one day:

A mother was telling a story to her daughter – the daughter was restless, it was getting late, and the mother was telling her a bedtime story to put her to sleep. The mother said. "There was a princess – very charming, beautiful...and very wise, very loving. The whole court of the king loved and respected her. She was very kind, particularly to animals.
"One day she came across a frog in the courtyard. She became afraid that somebody might tread on him, so she brought the frog into her bedroom. And in the morning she was surprised: the frog had turned into a beautiful prince! And the prince asked her hand in marriage."
At this point the mother looked at her daughter and felt that she was completely skeptical. Her eyes, her manner, her face – everything was saying, "No, I cannot believe it." Complete incredulity was on her face. So the mother said, "What? – don't you believe this?"
The girl said, "No...and I'll bet the princess' mother didn't either!"

Today's climate is one of skepticism. Even a child is doubtful – doubting, skeptical. In the old days, even old men were trusting; the whole climate was one of trust, faith. They were healthy people. Watch yourself – whenever you doubt, something shrinks in you; you become small and tiny. You become hard, you become dead and you are no longer flowing – frozen. Whenever trust arises, you are again flowing. The blocks are melting and you expand, you become vast. Whenever you trust you reach a peak of being alive, whenever you doubt you fall into death.

Because modern man is lacking in trust, drugs have started to have so much appeal for him. There seems to be no other way to have the feeling of an expanded being and consciousness. Drugs are chemical methods to feel, for a few moments or a few hours, an expansion of consciousness. Trust gives it to you easily and freely. Trust gives it to you not for a few moments – it becomes an eternal quality in you. And trust has no side-effects!

If you ask me, I will tell you trust is the only reliable drug if you want expansion of consciousness – those who have never known what expansion of consciousness is, have not lived yet. Consciousness can expand and can go on expanding...waves of bliss going to the very corners of existence ...expanding with the infinity of existence. When you expand you become part of the whole; when you shrink you become an island.

Those people were really simple, trusting:

> And Jesus, walking by the Sea of Galilee,
> saw two brethren, Simon called Peter,
> and Andrew his brother,
> casting a net into the sea:
> for they were fishers.
>
> And he saith unto them,
> "Follow me, and I will make you
> fishers of men."

Nothing is strange about his saying this. The strange thing is:

> And they straightway left their nets,
> and followed him.

Such deep trust. Not for even a single moment did they doubt, not for even a single moment did they say, "What do you mean – fishers of men?" Not for a single moment did they ask, "Who are you? By what authority do you speak?" No, it was not needed because they were simple fishermen. They must have looked at Jesus: his very presence was the authority.

If you have eyes of trust, nobody can deceive you. You are deceived because of your doubt and then you think that you need more doubt, otherwise people are going to deceive you more. Then you are deceived more and a vicious circle is created. You doubt so that you will not be deceived, but you are deceived because of your doubt. If you trust, nobody can deceive you. What do I mean when I say, "If you trust, nobody can deceive you?" Is your trust going to prevent somebody from deceiving you? No, but when you trust you have eyes to see, the deceiver will be revealed immediately – naked.

I would like you to remember this as a criterion: that a man who trusts cannot be deceived. If he is deceived then he must have some doubts within himself, because only when the eyes are full of clouds of doubt are you not able to see. When you are capable of seeing and your vision is clear, the very presence of the person says whether he is a deceiver or not.

They must have looked. The sun must have been rising on the sea, they were ready to throw their net into the sea. They must have looked back at this man: What manner of man is this Jesus? In that silent morning they must have felt the presence of this man Jesus. The presence was conviction; the presence was the proof. They threw away their nets, they straightway followed this man. In a single moment their whole life was turned completely upside down. In a single moment of vision they were converted.

Jesus says, "Come follow me, and I will make you fishers of men. How long will you go on throwing your nets into the sea? How long are you going to just catch fish? I will make you fishers of men." And he did make them.

It was almost unbelievable in those days — it is almost unbelievable even now — how Jesus transformed ordinary people into extraordinary beings. Buddha transformed Mahakashyapa, Sariputta, Mandgalyan, Ananda, but the credit goes more to Mahakashyapa, Sariputta, Ananda and Mandgalyan and less to Buddha because they were rare beings. If Mahavira transformed Gautam, Sudharma, the credit goes more to the disciples because they were rare beings.

But Jesus was tremendously powerful. Peter, a fisherman, uneducated, or Andrew or Matthew or Thomas or John — all poor, uneducated people who would have been lost in any crowd and you would not have been able to find them — they were just stones, ordinary pebbles on the way, and Jesus transformed them into *kohinoors*.

Mahakashyapa was a rare being in his own right; there is every possibility that even without Buddha he would have become a buddha. It would have taken a little longer, maybe he would have taken a little more time, but it seems almost certain that he would have become a buddha even without Buddha. But think of Simon called Peter, or his brother Andrew. Nobody can conceive that without Jesus they could have become anything whatsoever.

He not only promised, he *did* the miracle. *"Follow me, and I will make you fishers of men"* — and certainly more men have been caught in the net Jesus has thrown into the sea of humanity than in any other net. Half of the world is caught in the net. All the apostles, all twelve of the apostles, were very ordinary, uneducated, common people, and upon them he built the whole structure.

Peter, Simon called Peter – Jesus has made him the very rock on which the whole of Christianity stands. The word 'Peter' means rock. On Peter's rock the whole of Christianity stands and is supported by him. Yes, Jesus did make them fishers of men – and not only fishers of men. He delivered more than he promised: he made them fishers of God. *And they straightway left their nets, and followed him.*

When Mahakashyapa came to Buddha, he argued. When Mahakashyapa came to Buddha he had five thousand of his own disciples, he was a great teacher in his own name. When Sariputta came he had thousands of disciples of his own, he was a great scholar. For years he waited and argued. They were not men of trust, they were men of doubt and skepticism – very cultured minds, cultivated minds, geniuses in a way.

But Jesus worked with ordinary mud and transformed it into gold. You cannot find a greater alchemist than Jesus. *And they straightway left their nets, and followed him* – this is the miracle.

People went to Mahavira and argued, people went to Buddha and argued, because the whole Indian continent has been arguing for millennia. People have become trained here; they are born with philosophies. People come to me, very ordinary people, but they never come down below the level of *brahman*, the ultimate. They talk about brahman; it has become part of their blood.

But Jesus worked with very simple people. His very presence was the proof. In religion presence is first, proof is second. In philosophy proof is first, presence is second. Sariputta would open his eyes to Buddha only when Buddha had proved himself, argued for himself, when he had defeated Sariputta and his mind totally. Then he would open his eyes. Proof was first, presence was second.

But with Jesus and the people he worked with – they were

not theologians, they were not philosophers, not argumentative, no; they were simple people, ordinary people of nature, just like trees and rocks and rivers — for them presence is first, proof is later. In fact, presence is the proof. They fell in love — that's the only way to express it rightly. They looked at Jesus: they fell in love. When you fall in love, you follow. Then there is no question, then you simply follow, because your heart knows better than your mind can prove. Your heart has felt something, something of the mysterium, something of God. Your heart has felt the presence, something which is not of this earth. That is enough. You have tasted something...you simply follow. *And they straightway left their nets, and followed him.*

> And Jesus went about all Galilee,
> teaching in their synagogues,
> and preaching the gospel of the kingdom,
> and healing all manner of sickness
> and all manner of disease
> among the people.

This has to be understood in a totally new light — not the way Christians have been trying but in a totally new light, the new light that modern science has thrown on the phenomenon of disease.

A disease, any disease, first arises deep in the mind and then moves towards the body. It may take a long time to come to the body, it is a long distance. You are not aware of it when it is in the mind, you become aware of it only when it strikes ha rd at the roots of the body. You always feel the disease in the body, but it always originates in the mind. You are not aware of it then, so you cannot do anything about it. But when it comes to the body then of course you start seeking a physician, some help. The physician, seeing it in the body, starts treating it in the body. It can be treated in the body — but then some other disease will arise, because the treatment has not gone to the very source. You have been changing the effect and not the cause.

If it can be changed in the mind, then the disease will disappear from the body immediately. That's how modern research on hypnosis proves that every disease — at least in principle — can be transformed, changed, can be dropped, if the mind is changed. And the vice versa is also true: if the mind is convinced by hypnosis, then disease can be created also.

Just two or three days before, somebody sent me an article of deep significance. One man — one physician, a doctor in California — has treated many patients with cancer just through the imagination. This is the first clue which opens the door.... And not one patient, many. What he does is, he simply tells them to imagine. If they have cancer of the throat, he tells them to relax and imagine that the whole energy of their body is moving towards the throat and the tumor is being attacked by their energy, just like arrows from everywhere, all over, moving towards the throat and attacking the disease. Within three, four or six weeks the tumor simply disappears without leaving a trace behind. And cancer is thought to be incurable!

Cancer is a modern disease; it has come because of the stress, tension and anxiety of life. There has, in fact, been no cure for it up to now through the body. But if cancer can be treated through the mind, then everything can be treated through the mind.

Jesus' miracles happened because the people were very trusting. Once it happened: he was walking and a woman...a very poor woman, afraid and apprehensive about whether Jesus would treat her or not because he was always crowded by so many people....The woman thought to herself,"Just touch Jesus' garment from behind"...and she was cured.

Jesus looked back and the woman started thanking him. She fell at his feet and was very grateful. He said,"Don't be grateful to me, be grateful to God. Your faith has healed you, not I."

The world was deep in trust; people were rooted in faith. Then just the idea that "If Jesus touches my eyes they will be cured" – the very idea becomes the root cause of the cure. It is not that Jesus cures; if you are skeptical then Jesus can't help, then he will not be able to cure you.

I was reading a story.

One day Jesus was running out of a town. A farmer working in his fields saw him running, so he inquired, "What is the matter? Where are you going?" But he was in such a hurry that he would not answer.

So the farmer followed him, stopped him after a while, and said, "Please tell me, I have become too curious. If you don't tell me, then this will haunt me again and again. Why were you running? Where are you going? From whom are you escaping?"

Jesus said, "From a fool."

The farmer started laughing. He said, "What are you saying? I know well that you have cured blind people, you have cured people who were almost dying. I have heard that you have cured people who were dead already! Can't you cure a fool?"

Jesus said, "No. I tried, but I can't because he is a fool and he won't believe. I have cured all sorts of illnesses and I have never failed, but with this fool I have failed. He is following me and he says, 'Cure me,' but I have tried every way that I know and everything fails. That's why I am escaping from the town."

A fool cannot be cured...and a fool cannot be hypnotized. Ordinarily, amongst the common masses, the idea is prevalent that very intelligent people cannot be hypnotized. That is absolutely wrong. Only fools cannot be hypnotized, idiots cannot be hypnotized, mad people cannot be hypnotized. The greater the intelligence, the more possibility there is of your going deep into hypnosis – because in hypnosis your trust is needed, the first requirement is your trust. The first requirement is your cooperation, and an idiot, a madman, cannot cooperate and cannot trust.

Jesus could do miracles. Those miracles were simple; they happened because people were trusting. If you can trust, then the mind starts functioning from within, spreads to the body and changes everything. But if you can't trust, then nothing can help. Even ordinary medicine helps you because you trust it. There has been an observation that whenever a new medicine is invented it works very well for six months to two years – people are affected by it – but after six months, eight months, ten months, it doesn't work so well. Physicians have been worried – what happens?

Whenever a new medicine is invented you believe in it more than in an old medicine. Now you know the panacea is there "...and I will be helped by it." And you are helped! The trust in a new medicine, a new discovery, helps. They talk about it on TV, on the radio, in the newspapers, and there is a climate of trust and hope. But after a few months, when many people have taken it – and a few fools have also taken it, which cannot be helped – then a suspicion arises...."Because this man has taken the medicine and nothing happened." These fools then create an anti-climate, and after a while the medicine loses its effect.

Even more than medicine, the physician helps if you trust him. Have you watched that whenever you are ill and the doctor comes, if you trust the doctor then you feel relief just by his coming? He has not given any medicine up to now, he has just been checking your body – blood pressure, this and that – and already you feel that fifty percent of the disease is gone. A man you can trust has come. Now there is no need to carry the burden on yourself, you can leave it to him and he will see to it. If you don't trust the physician, he cannot do anything.

In medicine, they call a certain false medicine a placebo. It is just water or something which has nothing to do with the illness, but if it is given to you by a physician you trust it helps as much as the real medicine; there is no difference. Mind is more powerful than matter; mind is more powerful than the body.

> And Jesus went about all Galilee,
> teaching in their synagogues,
> and preaching the gospel of the kingdom,
> and healing all manner of sickness
> and all manner of disease
> among the people.
>
> And his fame went throughout all Syria:
> and they brought unto him
> all sick people that were taken
> with divers diseases and torments,
> and those which were possessed with devils
> and those which were lunatic,
> and those that had the palsy;
> and he healed them.
>
> And there followed him great multitudes of
> people from Galilee, and from Decapolis,
> and from Jerusalem, and from Judaea,
> and from beyond Jordan.

Jesus was less a teacher and more a healer. A healer not only of the body, not only of the mind, but of the soul also. He was a physician, a physician of the soul. That's how every master has to be.

You are divided within yourself, you are fragmentary, you are not whole. If you become whole, you will be healed. If the tensions for the future and the accumulated tensions of the past disappear from within you, you will be healed, your wounds will disappear. If you can be in the present you will be whole, fully alive, utterly alive, and a deep delight will happen to you.

Jesus is not a philosopher teaching some dogma to people. He is a physician, not a philosopher. He is trying to teach trust, and if trust happens everything becomes possible. He goes on saying: "If you have faith, faith can move mountains." It may not be the mountains that exist outside, but the mountains of ignorance, the mountains of ugliness, the mountains of unconsciousness that exist within. He does not have a creed, a dogma. He is, rather, releasing a healing force through himself. His whole effort is to help you to return to God. That's why he said, "Don't be thankful towards me. Thank God."

Then too, he says, "Your faith has healed you." Not even God can help to heal you – your faith. His insistence is on faith. And remember the distinction between belief and faith: belief is in an idea; faith is in total reality, faith is a reverence for the whole. Belief is of the mind; faith is of your totality.

When you believe in God, you believe in a God of philosophers. When you believe in God, God is an idea, a doctrine. It can be proved or disproved and it will not transform you. But if you have faith, it has already transformed you. I will not say that it *will* transform you. If you have faith, it has *already* transformed you. Faith knows no future, it is immediately effective. But faith is not of the head. When you have faith, you have faith in your blood, in your bones, in your marrow, in your heart. In your whole being, you have faith. A man of faith is a man of God.

Jesus' whole effort is how to bring you back home. Yes, God is shouting through him: "Enthrone me!" If you have faith you will become available and God will be enthroned in you. That is the only way of being blissful. Unless God is enthroned in you, you will remain a beggar, you will remain poor, you will remain ill. You will never be whole and healthy, and you will never know the ecstasy of existence. You will never be able to dance and laugh and sing and just be...only if God is enthroned in you – that means if you are dethroned and God is enthroned.

So there is this choice, the greatest choice that man ever encounters: either to continue on the throne yourself ...or dethrone yourself and let God come in.

Enough for today.

Chapter 6

You'll Never Forget The Jokes

THE FIRST QUESTION:

> Beloved Osho,
> What is the need for secrecy in master–disciple relationships and also in ordinary human relationships?

The being has two sides, the without and the within. The without can be public, but the within cannot be. If you make the within public you will lose your soul, you will lose your original face. Then you will live as if you have no inner being. Life will become drab, futile. It happens to people who live a public life: politicians, film actors. They become public, they lose their inner being completely, they don't know who they are except what the public says about them. They depend on others' opinion, they don't have a sense of their being.

One of the most famous actresses, Marilyn Monroe, committed suicide, and psychoanalysts have been brooding on the reason why. She was one of the most beautiful women ever, one of the most successful. Even the President of America, Kennedy, was in love with her, and she had thousands of lovers. One cannot think of what more you can have. She had everything. But she was public and she knew it. Even in her love chamber when President Kennedy would be there she used to address him as Mr. President – as if one was making love not to a man, but to an institution. She was an institution. By and by she became aware that she had nothing private. Once somebody asked her — she had just posed for a nude calendar and somebody asked, "Did you have anything on while you posed for the nude calendar?"

She said, "Yes, I had something on. The radio."

Exposed, nude, no private self. My feeling is that she committed suicide because that was the only thing left she could have done privately. Everything was public, that was the only thing left she could do on her own, alone — something absolutely intimate and secret. Public figures are always tempted towards suicide because only through suicide can they have a glimpse of who they are.

All that is beautiful is inner, and the inner means privacy. Have you watched women making love? They always close their eyes. They know something. A man goes on making love with open eyes, he remains a watcher also. He is not completely in the act, he is not totally in it. He remains a voyeur, as if somebody else is making love and he is watching, as if the love-making is going on on a TV screen or in a movie. But a woman knows better because she is more delicately tuned to the inner. She always closes her eyes. Then love has a totally different fragrance.

One day do one thing: run the bath and then switch the light on and off. When there is darkness you will hear the water falling more clearly, the sound will be sharp. When the light is on, the sound will be not so sharp. What happens in darkness? In darkness, everything else disappears because you cannot see. Only the sound and you are there. That's why, in all good restaurants, light is avoided; sharp light is avoided. They are candlelit. Whenever a restaurant is candlelit, taste is deeper…you eat well and you taste more. The fragrance surrounds you. If there is very bright light the taste is no longer there. The eyes make everything public.

In the very first sentence of his *Metaphysics*, Aristotle says that sight is the highest sense of man. It is not. In fact, sight has become too domineering. It has monopolized the whole self and it has destroyed all the other senses. His master – Aristotle's master, Plato – says that there is a hierarchy in the senses: sight at the top, touch at the bottom. He is absolutely wrong. There is no hierarchy.

All senses are on the same level and there should not be any hierarchy. But you live through the eyes: eighty percent of your life is eye-oriented. This should not be so; a balance has to be restored. You should touch also, because touch has something which eyes cannot give. But try: try to touch the woman you love or the man you love in bright light and then touch in darkness. In darkness the body reveals itself, in bright light it hides.

Have you seen Renoir's paintings of feminine bodies? They have something miraculous in them. Many painters have painted the feminine body, but there is no comparison with Renoir. What is the difference? All other painters have painted the feminine body as it looks to the eyes. Renoir has painted it as it feels to the hands, so the painting has a warmth and a closeness, an aliveness.

When you touch, something happens very close. When you see, something is far away. In darkness, in secrecy, in privacy, something is revealed which cannot be revealed in openness, in the marketplace. Others are seeing and observing; something deep within you shrinks, it cannot flower. It is just as if you put seeds down on the open ground for everybody to look at. They will never sprout. They need to be thrown deep into the womb of the earth, in deep darkness where nobody can see them. There they start sprouting and a great tree is born. Just like seeds need darkness and privacy in the earth, all relationships which are deep and intimate remain of the inner. They need privacy, they need a place where only two exist. There comes a moment when even the two dissolve and only one exists. Two lovers deeply in tune with each other dissolve. Only one exists. They breathe together, they are together; a togetherness exists. This would not be possible if there were observers. They would never be able to let go if others were watching. The very eyes of others would become the barrier. So all that is beautiful, all that is deep, happens in darkness.

In ordinary human relationships, privacy is needed. And when you ask about the relationship of a master and disciple, even more privacy is needed because it is a transmission of the highest energy possible to man. It is the highest peak of love, where one man pours himself into another and the other becomes a receptive womb. Even a slight disturbance – somebody watching – will be enough of a barrier.

Secrecy has its own reason to be there. Remember that, and always remember that you will behave very foolishly in life if you become completely public. It will be as if somebody has turned his pockets inside-out. That will be your shape – pockets turned inside-out. Nothing is wrong in being outside, but remember, that is only part of life. It should not become the whole.

I am not saying to move in darkness forever. Light has its own beauty and its own reason. If the seed remains in the dark for ever and ever, and never comes up to receive the sun in the morning, it will be dead. It has to go into darkness to sprout, to gather strength, to become vital, to be reborn, and then it has to come out and face the world and the light and the storm and the rains. It has to accept the challenge of the outside. But that challenge can only be accepted if you are deeply rooted within.

I am not saying to become escapists, I am not saying to close your eyes, move within and never come out. I am simply saying, go in so that you can come out with energy, with love, with compassion. Go in so that when you come out you are not a beggar, but a king. Go in so that when you come out you have something to share – the flowers, the leaves. Go in so that your coming out becomes richer and is not impoverished. And always remember that whenever you feel exhausted, the source of energy is within. Close your eyes and go in.

Make outer relationships; make inner relationships also. Of course there are bound to be outer relationships – you move in the world, there will be business relationships – but they should not be all. They have their part to play, but there must be something absolutely secret and private, something that you can call your own. That is what Marilyn Monroe lacked. She was a public woman – successful, yet failed completely. While she was at the top of her success and fame, she committed suicide. Why she committed suicide has remained an enigma. She had everything to live for; you cannot conceive of more fame, more success, more charisma, more beauty, more health. Everything was there, nothing could be improved upon, and still something was lacking. The inside, the within, was empty. Then, suicide is the only way.

You may not be daring enough to commit suicide like Marilyn Monroe. You may be very cowardly and you may commit suicide very slowly – you may take seventy years to commit it. But still it will be a suicide. Unless you have something inside you which is not dependent on anything outside, which is just your own – a world, a space of your own where you can close your eyes and move, and you can forget that anything else exists – you will be committing suicide.

Life arises from that inner source and spreads into the sky outside. There has to be a balance – I am always for balance.

So I will not say, like Mahatma Gandhi, that your life should be an open book – no. A few chapters open, okay. And a few chapters completely closed, completely a mystery. If you are just an open book you will be a prostitute, you will just be standing in the marketplace naked, with just the radio on. No, that won't do.

If the whole book is open, you will just be the day and no night, just the summer and no winter. Then where will you rest and where will you center yourself and where will you take refuge? Where will you move when the world is too much with you? Where will you go to pray and meditate? No, half and half is perfect. Let half of your book be open – open to everybody, available to everybody. Let the other half of your book be so secret that only rare guests are allowed there. Only rarely is somebody allowed to move within your temple. It should be so. If the crowd is coming in and going out, then the temple is no longer a temple. It may be a waiting room in an airport, but it cannot be a temple. Only rarely, very rarely, do you allow somebody to enter your self. That is what love is.

The second question:

> Beloved Osho,
> Sometimes I wonder what I am doing here, sitting before you. And then suddenly you are too much for me, too much light and love. Yet I want to leave you. Can you explain this to me?

Yes. The question is bound to happen to everybody some day or other. What are you doing here? The question arises because my emphasis is not on doing; I am teaching you nondoing. The question is relevant. If I was teaching you something to do, the question wouldn't arise because you would be occupied. If you go to somebody else — there are a thousand and one *ashrams* in the world where they will teach you to do something. They will not leave you unoccupied at all because they think that an unoccupied mind is the devil's workshop. My understanding is totally, diametrically opposite. When you are absolutely empty, God fills you; when you are unoccupied, only then you are. While you are doing something, it is just on the periphery. All acts are on the periphery — good and bad, all. Be a sinner — you are on the periphery; be a saint — you are on the periphery. To do bad you have to come out of yourself; to do good you also have to come out of yourself.

Doing is outside, nondoing is inside. Nondoing is your private self, doing is your public self. I am not teaching you to become saints, otherwise it would have been very easy: don't do this, do that; just change the periphery, change your acts. I am trying a totally different thing, a mutation — not a change from one part of the periphery to another part of the periphery, but a transmutation from the periphery to the center. The center is empty, it is absolutely void. There, you *are*. There, is being, not doing.

It is bound to happen to you sometimes: sitting before me you will wonder what you are doing here. Nothing — you are not doing anything here. You are learning how to just be, not to do — how not to do anything: no action, no movement...as if everything stops, time stops. And in that nonmoving moment you are in tune with the present, you are in tune with God.

Actions become part of the past. Actions can be in the future, they can be in the past. God is always in the present. God has no past and no future. And God has not done a thing.

When you think that he has created the world, you are creating his image according to yourself. You cannot remain without doing anything – you become too restless, it makes you too uneasy – so you have conceived of God also as a creator. Not only as a creator.... Christians say that for six days he created and on the seventh day, Sunday, he rested – a holiday. The Bible says God created man in his own image. Just the reverse seems to be the case: man has created God in his own image. Because you cannot remain unoccupied, you think: What will God do if he is not creating the world? And because you get tired by doing, you think God must also have got tired after six days – so on the seventh day he rested. This is just anthropomorphic. You are thinking about God just as you would think about yourself. No, God has not created the world; the world comes out of his nonactivity, the world comes out of his nondoing. The world is a flowering of God, just like a tree. Do you think a tree is creating the flowers – making much effort, doing exercises, planning, asking the experts? The tree is not doing anything at all. The tree is just there, absolutely unoccupied. In that unoccupied state, the flower flowers by itself. And remember, if some day trees become foolish – as foolish as man is – and they start trying to bring the flowers, then flowers will stop coming. They will not come because they always come effortlessly. Just watch a flower. Can you see anything of effort in it? The very being of a flower is so effortless, it simply opens. But we cannot conceive of it. The birds singing in the morning ...do you think they go to Ravi Shankar to learn? Do you think they are doing something in the morning when they start singing? No, nothing of that sort. The sun rises, and out of their emptiness arises the song. The greatest miracle in the world is that God has created without doing a thing. It is out of nothingness.

I was reading about the life of Wagner, a German composer and great musician. Somebody asked Wagner, "Can you say anything about the secret of why you have created such beautiful music – and how?"

Wagner said, "Because I was unhappy. If I had been happy, I would not have written down a single note. People who are unhappy have to fill their lives with imagination because their reality is lacking something." And he is right in many ways. People who have never loved write poetry about love. That is a substitute. If love has really happened in life, who bothers to write poetry about it? One would have been poetry himself; there would be no need to write it.

Wagner said, "Poets write about love because they have missed love." And then he made a statement which is tremendously meaningful. He said, "And I think God created the world because he was unhappy." A great insight – but the insight is relevant to man, not to God. If you ask me, God created the world…in the first place, he is not 'a creator' but 'a creativity'…but to use the old expression, God created the world not because he was unhappy, but because he was so happy that he overflowed; he had so much.

The tree is flowering there in the garden not because it is unhappy. The flower comes only when the tree has too much to share and does not know what to do with it. The flower is an overflowing. When the tree is not well-fed, not well-watered, has not received the right quota of sunlight and care and love, it doesn't flower because flowering is a luxury. It happens only when you have too much, more than you need. Whenever you have too much, what will you do? It will become a heaviness, it will be a burden; it has to be released. The tree bursts and blooms, it has come to its luxurious moment.

The world is the luxury of God, a flowering. He has so much – what to do with it? He shares, he throws it out, he starts expanding, he starts creating. But remember always, he is not a creator like a painter who paints. The painter is separate from the painting. If the painter dies, the painting will still live. God is a creator like a dancer: the dance and the dancer are one. If the dancer stops, the dance stops.

You cannot separate the dance from the dancer, you cannot say to the dancer, "Give your dance to me, I will take it home. I am ready to purchase it." The dance cannot be purchased. It is one of the most spiritual things in the world because it cannot be purchased. You cannot carry it away, you cannot make a commodity out of it. When the dancer is dancing, it is there; when the dancer has stopped, it has disappeared as if it never existed.

God is *creativity*. It is not that he created somewhere in the past and then stopped and rested – and since then what has he been doing? No, he is continuously creating. God is not an event, he is a process. It is not that once he created and then stopped. Then the world would be dead. He is continuously creating – just like birds are singing and trees are flowering and the clouds are moving in the sky. He is creating...and he need not take any rest because creativity is not an act; you cannot be tired. It is out of his nothingness.

This is the meaning in the East when we have said that God is emptiness. Only nothingness can be infinite; 'somethingness' is bound to be finite. Only out of nothingness is an infinite expanse of life, existence, possible – not out of somethingness. God is not somebody, he is nobody or more correctly, 'nobodiness'. God is not something, he is nothing or, even more correctly, 'nothingness'. He is a creative void – what Buddha has called *shunya*. He is a creative void. What am I teaching to you? I am teaching you the same: to become creative voids, nondoers, delighters in just being.

That is why the question is bound to come to everybody's mind sometime or other. You ask: "Sometimes I wonder what I am doing here." You wonder rightly – you are doing nothing here. Your mind may supply answers, but don't listen to them. Listen to my answer. You are not doing anything here; I am not teaching you to do something. Your mind may say that you are learning meditation: you are doing meditation, yoga, this, that or you are trying to achieve enlightenment, *satori*, *samadhi* – all nonsense.

This is your mind supplying because the mind is an achiever, the mind cannot remain without activity. The mind goes on creating some activity or other. Earn money; if you are finished with that, then earn meditation – but earn. Achieve something, do something.

You become afraid when you are not doing anything, because then suddenly you are face-to-face with the creative void. That is the face of God: when you are in a chaos and you are falling in an infinite abyss and you cannot see the bottom – there is none.

Sitting before me, what are you doing? Just sitting. That is the meaning of *zazen*. In Zen they call meditation 'zazen'. Zazen means just sitting, doing nothing. If you can just sit near me that is enough, more than enough; nothing else is needed. If you can just sit without doing anything – not even doing a thought, not even thinking or dreaming – if you can just sit near me, that will do everything. "Suddenly you are too much for me," you say. Yes, if you just sit I will be too much – because if you just sit, suddenly I will be flowing within you. If you just sit, you will immediately become aware of light and love. And then you say, "I want to leave you," because you are afraid of love and light.

You have become a denizen of darkness. You have lived in darkness so long that your eyes are afraid. No matter what you say – that you would like to live in the light – your deep-rooted habits shrink and say, "Where are you going?" You have a great investment in darkness. All your knowledge is related to darkness. In light you will be absolutely ignorant. All your wisdom and experience is out of darkness; in light you will be naked, nude. All that you know belongs to darkness; in the light you will find yourself just like an innocent babe, a small child, not knowing anything.

You have lived in bondage and now you are afraid to be free. You go on talking about freedom and *moksha* – absolute freedom – but if you watch yourself you will know that whenever freedom comes your way, you escape. You become afraid. Maybe you talk about freedom just to deceive yourself; maybe it is a substitute, the substitute Wagner is talking about. You are in bondage; you have never known freedom. You talk about freedom, you sing songs of freedom and through those songs you have a vicarious satisfaction – as if you have become free. It is an 'as if' freedom. But with me it is not going to be 'as if', it is going to be a reality. You become afraid of the reality.

You go on asking for love, but when it comes you escape because love is dangerous. One of the greatest dangers in life is love. The mind can become settled with marriage, but not with love. The mind always wants law, not love. The mind always loves order, not the chaos that love is. The mind wants to remain in security, and love is the greatest insecurity you can come across. Whenever love comes you become afraid to the very roots, you shake and tremble because that love, if allowed to enter in you, will destroy your mind. The mind says: "Escape! Escape immediately!" The mind is trying to save itself.

You have lived too deeply in contact with the mind and you have become too attached. You think that whatever the mind says is right; you think that whatever is security for the mind is security for you. There is the whole misunderstanding. The death of the mind will be life for you, and the life of the mind is nothing but death for you. The identity has to be broken. You have to become aware that you are not the mind. Only then can you be near me, only then will the effort to leave and escape dissolve. Otherwise you can find reasons to leave, but those reasons will all be phony. The real reason will be this: that you were not able to let light come in, you were not able to let love come in and destroy your mind and destroy your ego and give you a rebirth.

The third question:

> Beloved Osho,
> Your teaching seems to be:
> to be absolutely oneself.
> This is beyond me. How can one be
> oneself if one is not oneself?

Let me ask you another question: How can you not be yourself? You can believe it, but you cannot be anything other than yourself. You can think that you are somebody else, you can imagine that you are somebody else, but all the time you are just yourself, nothing else. Whether you believe you are yourself or not is irrelevant. You remain, all the time, yourself. You can go on running and chasing shadows, but one day or the other you will have to realize that you have just been doing an absurd thing.

How can you be other than yourself? How? You ask me how one can be oneself. I ask you, how one can be other than oneself? – and in my questioning is the answer. Nobody has even been other than himself; nobody can ever be other than himself. To be oneself is the only way to be, nothing can be done about it.

You can believe.... It is just like you sleep at night in Pune and you dream that you are in Philadelphia. That doesn't make any change in reality. You remain in Pune – here, somewhere, in Mobo's. You remain in Pune; Philadelphia remains just a dream. In the morning you will not wake up in Philadelphia, remember. You will wake up in Mobo's, in Pune. Howsoever miserable, but it is the case! Nothing can be done about it; at the most you can again dream of Philadelphia.

You are gods. That is your reality. You can believe...you have believed in many things. Sometimes you believed you were a tree – many trees are still believing that. Sometimes you believed you were an animal...a tiger, a lion. There are a few people who belong to Lion Clubs – Lion Bhabhutmal Sanghvi. They are not satisfied in being men – lions! Sometimes you believed that you were a lion, and then you *were* a lion: a dream. Sometimes you believed that you were a rock and you *were* a rock: a dream. You have been changing your dreams.

Now the time has arrived. Wake up! I'm not giving you another dream, remember. You hanker for it, you would like me to give you another dream, but I am not going to give you another dream. That's why to be with me is difficult and arduous – because I am insisting that you wake up. Enough is enough. You have dreamed a lot; you have been dreaming since eternity . You have just been changing dreams. When you get fed up with one dream you start changing it; you dream another dream. My whole effort is to shake you, to shock you – to wake you.

It is not a question of achieving any new thing; it is already your being. Just opening the eyes, just dropping the dreams, just dropping the clouds and the vision – it is a question of clarity and understanding, that's all. Between you and Jesus, between you and me, between you and Buddha there is no difference of being – nothing. You are exactly the same. The difference, at the most, is that you are asleep and Jesus is not asleep, that's all.

So don't ask me how to be oneself; you cannot be otherwise. Just ask me how to be awake. You are yourself *all the time!* Just become a little more alert, just bring a new quality of waking consciousness – just watch. Don't try to be anything because that will again be a dream. Just watch: whosoever you are, wheresoever you are, just watch and be...and allow it. Then the happening, the sudden happening, can come any moment. The heavens can open and the spirit of God, like a dove, can enter in you.

In fact, this is just a way of saying something that cannot be said. It can be said in just the opposite terms also. Let me say it: that when John the Baptist initiated, baptized Jesus, Jesus opened and the spirit of God, like a dove, was released from him and flew into the infinite sky. That is also exactly the same truth. It is just a way of saying it from two polarities.

You are gods and you have never been anything else. That's why I am not worried if you want to sleep a little longer. Nothing is wrong; the choice is up to you. You can have a little more sleep – turn over and have a little more sleep, snore a little longer – nothing is wrong. But don't try to improve, don't try to achieve anything. Don't try to become anything because you are already that which you can become! The being is your only becoming, you carry your destiny within yourself. Relax...and be.

The fourth question:

> Beloved Osho,
> Are you still learning too?

Yes, because if learning stops, you are dead. Learning is life. You can ask me, "Are you still alive?" – that will be the same question.

The ego is a perfectionist and the ego thinks that when you have attained, when you have become enlightened, then there is no learning, then you know all. But if you know all, that 'all' will be finite. Just by being known it has become finite. You cannot know the infinite. The infinite simply means that you can go on learning and learning and learning and the end never comes, it is an eternal journey. It begins, but it never ends. But then the ego thinks: then what is the difference when we are also learning? The difference is that you are learning while fast asleep, unconscious, and a man who is enlightened learns consciously. Your learning is not knowing; your learning is knowledge, dead information. A man who is awakened – his learning is not like knowledge, his learning is simply knowing.

He is like a mirror. The mirror goes on mirroring. A bird flies before a mirror and the mirror mirrors it. Is there a point where you can say, "Now the mirror is perfect. It mirrors nothing"? When the mirror is perfect it will mirror perfectly, that's all.

When you are awakened, you learn perfectly. Not that you stop learning, not that you have become perfect and now there is nothing more to know – just the contrary. The more you know, the more there is to know; the more you open your eyes, the more the infinite surrounds you. It is an infinite journey. I am still learning. And I am happy,

I would not like it to be otherwise. I would not like to come to a point where I could say, "I have known all," because that would be death. Then what? – then the river is frozen, then it no longer flows. No, a perfect river goes on flowing, it is never frozen. I will go on learning, Buddha and Jesus are still learning. It has to be so.

Mahavira is still learning, notwithstanding what Jainas say. They say that he has known all, he has become all-knowing – because their ego is involved. Their master: how can he still be learning? Doesn't that mean he is still not perfect? So Jainas say Mahavira has known all, he has become a *sarvagya* – all-knowing, omniscient. This is their ego, not Mahavira.

If you say to Christians that Jesus is still learning, they will be very angry. The son of God, the only begotten son of God – how can he be still learning? He knows all! But I tell you, he is still learning because he is still alive, alive with the infinity – learning infinitely, but of course learning perfectly.

This is very difficult to understand because your ego always seeks goals and if learning continues for ever and ever, then there is no goal. But I tell you, that's how life is. Life has no goal, it is an ever-flowing river: always reaching, but never reaching; always arriving – but every arrival becomes a new departure. Go to the Himalayas. You trek, you move, you go high to the peak. All the time you were trekking up, there was no peak beyond it. Then you reach the peak and many more peaks are revealed. You go on and on and on; it is an ongoing process.

God is the process. Even God is learning. It has to be so, otherwise he will be stupid. He is not stupid, he is learning. He is evolving – and that's beautiful. Nothing is static, everything is dynamic. That's what I mean when I say: don't say, god is, always say god is happening. Don't use a static term; don't use a noun for him – use a verb. Say he is happening; say he is learning; say he is evolving; say he is a process, he is a river and you will have struck truth.

Yes, I am continuously learning. Every moment life is so tremendously beautiful and so tremendously vast, so tremendously infinite and so tremendously mysterious. To say that one has known all will be sacrilegious.

The fifth question:

> Beloved Osho,
> Why did Jesus constantly talk in
> obscure parables which baffled even
> his disciples most of the time? Was this
> a deliberate technique? Why couldn't he
> be more straightforward like you?

Whoever told you that I am straightforward? While listening to me you may get that impression. Think and meditate on it later on: you will find me more baffling than Jesus. At least he is consistent!

And never ask such questions because these questions show that you are sitting as a judge. Why did Jesus do this or that? If you cannot leave even Jesus out of your judgment, how will you be able to leave out anybody else? Why can't you accept things as they are? "Why is this flower white and not red?" – is it not a foolish question? This flower is red, that flower is white – why?

A small child was walking with D. H. Lawrence in a garden and the child asked, "Why are the trees green?"

D. H. Lawrence looked at the child and said, "They are green because they are green!"

Jesus is Jesus, I am me. Jesus is not there to follow me,

nor am I there to follow him. And it is good that everybody is unique, otherwise life would be a boredom, a monotony. But people are foolish – they go on coming to me and asking me, "Why did Buddha say this, why did Mahavira never say this?" But Mahavira is Mahavira, Buddha is Buddha. The Ganges flows towards the east and the Narmada goes on flowing towards the west – what to do? If all the rivers were flowing towards the east do you think the world would be better? Just think of a world with four thousand million buddhas – can you think of anything more boring? They would start committing suicide: wherever you went you would meet your replica, wherever you would look it would be as if you were always looking in the mirror – only people exactly alike.

No, it is good that everybody is unique. Why do you hanker after such things? Jesus is beautiful in his parables; without parables he would not be beautiful, without parables something would be missing. He is one of the most beautiful storytellers.

And of course the beauty of a parable is that it baffles the reason. But you are childish: you think that a story is perfect when the story gives you the conclusion, the motto. You are just like schoolchildren who can't be satisfied unless the story comes to a conclusion and gives an exact mathematical conclusion to it. Then they are satisfied, but then the story is dead. A perfectly concluded story is dead.

A parable tries to show something, not to say it. It indicates very indirectly; the conclusion has to be supplied by you. It leaves a gap, it gives you some space to find out the conclusion. A parable is creative. When a story is totally complete – like two plus two equals four – then it gives no scope for your imagination, no scope for your meditation.

Then it is simply mathematical. It is no longer poetic, it is dead.

You would like for somebody to say absolutely, exactly, what he means, but then that which is the ultimate meaning cannot be shown to you. The ultimate meaning is always going to be indirect, indicated – said, and yet not said. You feel a vague something, but it is never concrete. If it becomes concrete, it is of this world. If it remains vague and you follow it and you try to find out the clue, in the very effort to find the clue you rise above it – you have already entered into another world.

A parable is not an ordinary story; it is symbolic, it is creative. If you listen to it, if you try to understand it, your understanding will become higher than it was before you heard it. An ordinary story remains below your understanding; you can understand it perfectly because it has nothing beyond it. Parables are of the beyond: one step within your mind, one step without, another step beyond. It is a persuasion.

Jesus constantly talks in parables. He really wants to baffle you because he is talking about something which is ineffable, elusive – mysterium. He is talking about the mysterious. Gaps have to be left for you to fill. Parables should be like puzzles which challenge you, and through the challenge you grow.

And never compare: Why is Jesus like this? The trees are green because they are green. Jesus is just Jesus-like, and he is not like anybody else. That is what I have been insisting continually for you to be also: just be yourself, never be anybody else. Never be a Christian, never be a Hindu, never be a Jaina, because then you are following a pattern and you will miss your soul. The soul is yours – individual, unique – and the pattern is public, collective, social. Never try to be somebody else. Just try to find out who you are and allow it, accept it, welcome it, delight in it, relish it so that it is nourished, so that it grows. Through you, God is trying to become somebody he has never tried before.

God is not repetitive; his creativity is infinite. He never drives the same model again – he is not a Henry Ford. He is absolutely inventive; every day he goes on trying the new, the fresh. He never bothers to repeat a model again, he always goes on improving. He is a great innovator. That's what creativity is. So don't try to become a Jesus – because then God won't receive you.

One Hassid was dying. His name was Josiah. Somebody asked him, "Have you prayed to God, have you made your peace with God? Are you certain that Moses will be a witness to you?"

Josiah looked at the questioner and said, "I am not worried about Moses because when I am facing God I know perfectly well that he will not ask me, 'Josiah, why were you not a Moses?' He will ask me, 'Josiah, why were you not a Josiah?' So I am worried about myself. Stop talking nonsense! Moses – what am I to do with Moses? My whole life has been wasted in it. Now I am dying and I am facing the real question that he will ask me: 'Were you a Josiah or not? I had made you to be somebody special, somebody unique. Did you achieve that peak or not, or have you missed the opportunity?'"

God will certainly ask you, "Were you able to become yourself?" No other question can be asked.

Don't ask such questions: "Why did Jesus constantly talk in obscure parables?" He loves it that way! And a parable has to be obscure, dim, candlelit. Too bright a light kills a parable, too much analysis kills it. It is poetry.

"Was this a deliberate technique?" You can never go beyond the technique, you are too obsessed with the technique. Everything becomes a technique to you. This is the way Jesus is, it is not a question of technique. He is not following a certain technique – he is not a follower of Dale Carnegie. He has never read the book *How to Win Friends and Influence People*. He is not following a technique, he was not an American.

In America, everything has become a technique. Even if you want to make love you go and learn the technique. Can you imagine a more unfortunate day for humanity? Even animals don't ask. They know perfectly well how to make love, they don't go to a school to learn the technique. But in America everything has become a technique. How to be friendly – even that has to be learned. Is man so completely lost that even friendship has to be learned?

People come to me and I go on saying to them, "Laugh!" They ask me how to laugh. How to laugh? – learn from Swami Sardar Gurudayal Singh, he is a perfect master! But I have come across the rumor that people don't allow him to laugh. They say, "Our meditation is disturbed." Your meditation is disturbed by laughter? Then it is not worth anything.

You have to learn *everything*. I think sooner or later you will have to learn how to breathe. It is possible because you follow many other things in the same way. You have to ask how to sleep, how to relax. They were natural once, just like breathing.

Go and ask a primitive. He will simply laugh if you ask, "How do you go so deeply into sleep?"

He will say, "What a foolish question! I simply put my head down and go. There is no *how* to it."

But you will say, "Still, there must be a trick because I try hard and nothing happens. You must be knowing a secret which you are hiding."

He is not hiding anything; that's how it happens. He simply puts down his head and goes to sleep. There is no gap between these two states.

One day or another, man is going to ask how to breathe and then if you say, "You just breathe; there is no *how* to it," he will not believe you. How to love, how to live, how to laugh, how to be happy – these are all simple things, no *how* is needed. These are natural things, they are not techniques.

This is how Jesus is. He loves...the way he says his parables, he loves it! He knows he has an intrinsic knack of how to tell a parable.

A parable is not arithmetic. It should not be too clear, otherwise the point is lost. It should be a persuasion, it should not be an advertisement. It should not argue, because then the point is lost. Then why not argue – why say a parable? It should not give proofs, it should only supply hints, and that too, not completely. Just a few hints so that your being is challenged, you become alert.

I have heard about Chuang Tzu that he was talking to his disciples, and as disciples are, many of them were fast asleep. It must have been late in the night and they were tired and Chuang Tzu was saying difficult things that were beyond them. When something is beyond you, it seems better to rest and sleep than to bother with it. Suddenly Chuang Tzu became aware that many of them were fast asleep and it was useless. They were even snoring and disturbing him. So he told a parable.

He said: "Once it happened that a man had a donkey, and he was traveling on a pilgrimage towards some holy place. But he was very poor, and it came to pass that he was hungry. No money was left, so he sold the donkey on which he was riding to another traveler who was rich. But the next afternoon, when the sun was very hot, the first owner rested in the shadow by the side of the donkey.

"The second owner said, 'This is not good. You have sold the donkey.'

"The first owner said, 'I have sold the donkey, but not the shadow.'"

Everybody became alert — nobody was asleep, nobody was snoring. When you talk about donkeys, donkeys hear it immediately! Chuang Tzu said, "I am finished with the story. Now I come to my point."

But they all said, "Wait! Please finish the story."

Chuang Tzu said, "It was a parable, not a story. You are more interested in donkeys than you are in me."

Now everybody was throbbing with excitement: "What happened? Then what happened?" — but Chuang Tzu left it there, he never completed it. It was not meant to be completed, it was just an indication that the human mind is more interested in stupidities than in higher values and higher things, more interested in foolish things.

But I loved it. It was beautiful of him. He brought all the stupid minds to a certain point — to an indication, to a hint.

Jesus talks in parables for many reasons. But those reasons are not techniques. You can think about them, but they are not techniques. It simply happened naturally to him, he was a good storyteller. But you can think about the reasons he talked in parables. The first: great things can be said if you create a drama around them. If you say them without the drama they fall flat.

That's why stories have a tendency to live, to live forever and ever. The Vedas may disappear, but *Ramayana*, the story of Rama, will not disappear. It is a story; it will be preserved. The Upanishads may disappear, but the parables of Jesus will remain. They hang around you, they become a climate.

You never forget a beautiful story. It is just like...if you sing a beautiful song you will remember it better than if it were prose. If it is poetry, it is remembered well. Somehow it fits with the deepest quality of your mind. If it is a parable, if there is a drama in it, it has a tendency to cling to you. It will come again and again and again; it will become an inner climate.

Bare principles are soon forgotten. And in the days of Jesus, books were not written. All that Jesus was saying was recorded many, many years afterwards. For those many, many years it was just in the memory of the people who had heard him.

A parable can be remembered well. You will forget what I say, but you will never forget the parables, the anecdotes, the jokes. You may forget Mahavira and Moses, but you will not forget Mulla Nasruddin. Mahavira is too far away; Mulla is your neighbor. Mahavira may be somewhere in *moksha*, Mulla is just within you. He is you, you can recognize yourself in him.

So there may be reasons, but don't be bothered about them. It is Jesus' way, and it is good that he never tried anybody else's way. In Judaism there were prophets, great prophets: Jeremiah, Ezekiel.... They had their own way. Even John the Baptist never used any parable.

This has to be understood. Prophets are something special to Judaism. They don't exist anywhere else. Mystics are everywhere: Buddha is a mystic, not a prophet; Mahavira is a mystic, not a prophet. A mystic is one who has attained to God; a prophet is one to whom God has come. It exists only in Judaism – the concept of prophets –

because only in Judaism does God seek man. In all other religions, man seeks God.

When man seeks God and finds him, he is a mystic. When God seeks man and finds him, he is a prophet. When man comes to God he is a mystic; when God comes to man he is a prophet. When the drop drops into the ocean he is a mystic. When the ocean drops into the drop then he is a prophet.

A prophet is a very mad and fiery man. Of course, he has to be: the ocean has come to him. Jeremiah, Ezekiel, John the Baptist – they are prophets, mad people, mad people of God. They speak fire, they don't talk in parables. Their sentences are acidic; they will burn you. They cannot soothe you.

Buddha is very soothing, Krishna is just like a lullaby that surrounds you, soothes you, consoles you, heals you. A prophet simply burns you with an unknown desire, makes you mad. Jesus is both a prophet and a mystic, one who has come to God and one to whom God has also come. Sometimes he talks like John the Baptist and sometimes he talks like Krishna. Sometimes he soothes and sometimes he wounds. He is a very deep balancing phenomenon: a prophet and a mystic both. That's why you will find in him a synthesis. You will find in him all that is in Judaism – all that is beautiful and great – and you will find in him all that is beautiful in Krishna, Buddha, Mahavira; Jainism, Hinduism, Buddhism.

Jesus is a culmination point, as if all the religions of the world meet in him and reach to a crescendo. He talks sometimes as a prophet: he invokes, provokes – he calls you. But that is not his only quality. He soothes; he says parables, he consoles, he gives you a lullaby. He wakes you, and he helps you to sleep also. But that is the way he is. All explanations are explanations after the fact, remember.

The basic thing is that this is the way he is, and no other way is possible for him.

Socrates was poisoned. The court decided that he should be murdered, but the people loved him very much – even in the court almost half of them were in favor of him. So they gave him an opportunity. They told him, "If you stop talking about the truth, if you keep quiet, you can be pardoned and your death can be avoided."

Socrates said, "That will be impossible. That will be more deathly than death, because to talk about truth is the only way I know to be. It will be worse than death. So please kill me, because if you leave me and you say I have to keep quiet, it will be impossible.

That's not the way I am. To talk about truth is the only business I know – the *only* business I know. It is the only way I am. I cannot promise that I will stop talking truth because even if I stop, even in my silence only truth will be spoken. So I cannot promise that. You had better kill me."

And he was killed.

This is very meaningful. A Socrates is a Socrates. A Socrates is a Socrates, and there is no other way. All explanations are explanations *after*. But don't be bothered about them. Love if you can – and if you cannot love Jesus, forget about him and find somebody else you can love. Don't be bothered about explanations and reasonings and proofs.

Only love will help you to understand, nothing else. When you love a person – whosoever he is: Jesus or Krishna – when you love a person, you immediately understand him, that that's the way he is. Then you don't want him to be otherwise. Love never wants to change anybody. Love accepts, understands.

The last question:

> Beloved Osho,
> Is there any mystery behind your answer when you also tell the name of the questioner? Please explain it – but please don't tell my name because sometimes it is too heavy.

This is from a sannyasin.... I will not tell you the name, because deep down she wants her name to be told. This is not the first time she has asked the question; I have been avoiding this question many times.

Deep down she wants her name to be told so that it becomes a part of history, part of the record. This is her last effort now. She is trying to play a trick by saying, "Please don't tell my name," so that I can be provoked.

But you cannot provoke me....

Enough for today.

CHAPTER 7

Have Mercy And Not Sacrifice

**Have Mercy
And Not
Sacrifice**

Matthew 9

9 And as Jesus passed forth from thence,
he saw a man, named Matthew,
sitting at the receipt of custom:
and he saith unto him,
"Follow me."
And he arose, and followed him.

10 And it came to pass,
as Jesus sat at meat in the house,
behold, many publicans and sinners
came and sat down with him
and his disciples.

11 And when the Pharisees saw it,
they said unto his disciples,
"Why eateth your Master
with publicans and sinners?"

12 But when Jesus heard that,
he said unto them,
"They that be whole need not a physician,
but they that are sick."

13 "But go ye and learn what that meaneth,
I will have mercy, and not sacrifice:
for I am not come to call the righteous,
but sinners to repentance."

Luke 9

23 And he said to them all,
"If any man will come after me,
let him deny himself, and take up
his cross daily, and follow me."

24 "For whosoever will save his life shall lose it:
but whosoever will lose his life for my sake,
the same shall save it."

25 "For what is a man advantaged,
if he gain the whole world,
and lose himself, or be cast away?"

Religion is basically, essentially, a rebellion. It is not conformity, it is not belonging to any organization, society, church, because all belonging comes out of fear – and religion is freedom. There is fear in being alone. One likes to belong – to a nation, to a church, to a society, because when you belong to the crowd you forget your loneliness. It does not disappear, but you become oblivious to it. You deceive yourself, you create a dream around you, as if you are not alone. You remain alone all the same; this is just an intoxicant.

Religion is not an intoxicant. It does not give you unconsciousness, it gives you awareness. And awareness is rebellious. When you become aware, you cannot belong to any society, to any nation, to any church, because when you become aware you become aware of the austere beauty of aloneness. You become aware of the music that is continuously happening within your soul...but you have never allowed yourself to be alone to hear it, to be in rapport with it, to be one with it.

Religion is not conformity because all conformity is mechanical. You do certain things because you are expected to do them. You do them because you have to live with people and you have to follow their rules; you do them because you have been conditioned to do them. You go to church, you go to the temple, you pray, you follow rituals, but everything is empty. Unless your heart is in it, everything is dead and mechanical. You may do everything exactly as it is prescribed, with no error — it may be perfect — but then too, it is dead.

I have heard that President Kennedy had to sign so many letters, autographs and personalized pictures that a small mechanism was invented for him. The machine used to sign for him, and the signature was so perfect that no expert was able to say which was mechanical and which was true — not even President Kennedy himself was able to say which was false and which was true. Malcolm Muggeridge reports that when Kennedy was killed they forgot to turn the machine off, so it continued. The President continued to sign personalized letters even when he was dead. A mechanism is a mechanism.

You become a Christian: then you become a mechanism. You go on behaving as if you really loved Christ, but that 'as if' has to be remembered. You become a Buddhist: you go on behaving as if you follow Buddha, but that 'as if' has not to be forgotten. Your signature may be perfect, but it is coming out of a dead mechanism.

Religion is not conformity. Conformity is between the individual and the past, and religion is something between the individual and the present — poetry is something between the individual and the future. Conformity means to conform with those people who are no more, the dead — to conform with Moses, with Mahavira. Now to conform with Jesus is a dead thing; you are conforming with the past. If you relate to the present, it is totally different. It revolutionizes you; it gives you a rebirth.

Conformity is between the individual and the society. Religion is something between the individual and existence itself. Society is our creation. God created Adam — not humanity; God created Eve — not humanity. God creates individuals; humanity is our fiction. But the fiction can take possession of you and you can forget the real and you can cling to the fiction. I know persons who want to love humanity and they cannot love a human being. Where is humanity and how are you going to love humanity? You can only make empty gestures in the air. Humanity is nowhere. Wherever you come across it, you will come across real, concrete human beings. Humanity is an abstraction, a mere word. It has no reality in it – a soap bubble, nothing more. You can only come across real human beings. To love a real human being is very difficult, but to love humanity is very easy. It is almost as if you love nobody. To love humanity is equal to loving nobody. Then there is no problem, no difficulty.

Religion is something that happens between you and the concrete existence. It is not about fictions. Also, religion is not about tradition. Tradition belongs to time; religion belongs to eternity. To move into religion you have to move in the eternal now. Religion has no history – there the West has to learn something from the East.

In the East we have never bothered about history. The reason...? The reason is simple. All history is about time, that which happens in time is recorded in history. History is a dead book. We have never bothered about history because religion belongs to eternity: you cannot record it as an event; it is an eternal process. You can only record the essential fact of it, the essential truth of it, not the ripples that are made in the river of time. That's why if you go to a Jaina temple and see the twenty-four *tirthankaras* you will be confused about who is who. They all look alike. You will not be able to make any sense out of it – why do these twenty-four tirthankaras of the Jainas all look alike? They cannot be alike...they existed in different ages, they were different individuals. But we have not bothered about events in time.

'Body' is an event in time. The difference in bodies is past history, but the innermost being, which is in eternity, is the same within me, within you, within everybody. The form differs, but the innermost center is the same. Those twenty-four tirthankaras in the Jaina temples say something about the innermost being, that's why they have been sculpted to be similar. Look at Buddha. He also looks like Mahavira; there is no difference. They are not facts, they are truths. Religion is not concerned about facts, it is concerned about truth.

The facts can be learned from books – truth, never. If you become too involved with the facts, your eyes will be clouded and confused and you will not be able to know the truth. Beware of facts! – they can lead you astray. Sort out the truth. Always try to find the truth; don't be bothered too much about facts. Facts are irrelevant. That which changes is the fact and that which remains always the same is the truth. Your body is a fact: one day you were a child, now you are a young man or an old man; one day you were born, one day you will die – the body changes. But the *you* who abides in the body, who has made it a temporary abode – that 'you' is eternal, that is the truth. It is formless, it has no qualities. It is immortal, it is eternity.

Religion is not a tradition, so you cannot borrow religion. You will have to risk yourself, you will have to earn it. You will have to stake your life for it; that is the only way there is. You cannot get it cheap. If you want to get it cheap, you will get a counterfeit.

Religion is not consolation. It is, on the contrary, a challenge: God challenges man, God haunts man, God goes on crying, "Return! Enthrone me." He will not leave you at rest. He will go on knocking at your doors, he will go on creating storms in your being, in your spirit. He will go on stirring you. He will not allow you to settle for less. Unless you attain to the ultimate you will not be allowed to rest. Religion is a challenge, it is a great storm. It is like death. It is not a consolation.

But the so-called religions, the organized religions, are consolations. They console you, they hide your wounds. They don't stir you, they don't call and invoke you. They don't ask you to be adventurous, they don't ask you to be daring, they don't attract you to move in a dangerous life. They are like lubricants.

In a society with so many people you need lubricants around you so that there is not so much conflict. You can move easily, movement is not very difficult, and you don't rub against the neighbor. No conflict arises – the lubricant goes on flowing around you. You go to church as a lubricant. It helps, it helps in a social way; it is a formality. Filled full, you become respectable. It is just like becoming a member of the Rotary Club – it is respectable, it helps. You become a member of a church, that too helps. You become a member of a religion, that too helps. People think you are religious, and when people believe you are, you can deceive them more easily. When you have a garb around you that you are religious, you have a potential weapon with you. Your religion is a consolation to yourself and a respect-ability. In fact, it is politics, a diplomacy – part of your struggle to survive, part of your ambition, part of the whole politics of the ego. It is power politics.

These things have to be remembered when you try to understand Jesus. Also religion is not morality. Morality, again, is just the rules of the game. Those who want to play the game of the society have to follow the rules of it – just like when you play cards you have to follow certain rules. Not that those rules have any ultimacy about them, not that they come from God. You create the game, you create the rules, you follow the rules. But if you want to play, you have to follow the rules.

Morality has nothing ultimate in it. That's why every society has its own morality, every culture has its own morality. One thing can be moral in India and can be immoral in America; another thing can be moral in America and may be immoral in India. If morality is really real, then it cannot differ.

In India, to divorce a woman or a man is immoral. It is not thought to be good. Once you are married you have to live with your partner. But in America, if you live with a woman you don't love it will be thought immoral. If you don't love, then it is immoral to sleep with that woman. Only love, only a deep love allows you to be with the woman. Otherwise, leave her. Don't deceive her, don't waste her life.

Morality is a game; it changes. From society to society, age to age, period to period, it goes on changing. It depends, it has nothing ultimate about it.

But religion is ultimate. It has nothing to do with America or India. It has something to do with a new consciousness within the individual. It is a sunrise in the individual, it is a new being arising and expanding in the individual. You have a new look, you have new eyes through it. You can see the old problems, but they disappear. Not that they are solved – they simply disappear, they dissolve. With a new eye, they cannot be there. You have a new vision, a new dimension. These things have to be remembered because when a Jesus – a man like Jesus – comes, these things become the problem.

I have heard an Arabian proverb: it says – "Show a man too many camels' bones or show them to him too often, and he will not be able to recognize a camel when he comes across a live one."

"Show a man camels' bones too many times, or too often, and" – the Arabian saying says – "that man will not be able to recognize a camel when he comes across a live one." This happens when a Jesus comes to the world. You have seen so many phony priests, you have seen so many hocus-pocus preachers, you have seen so many scholars, not knowing anything but creating much fuss about it, that when a Jesus comes you cannot recognize him. Whenever a Jesus or a Buddha comes, it becomes almost impossible to recognize him. For the majority, it is almost impossible. Only a few rare beings who have some potentiality, or who are a little alert, only they can have a few glimpses.

To recognize a Jesus is a great achievement because that means you have a certain consciousness which can relate to Jesus. You have a certain quality which can relate to Jesus: you are already on the way to becoming a Jesus yourself. You can only recognize that which you already have within you – opening, flowering. It may be just a bud, but you can recognize a little bit, your eyes are not completely closed.

There are priests who are pretenders. To them, religion is a trade. It is a livelihood, not their life. To Jesus, religion is life; to the rabbis, to the priests, it is a livelihood. Then there are scholars who go on talking about nothing – and they can talk so much, they are so articulate, that you will never be able to recognize the fact that, deep within, they are empty.

I have heard about one international competition. A competition was arranged, essays were invited, from many countries. The subject of the competition was 'The Elephant'. The Englishman immediately went to South Africa with cameras and a group of followers, and he investigated the whole thing. He came back after six months and wrote a book – well-printed, illustrated. The title of the book was *Hunting the Elephant in South Africa*.

The Frenchman never went anywhere. Every day he simply went to visit the elephant house in the zoo in Paris. After two, three weeks he started to write a book – a very carelessly printed book, not even hard-cover, just a paperback. The title of the book was *The Love Life of the Elephant*.

The Indian, who had been appointed by the Indian Government, was a man who had never seen an elephant because he had always remained in the Himalayas. He was a great *yogi* and poet and Sanskrit scholar. He never even went to the zoo. He wrote a big book, a great treatise. The title was *The Divine Elephant*. It was written in the form of poetry and he quoted great Sanskrit books, from the Vedas up to Shree Aurobindo. Anybody who read the book had the impression that this man had never seen an elephant. He was a poet, he may have seen one in his dreams. He talked about the elephant which was seen by Buddha's mother before he was conceived...mythology, a white elephant.

And last of all, the Germans. They appointed six professors of philosophy to write the book. They went to all the museums and libraries, all over the world to study everything that is written about the elephant. They never went to see any elephant or any zoo – just museums and libraries. They searched all over, they took almost six years, and they wrote a book – twelve volumes, almost an *Encyclopaedia Britannica*. The title of the book was *A Short Introduction to the Study of the Elephant*. Professors of philosophy – what do they have to do with elephants? And that too, a short introduction – a prolegomenon. It was not even about the elephant! It was just an introduction to the study of the elephant.

When a Jesus comes, you are already too much in the know. You have read the books, you have listened to the scholars, you have listened to the priests, you are too full of ideas, and when Jesus or a man like Jesus comes, you simply cannot recognize him. The live animal is there and you have become too addicted to the dead bones. To recognize Jesus means you will have to put aside all that you know already.

Jesus was not murdered by bad men, he was not murdered by criminals; he was murdered by very respectable rabbis. In fact, religious people killed him. Religion is never in danger from irreligious people because they don't bother about it. Religion is always in danger from the so-called religious, because their whole life is at stake. If Jesus is right, then all the rabbis are wrong. If Jesus is right, then the whole tradition is wrong. If Jesus is right, then the whole Church is wrong.

Everybody stands against Jesus. Jesus is always alone, very alone. You cannot understand his aloneness. Whatsoever you know about aloneness is a physical aloneness. Sometimes no one is in the house, the house is dark and you are alone. The electricity has also gone so you cannot put on the light, you cannot put on the radio or the TV. You are suddenly thrown into aloneness. But this is a physical sense of aloneness; you don't know what Jesus feels.

He is spiritually alone, amidst strangers, where it is so difficult to find a friend who will recognize you. He goes on looking into each and everybody he meets on the path, penetrating, gazing deep in the eyes. Nobody recognizes him, nobody understands him. Rather, people misunderstand him. They are ready to jump into misunderstanding, but nobody is ready in any way to understand him.

Whenever there is a religious being, the so-called religious are all against him. They would like to kill him immediately so the danger is avoided and their security again becomes certain.

Remember, he was killed by very good people! You go…it is still the same. Go around Pune and ask the so-called good people: you will always find them against me. They have to be – their whole way of life is in danger! They are afraid to even listen to me, because who knows? – a truth may strike home. They won't come near me, they won't read my books; they cannot take that much risk. They always have opinions of their own.

One day it happened, I witnessed a beautiful scene.

A man was talking to Mulla Nasruddin. The man said, "Why are you so miserly and so stingy towards your wife?"

Mulla said, "You must have heard something wrong about me because, as far as I know, I am generally a very generous man."

The man became angry, because whenever you challenge anybody's opinion he becomes angry. He became angry and he said, "Stop defending yourself. Everybody in the whole town knows that you are too hard on your wife. Even for day-to-day expenses she has to beg you like a beggar. And stop defending yourself. Everybody knows it!"

Nasruddin said, "Okay, if you are so angry, I will not defend myself. But can I say one thing, just one thing?"

The man said loudly, "What?"

Nasruddin said, "That I am not married."

Since that day that man is against Nasruddin.

Once I met him and I told him that since Mulla Nasruddin is not married, the whole thing is baseless. "Your whole argument is baseless. Why are you angry?"

He said, "It makes no difference, it is only a question of time. Wait, sooner or later he will be married and then I will be right! I am still telling the truth. It is only a question of time. Wait, my opinion cannot be wrong."

People cling to their opinions – baseless – but still they cling. The more baseless the opinion, the more people cling to it.

If it is based on right grounds there is no need to cling; it is true in itself. When it is baseless, your clinging is needed because only your clinging can become the base. Remember always, if you know something is true, you never get angry if somebody contradicts it. You get angry in the same proportion as you know it is not true. Anger shows that you have just a mere opinion, no knowledge.

People were very much against Jesus because he was ruining all their edifices. They were thinking their houses were built on rocks and just his presence showed them that their houses were built on sand, they were already falling. They jumped on him, they killed him. He was not killed by the political powers, he was killed by the pseudo-religious powers, by the priests.

This is my understanding: that if religion has disappeared in the world today, it is not because of science – no, it is not because of atheists – no, it is not because of rationalists – no. It is because of pseudo-religion. There is too much pseudo-religion and it is so bogus, phony, that only people who are phony can be interested in religion. People who have even an iota of reality will go against it, they will rebel.

Real people have always been rebellious, because reality wants to assert its being, to express its freedom. Real people are not slaves. Remember this, then we will enter into the sentences.

> And as Jesus passed forth from thence,
> he saw a man, named Matthew,
> sitting at the receipt of custom:
> and he saith unto him,
> "Follow me."
> And he arose, and followed him.

The whole thing seems to be a little unreal. The world has changed so much it looks more like drama than real life. Jesus comes and says to a man who is sitting in the customs, working there — maybe a clerk or somebody — he simply looks at him and says, "Follow me." *And he arose, and followed him.* It looks like a drama, not reality, because the reality that we know today is absolutely different. The world has changed, the human mind has changed.

For these past three centuries the human mind has been trained to doubt. Before Jesus, for centuries continuously, the human mind lived on trust, lived on the simplicity of the heart. People's eyes were clear. This Matthew, an ordinary man, must have looked into Jesus' eyes...the way he walked, the presence that he brought with himself, the penetrating look that stirred the heart — he touched something deep.

It rarely happens today. I come across so many people, but rarely do I see a person so open that whatsoever I say simply reaches to the heart and becomes a seed immediately, with no time wasted. Otherwise, people are protecting. They come to me and they say they would like to surrender, they would like to follow me, but I see a great armor around them — very subtle, but they are protecting from everywhere. They won't allow any space for me to enter in them. If I try too hard, then they become too protective. They go on saying that they would like to relax and let go: their mouths say something, their bodies show something else. Their thoughts are something, but their reality is just contradictory.

People were simple in Jesus' time. They must have just looked, and when Jesus said, "Follow me," they simply followed. It was natural. When these gospels were written, those who were writing these gospels were not aware that some day these things would look fictitious. It was so natural in those days that the gospel writers could not imagine that some day the thing would look false, would not sound real – it is happening now all over the world.

Move with Buddha: a different quality of humanity surrounds him.

Prasanjita, a king, came to see Buddha. He was Buddha's father's friend – both were kings – and when he heard that his friend's son had renounced the world, he was very worried. When Buddha came to his capital town, he went to see him and to persuade him.

He said to Buddha, "What have you done? If you are not happy with your father, come and be in my palace. Get married to my daughter, I have only one daughter, and this kingdom will be yours. But don't move like a beggar; it hurts. You are the only son of your father – what are you doing? Both these kingdoms will be yours. Come to my home."

Buddha looked into Prasanjita's eyes and said, "Just one question. Have you attained to any happiness through your kingdom? Just say yes or no. If you say yes, I follow you. If you say no, then you have to follow me."

Prasanjita fell to Buddha's feet and said, "No. I renounce. Initiate me. I leave all this." A very different quality of immediacy.

The same thing happened to me, the same. One of my father's friends was a lawyer, a very cunning lawyer. When I came back home from the university, of course my parents were worried. They wanted me to get married and settle, but they didn't want to say it directly to me. They knew that to say it directly would be like interfering in my life, and they are very nonaggressive, silent, simple. So they thought about their friend and they asked the friend to come.

He came with all his arguments ready – he was a lawyer!

He said, "If I convince you that marriage is a must, will you get married?"

I said, "Of course. But if you cannot, then are you ready to leave your wife and children?"

The man had not thought of that! He said, "Then I will have to think."

He never came back. The quality of the mind has changed — otherwise there was an opportunity for him, an opening of the sky. I waited and waited, but he never came. He became afraid because everybody knows that life as you have lived it has not given you anything. But one needs courage to say that, because just in saying that a deep renunciation happens. You have already moved on another path once you realize the fact that life as you have lived it has been futile, fruitless, irrelevant.

Saith Jesus unto him: *"Follow me." And he arose, and followed him.* What a beautiful world, what a beautiful consciousness! You can have that consciousness, and through it everything becomes possible, even the impossible becomes possible.

Try. Drop the doubts, because whenever you doubt you are destructive. Doubt is destructive; trust is creative. Doubt kills, doubt is poison. Trust gives you life, life abundant, infinite life, because when you trust you relax.

In trust there is no fear, in trust there is no need to defend, in trust there is no struggle. You let go, you flow with the river. You don't even swim, the river takes you to the ocean. It is already going to the ocean. You fight unnecessarily, and through fight you destroy your energy. Through fight you get frustrated, and through fight the whole opportunity is lost in which you could have danced, in which you could have celebrated. The same energy becomes a struggle…the same energy can become surrender.

> And it came to pass,
> as Jesus sat at meat in the house,
> behold, many publicans and sinners
> came and sat down with him
> and his disciples.

This has to be understood. It is a very delicate point that whenever a man like Jesus is on the earth, sinners recognize him before your so-called righteous people — because sinners have nothing to lose except their sins. Sinners don't have opinionated minds; they don't have theologies and scriptures. Sinners have a sense that their lives have been futile, sinners have an urgency to repent and return. But the so-called respectable people — trustees of temples and churches, mayors, politicians, leaders, pundits, scholars — have much to lose and no urgency of being, no intensity to transform themselves, no desire in fact. They are dull and dead. Sinners are more alive than your so-called saints, and sinners are more courageous than your so-called saints. To come near, to come close to Jesus needs courage.

Have you watched that your so-called saints are not really religious, but simply people who are afraid? Afraid of hell, afraid of God's punishment...or greedy, greedy and ambitious to achieve heaven: the awards and blessings of God. But they are not truly religious. When you are truly religious you don't bother about hell and heaven, you don't bother about anything. This very moment you are so deeply in heaven — who bothers about the heaven which comes after death?

Sinners are more courageous, they risk. And, *behold, many publicans and sinners came and sat down with him and his disciples.*

> And when the Pharisees saw it...

— the respectable people, the righteous —

> ...they said unto his disciples,
> "Why eateth your Master
> with publicans and sinners?"

Their mind is always concerned with such foolish things: with whom you are eating, with whom you are sitting. They don't look directly into Jesus; they are more interested in with whom he is sitting. He is sitting with sinners — now, that is their problem. Jesus does not create any ripple in their being, but the sinners create anxiety. How can they come and sit with this master?

Sinners are there. The condemned people, for whom they have invented hell, are sitting there. Your so-called saints won't allow those sinners to be so close — never. They would not like to be in their company at all. Why? Why are your saints so afraid of sinners? They are afraid of their own inner fear, afraid that if they are with sinners it is more possible that the sinners will convert them than the possibility of the sinners being converted by the saints. They are afraid. They are afraid of their own sinner inside them. That's why there is the fear of the sinner outside. Always remember that whatsoever you say ultimately refers to you, not to anything else. If you are afraid to go to a place where drunkards gather together, it shows simply that you have a certain tendency towards alcohol, intoxicants, and you are afraid. Otherwise why fear? — you can be at ease there. Nobody can corrupt you except yourself.

They said unto his disciples.... This too has to be remembered: they didn't say it to him. I know those Pharisees who are around. They will say it to you, they will not come to say it to me. They say it to the disciples — because even to come to Jesus to say it is dangerous. The man may hypnotize you, it is risky – just talk to the disciples. Such impotent people have become so important; they hold all the key posts in the world, they hold all power, and they are absolutely impotent. They are not even ready to come and face Jesus.

"Why eateth your Master with publicans and sinners?" – as if sinners are not human beings. And as if these people themselves are not sinners. Who is there who can say that "I am not a sinner"? To be here in this world is to be somehow or other involved in sin. Nobody can claim otherwise.

When the whole humanity is involved in sin, how can you be out of it? You are part. If sin is happening somewhere, I am part of it because I am part of humanity. I create the climate – maybe a very tiny part of it, but I also create the climate. A Vietnam happens: I am part of it; I am the sinner. How can I think of myself as out of it? Whatsoever any human being is doing anywhere, he is part of me and I am part of him. We are members of each other.

A real saint always feels humble because he knows that he is also a sinner. Only a false saint feels proud and thinks that he is above. Nobody is above. If there is any God, he must be part of your sin also. And he knows it, because he is involved in you. He beats in your heart, he breathes in you, and if you commit sin, he is a part of it. Only so-called saints – dummies, not real – can think otherwise and be proud.

> But when Jesus heard that,
> he said unto them,
> "They that be whole need not a physician,
> but they that are sick."

He simply said, "Those who are sick need the physician. I am the physician, so the sick people have come to me." It should be the criterion: around a saint, sinners will gather together. This should be the criterion. If you see a saint and only respectable people are around him, he is no saint at all. The physician is false, because whenever a great physician comes into the world, people who are ill are bound to rush to him. They are bound to crowd the man because their need is there. They want to be whole and healed, and the physician has come.

"They that be whole need not a physician, but they that are sick."
But the reverse is not true, remember. A sinner needs a saint, but if you think that you don't need a saint, it does not mean that you are not a sinner. A sick man seeks a physician and there is no need for a healthy man to seek a physician, but just by not seeking a physician, don't deceive yourself that you are healthy. Remember that the reverse is not true. That's why in the next sentence Jesus says:

"But go ye and learn what that meaneth…"

He said, "This is the truth: sinners are bound to seek me and sick people are bound to come to me. I am a physician of their soul. Those who are healthy, I am not for them; they need not come. *"But go ye and learn what that meaneth…"* it is not simple. Go and meditate over it. You may be ill yourself and you need me, but you have just been thinking that you are not ill."

The greatest illness that can happen to a man is when he is ill and thinks that he is not ill. Then nobody can cure him, then no medicine will help him. Then the physician may be next door, but the man will die uncured. This is the greatest misfortune that can befall a man: to be sick and to think himself healthy.

"But go ye and learn what that meaneth,
I will have mercy, and not sacrifice…"

This is one of the most significant sayings that Jesus has ever uttered. This is his whole secret: *"I will have mercy, and not sacrifice...."* Mahavira is not so merciful, Mohammed not so merciful, even the compassionate Buddha is not so merciful as Jesus, because they all say that you will have to sacrifice, you will have to change your ways and you will have to account for your past *karmas*.

In India we have talked about compassion long enough, but we have continuously been talking about karma. One has to keep all accounts and whatever bad deeds you have done, you will have to cancel them by good deeds. You will have to come to a balance, only then can the accounts be closed. This is what Jesus means by sacrifice.

He says: *"I will have mercy...."* This is his key secret. What does he mean when he says *"I will have mercy..."*? He means that it is almost impossible for you to cancel all the bad karmas that you have committed because the whole thing is tremendous, vast. Millions of lives you have been doing things and all that you have done has been wrong, has to be wrong, because you have been unconscious. How can you do anything good while unconscious? You have done millions of things, but all are wrong.

While one is asleep one cannot do anything that is good. Virtue is impossible in unconsciousness, only sin is possible. Unconsciousness is the source of sin. You have done so many sins that it seems almost impossible: how will you get out of this? The very effort doesn't seem probable, the very effort seems hopeless. Jesus says, "Mercy will do it. Just surrender to me." Jesus says: "and I will have mercy." What does he mean? He simply means that "If you can trust me and trust that you have been forgiven, you are forgiven" – because all those karmas have been committed in an unconscious sleep. You are not responsible for them.

This is the key message of Jesus: that man is not responsible unless he is alert. It is as if a child has committed a sin. No court will punish the child because they will say the child doesn't know, he has done it unaware. He had no intention of doing it, it has simply happened, he is not responsible. Or a madman has committed a crime, murdered somebody. The court, once it is proved that the man is mad, has to forgive, because a madman cannot be responsible. Or a drunkard has done something and it is proved that he was drunk, absolutely drunk. You can, at the most, punish him for his drinking. You cannot punish him for the act.

Jesus says, "I have come. I will have mercy." It does not mean that it is up to Jesus to forgive you, remember. That has been a mistake. Christians have been thinking that since Jesus is the only begotten son of God, and he is merciful, there is no need to do anything. Just pray to him, confess your sin. He is merciful, he will forgive you.

In fact, Jesus is just an excuse. He is saying this: that if you become alert and become aware that you were unconscious in whatsoever you have been doing up to now, hitherto, the very awareness that you were unconscious, the very realization, forgives, becomes the forgiveness. Not that Jesus is doing anything.

It is just like when I promise you that if you surrender to me, I will transform you. There is no promise and I am not going to do anything. You surrender, that's all, and the transformation happens. But it will be difficult for you to surrender if there is nobody to surrender to. Then you will say, "To whom do I surrender?" It will be almost impossible, absurd. Just surrendering, without anybody there to surrender to? You will feel yourself absurd: what are you doing? – somebody is needed to surrender to. That is just an excuse.

When I say, "I promise I will transform you," I am not going to do anything, because nobody can transform you. But if you surrender...in the very *effort*....When you surrender, the ego is surrendered and transformation happens because the ego is the only barrier. It is because of the ego that you are not changing; it is because of the ego that your heart is burdened by rock and you are not throbbing well. Once the rock is put away....

You have become so addicted to the rock that you say, " Unless I find some golden lotus feet, I am not going to surrender this rock." So I say, "Okay, let my feet be the excuse." You have become so addicted to the rock that you think that unless you find lotus feet, golden feet, unless you find a god you are not going to surrender, because the rock is very valuable. It is because of your foolishness that I have to play god. So I say, "Okay, let me be the god. But please, surrender your rock so your heart starts throbbing well – you start feeling, loving, being."

When Jesus says, *"I will have mercy...,"* he is saying the same thing. He is saying, "I am here to forgive you. You just surrender. Come follow me, and...

> "...I will have mercy, and not sacrifice:
> for I am not come to call the righteous,
> but sinners to repentance."

This is tremendously beautiful. Every time a Buddha, a Jesus or a Krishna happens, this is what they come for.

"I am not come to call the righteous...." In the first place, they never listen to the call. The righteous are dead people; they are deaf, they are too full of their own noise. They are so certain about their virtues. They don't have any earth to stand on, but in their beliefs, in their imagination, they think that they are standing on a well-founded ground. They have no foundation – their edifice is just as if a child has made a house of playing cards: a little breeze

and the house will be gone. But they believe in it. The house exists only in their imagination.

In the first place, they will not listen to the call. In the second place, if you insist too much they will get angry. In the third place, if you are stubborn, as Jesus was, they will kill you. And in the fourth place, when you are dead they will worship you. This is how things go.

"For I am not come to call the righteous, but sinners to repentance." In fact, to realize that you are a sinner is already a transformation. The moment you recognize that you are a sinner, you have repented. There is no other repentance.

Look at it in this way. In the night you are fast asleep and dreaming. If you realize that you are dreaming, what does it mean? It means that now you are no longer asleep. Once you become aware that you are dreaming, you are awake. Once you become aware that you are asleep, you are no longer asleep – finished. The sleep has already left you.

To remain a sinner one needs to continuously think to himself that he is not a sinner, he is a virtuous man. To hide the sin, one needs the confidence that one is righteous, not a sinner. Sometimes the people who call themselves righteous think that even if they sin sometimes it is just to protect their virtue, to protect their righteousness.

It happened:

India and Pakistan were at war and everybody was in a war mood. Even Jaina saints were in a war mood. At least *they* shouldn't have been – they have been preaching nonviolence for centuries. But I came across the news that Acharya Tulsi, one of the greatest Jaina *munis*, had given his blessings to the war. What did he say?

He said it was "to protect the country of nonviolence. Even if violence has to be done, it has to be done – to protect the country of Buddha, Mahavira, Gandhi."

Do you see the trick? Nonviolence has to be protected by violence. One has to go to war so that peace reigns. I have to kill you because I love you; I am doing it for your sake.

A man who thinks he is a sinner has already surrendered. He realizes the fact that "I am a sinner and I have done nothing else except sin and sin. It is not that sometimes I have committed a sin. Rather, on the contrary, I am a sinner. It is not a question of actions; it is a continuity of unconsciousness. I am a sinner and whether I have done something wrong or not is irrelevant. Sometimes I don't do anything wrong, but still I am a sinner."

'The sinner' is a quality of unconsciousness. It has nothing to do with actions. For twenty-four hours you may not have done anything wrong – you may have remained in the house, fasting, sitting silently, meditating; you have not done anything wrong – but still you remain a sinner. If you are unconscious, you are a sinner.

Your being a sinner is not the result of your sins you have committed. Your being a sinner is simply the state of unconsciousness. You are not a sinner because you do sins. You do sins because you are a sinner. It is a continuity of unconsciousness – a continuum, without any gap. Once you realize this, the very realization is an awakening. The morning has come, it has knocked on the door of your home: you are aware. Yet awareness is fragile, very delicate: you can fall asleep again – yes, that is a possibility – but still you are aware. You can use this moment and come out of the bed.

> "...for I am not come to call the righteous,
> but sinners to repentance."
>
> And he said to them all,
> "If any man will come after me,

let him deny himself, and take up
his cross daily, and follow me."

"*If any man will come after me...*if you have decided to come after me, then this is what you have to do." This is the discipline, the only discipline Jesus ever gave: *"...let him deny himself...."* When you come to a man like Jesus, you have to drop your own ideas and the ego. You have to drop completely your own decisions because only if you drop your ideas, decisions, ego, can Jesus penetrate you. Soon you will not need Jesus – once you have dropped your ego, things will start happening to you on your own – but as a first step: *"...let him deny himself...."*

Look...you can come to me and surrender. But it is possible that the surrender may be your idea. Then it is no longer a surrender. The surrender is surrender when it is my idea, not yours. If it is your idea, then it is not surrender – you are following your idea.

It happens every day. Somebody comes here and I ask him, "Would you like to move into sannyas?"

He says, "Wait, I have to think about it."

I say to him, "If you think about it, then it will be your sannyas, not mine."

Then you think and you come to a conclusion, but it is your ego thinking and coming to a conclusion. Then you take sannyas, but you have missed the opportunity. The opportunity was there when I had asked you to take a jump. Had you taken it without any consideration on your part that would have been a repentance, a turning, a conversion. If you think, it's okay, but it is simply okay, nothing more. You have come in, it is your idea you are following. There is no surrender in it. Deny yourself.

And the second thing: *"...and take up his cross daily...."* A life with Jesus is a life moment to moment. It is not a planning for the future. It has no plan; it is spontaneous. One has to live moment to moment *"...and take up his cross daily...."*

And why a cross? – because surrender is death. And why a cross? – because surrender is pain. Why a cross? – because surrender is suffering. Your whole ego will suffer and burn. Your ideas, your past, your personality, will be on fire continuously. Hence, the cross. The cross is a symbol of death ...and until you die, nothing is possible; until you die, the resurrection is not possible.

"...Let him deny himself, and take up his cross daily...." This has to be done daily, every morning. You cannot think that "Yes, I have surrendered once. It is finished." It is not so easy. You will have to surrender a million times. You will have to surrender every moment because the mind is very cunning. It will try to reclaim you. If you think that you have surrendered once and it is finished, the mind will recapture you. It has to be done every moment – until you are completely dead and a new entity has arisen, until a new man is born within you, until you are no more continuous with the past: a breakthrough has happened.

You will know it because you will not recognize yourself. Who are you? You will not be able to see how you were connected with the past. You will recognize only one thing – that there has been a sudden gap. The line broke, the past disappeared, and something new entered within you which has nothing to do with the past, which is not at all connected with it. The religious man is not a modified man, the religious man is not a decorated man. The religious man has nothing to do with the past. It is absolutely new...

> "For whosoever will save his life
> shall lose it..."

– don't cling to the ego.

> "For whosoever will save his life shall lose it: but whosoever will lose his life for my sake, the same shall save it."

Lose it and you will have it; cling to it and you will lose it. Looks paradoxical, but it is a simple truth. The seed dies in the soil and becomes a great tree. But the seed can cling to its own self, go on protecting itself and defending itself, because for the seed it looks like death. The seed will never be able to see the plant, so it is death.

You will never be able to see the man I am talking about, so it is a perfect death. You cannot imagine that man because if you can imagine that man it will be your continuity. You cannot hope about that man because if it is your hope then your hope will be the bridge. No, you are completely in the dark about that new man – that's why trust is needed.

I cannot prove it to you, I cannot argue about it, because the more I argue about it and prove it to you, the more it will become impossible for you. If you become *convinced,* then the barrier is perfect because your conviction will be *your* conviction. And the new will come only when *you* have gone totally; all your convictions, ideologies, arguments, proofs you are gone, wholesale – and only absence is left. And in that absence, the heavens open and the spirit of God descends like a dove, lights on you.

"*...But whosoever will lose his life for my sake, the same shall save it."* Why does Jesus insist: 'for my sake'? Look at the problem: if you are going to die completely and a new man is going to come only when you are no more, then who will be the bridge between you and the new? Who will be the bridge? You cannot be the bridge otherwise the new will not be new; it will be just a modified old.

There the master becomes the bridge. He says, "Die silently. I am there to look after you. You move into death; I will take care of the new coming into you. Don't be worried, you relax...*for my sake....*"

That's why religion will never become a philosophy, it will never become a theology. It will never be based on arguments; it cannot be, the very nature of it forbids it. It will remain a trust. If you trust me, you can die easily without fear. You know I am there, you love me and you know that I love you, so why fear?

It happened: a young man, recently married, was going on his honeymoon. He was a *samurai*, a Japanese warrior. They were going on a boat to an island when suddenly a storm came. The boat was small and the storm was tremendously terrible, and there was every possibility that they would be drowned. The wife became very much afraid, started trembling. But she looked at the samurai, her husband. He was sitting silently as if nothing was happening. And they were in the throes of death! And any moment the boat would be gone under the sea.

The woman said, "What are you doing? Why are you sitting like a statue?"

The samurai pulled his sword out of its sheath – the wife could not believe it, what was he doing? – and he put his naked sword just near the throat of the wife. She started laughing, and he said, "Why are you laughing? The sword is so near your throat – just a little move and your head will go."

The wife said, "But it is in your hands, so there is no problem. The sword is dangerous, but it is in your hands."

The samurai put his sword back and said, "The storm is in my God's hands. The storm is dangerous, but it is in the hands of somebody whom I love and who loves me. That's why I am unafraid."

When the sword is in your master's hand and he is going to kill you, if you trust him, only then will you die peacefully, lovingly, gracefully. And out of that grace...and out of that peace...and out of that love...you will create the possibility where the new arrives. If you die afraid, the new will not arrive. You will simply die. That's why Jesus says: *"...for my sake..."* – let me be the bridge.

> "For what is a man advantaged,
> if he gain the whole world,
> and lose himself, or be cast away?"

And remember, you can gain the whole world and lose yourself – as people are doing all over the world throughout time: gaining the world and losing themselves. Then one day they suddenly find that all they have gained is not theirs. Empty-handed they come; empty-handed they go. Nothing belongs to them. Then anguish takes over.

"For what is a man advantaged, if he gain the whole world, and lose himself, or be cast away?" The only way to be really intelligent in the world is first to gain yourself. Even if the whole world is to be lost, it is worth it. If you gain your own being, your own soul, your own innermost core, and the whole world is lost, it is worth it. To gain that innermost core you will not only have to lose the world. You will have to lose the idea of yourself – because that is the innermost barrier: the ego. The ego is a false identity. Not knowing who you are, you go on thinking that you are somebody. That somebody – the false identity – is the ego. And unless the false goes, the true cannot enter.

Let the false go and the true is ready. Repent, return, answer – the kingdom of God is at hand!

Enough for today.

CHAPTER 8

I Treat Jesus
As A Poet

THE FIRST QUESTION:

> Beloved Osho,
> How is one who has been trained all his
> life to analyze and question and doubt,
> brought to bridge the gap
> between doubt and trust?

Doubt is beautiful in itself. The problem arises when you are stuck in it, then doubt becomes death. Analysis is perfect if you remain separate and aloof from it. If you become identified then the problem arises, then analysis becomes a paralysis. If you feel that you have been trained to analyze, question and doubt, don't get miserable. Doubt, analyze, question, but remain separate. You are not the doubt; use it as a methodology, a method. If analysis is a method, then synthesis is also a method. And analysis in itself is half; unless it is complemented by synthesis, it will never be the whole. And you are neither analysis nor synthesis, you are just a transcendental awareness.

To question is good, but a question is obviously the half. The answer will be the other half. Doubt is good, but one part; trust is another part. But remain aloof. When I say 'remain aloof', I say, remain aloof not only from doubt but from trust also. That too is a method. One has to use it, one should not allow oneself to be used by it – then a tyranny arises and the tyranny can be either of doubt or of trust.

The tyranny of doubt will cripple you. You will never be able to move a single step, because doubt will be everywhere. How can you do anything while there is doubt? That will cripple you. And if trust becomes a tyranny – and it can become, it has become for millions: the churches, the temples, the mosques are full of those people for whom trust has become a tyranny – then it doesn't give you eyes, it blinds you. Then religion becomes a superstition.

If trust is not a method and you are identified with it, then religion becomes superstition and science becomes technology. Then the purity of science is lost and the purity of religion is also lost. Remember this: doubt and trust are like two wings. Use both of them, but you are neither.

A man of discretion, a man who is wise, will use doubt if his search is towards matter. If his inquiry is about the outside, the other, he will use doubt as the method. If his search is towards the inner, towards himself, then he will use trust. Science and religion are two wings.

In India we have tried one foolishness. Now the West is committing another. In India we have tried to live only by trust; hence the poverty, the starvation, the misery. The whole country is like a wound, continuously suffering. And the suffering has been so long that people have even become accustomed to it, they have accepted it so deeply that they have become insensitive to it. They are almost dead: they drift, they are not alive. This happened because of the tyranny of trust. How can a bird fly with one wing?

Now, in the West, another tyranny is happening, the tyranny of doubt. It works perfectly well as far as objective inquiry is concerned: you think about matter, doubt is needed; it is a scientific method. But when you start moving inwards it simply doesn't work, it doesn't fit. There, trust is needed.

The perfect man will be a man who has a deep harmony of doubt and trust. A perfect man will look inconsistent to you. But he is not inconsistent, he is simply harmonious. Contradictions dissolve in him. He uses everything.

If you have doubt, use it for scientific inquiry. And watch great scientists: by the time they reach their age of understanding and wisdom, by the time their youthful enthusiasm is gone and wisdom settles, they are always very deep in trust. Eddington, Einstein, Lodge – I'm not talking about mediocre scientists, they are not scientists at all – but all the great pinnacles in science are very religious. They trust because they have known doubt, they have used doubt, and they have come to understand that doubt has its limitations.

It is just like: my eyes can see and my ears can hear; if I try to hear from my eyes then it is going to be impossible, and if I try to see by my ears then it is going to be impossible. The eye has its own limitation, the ear has its own limitation. They are experts, and every expert has a limitation. The eye can see – and it is good that it can only see because if the eye could do many things then it would not be so efficient in seeing. In the eye the whole energy becomes sight, and the whole energy in the ear becomes hearing.

Doubt is an expert. It works if you are inquiring about the world. But when you start inquiring about God through the same method, then you are using a wrong method. The method was perfectly suited to the world, to the world of law, but it is not suited to the world of love. For the world of love, trust is needed.

Nothing is wrong in doubt, don't be worried about it. Use it well, use it in the right direction. If you use it in the right direction and use it well, you will come to an understanding: you will come to a doubt of doubt itself. You will see – you will become doubtful of doubt. You will see where it works and where it doesn't work. When one comes to that understanding, one opens the door of trust.

If you are trained for analysis – good. But don't be caught in it, don't allow it to become a bondage. Remain free to synthesize also, because if you go on analyzing and analyzing and you never synthesize, you will come to the minutest part but you will never come to the whole.

God is the ultimate synthesis; the atom, the ultimate analysis. Science reaches to the atom: it goes on analyzing, dividing, until finally it comes to the minutest part which cannot be divided anymore. And religion comes to God, godliness: it goes on adding, synthesizing. God is the ultimate synthesis; more cannot be added to it. It is already the whole. Nothing exists beyond it. Science is atomic; religion is 'wholly'. Use both.

I am always in favor of using everything that you have. Even if you have some poison I will say, "Preserve it, don't throw it." In some need it can become medicinal – it depends on you. You can commit suicide by a poison, and by the same poison you can be saved from dying. The poison is the same; the difference is right use. Everything depends on right use. So when you go to the lab use doubt, when you come to the temple use trust. Be loose and free so that when you go from the lab to the temple you don't carry the lab around with you. Then you can enter the temple totally free of the lab – pray, dance, sing. And when you move towards the lab again leave the temple behind, because dancing in the lab will be very absurd – you may destroy things.

Bringing the serious face that you use in the lab to the temple won't be appropriate. A temple is a celebration, a lab is a search. Search has to be serious, a celebration is a play. You delight in it, you become children again. A temple is a place to become children again and again, so you never lose touch with the original source. In the lab you are an adult, in the temple you are a child. And Jesus says, "The kingdom of God is for those who are like children."

Remember always not to throw away anything that God has given to you – not even doubt. It must be he who has given it to you and there must be a reason behind it, because nothing is given without reason. There must be a use for it.

Don't discard any stone, because many times it has happened that the stone that was discarded by the builders became the very cornerstone of the building in the end.

The second question:

> Beloved Osho,
> The Bible uses the word 'repent'.
> Sometimes you translate it as 'return',
> sometimes as 'answer' and sometimes
> you leave it as 'repent'. Do you change
> the meaning as you need it?

I am not talking about the Bible at all. I am talking about me. I am not confined by the Bible; I am not a slave to any scripture. I am totally free, and I behave as a free man.

I love the Bible, the poetry of it, but I am not a Christian. Neither am I a Hindu, nor am I a Jaina. I am simply me. I love the poetry, but I sing it in my own way. Where I should emphasize what, is finally decided by me, not by the Bible. I love the spirit of it, not the letter. And the word that I translate sometimes as 'repent', sometimes as 'return' and sometimes as 'answer' means all three things. That is the beauty of old languages. Sanskrit, Hebrew, Arabic – all the old languages are poetic. When you use a poetic language it means many things. It says more than the words contain and it can be interpreted in different ways. It has many levels of meaning.

Sometimes the word means repent. When I am talking about sin and I use the word 'repent', it means repent. When I am talking about God calling you, then the word 'repent' means answer, it means responsibility: God has asked, you answer. And when I say that the kingdom is at hand, the word means return. All three meanings are there. The word is not one-dimensional, it is three-dimensional. All the old languages are three-dimensional. Modern languages are one-dimensional, because our insistence is not on poetry, but on prose. Our insistence is not on multi-meaningfulness, but exactness. The word should be exact: it should only mean one thing so that there is no confusion. Yes, that's right. If you are writing about science the language has to be exact, otherwise confusion is possible.

It happened in the second world war: the American general wrote a letter to the emperor of Japan, before Hiroshima and Nagasaki. The letter was in English and it was translated into Japanese which is more poetic, more flowery – and one word means many things.

A certain word was translated in a certain way. It could have been translated in some other way also; it depended on the translator. Now they have been inquiring about it, and they have come to the conclusion that if it had been translated in the other way that was also possible, there would have been no Hiroshima and no Nagasaki.

The American general meant something else, but the way it was translated it was felt to be an insult. The Japanese emperor simply declined to answer it; it was too insulting. And Nagasaki and Hiroshima happened, the atom bomb had to be thrown. If the emperor had replied to it, then there would have been no need for Hiroshima and Nagasaki. Just a word translated in a different way and one *lakh* people died within minutes, within seconds. Very costly — just a single word. Words can be dangerous.

In politics, in science, in economics, in history, words should be linear, one-dimensional. But if the whole language becomes one-dimensional, then religion will suffer very much, poetry will suffer very much, romance will suffer very much...because for poetry a word should be multi-dimensional, it should mean many things so that the poetry has a depth and you can go on and on and on.

That's the beauty of old books. You can go on reading the Gita every day, you can go on reading the gospels every day, and every day you can come upon a new and fresh meaning. You may have read the same passage a thousand times and it never occurred to you that this can be the meaning. But this morning it occurred, you were in a different mood — you were happy, flowing — a new meaning arises. Some day you are not so happy, not so flowing — the meaning changes. The meaning changes according to you, according to your mood and climate.

You carry an inner climate that goes on changing, just like the outer climate. Have you watched it? Sometimes you are sad and you look at the moon and the moon looks sad, very sad. You are sad and a fragrance comes from the garden and it seems very sad. You look at the flowers: rather than making you happy, they make you heavy. Then in another moment you are happy, alive, flowing, smiling — the same fragrance comes and surrounds you, dances around you, and makes you tremendously happy. The same flower...and when you see it opening, something opens within you also. The same moon, and you cannot believe how much silence and how much beauty descends on you. There is a deep participation: you become partners in some deep mystery. But it depends on you. The moon is the same, the flower is the same — it depends on you.

Old languages are very flowing. In Sanskrit there are words.... One word can have twelve meanings. You can go on playing with it and it will reveal many things to you. It will change with you, it will always adjust to you. That's why great works of classical literature are eternal. They are never exhausted.

But today's newspaper will be worthless tomorrow, because it has no vitality of meaning. It simply says what it means; it has nothing more in it. Tomorrow you will look foolish reading it. It is ordinary prose; it gives you information but it has no depth, it is flat.

Two thousand years have passed since Jesus spoke and his words are still as alive and fresh as ever. They are never going to be old. They don't age, they remain fresh and young. What is their secret? The secret is that they mean so many things that you can always find a new door in them. It is not a one-room apartment. Jesus says, "My God's house has many mansions." You can enter from many doors, and there are always new treasures to be revealed, to be discovered. You never come on the old landscape again. It has a certain infinity. That's why I go on changing. Yes, whenever I feel, I change the meaning. But that is the way Jesus himself has done it.

In translating the Hebrew Bible into English, much has been lost. In translating the Gita into modern languages, much has been lost. In translating the Koran, the whole beauty is gone because the Koran is a poetry. It is something to be sung, it is something you should dance with. It is not prose. Prose is not the way of religion; poetry is the way.

Remember this always and don't get confined. Jesus is vast and the English Bible is very small. I can understand the resistance of old people that their books should not be translated. It has a deep significance. You can translate prose, there is no trouble. If you want to translate a book on the theory of relativity into any language it may be difficult, but the difficulty is not the same as it is with the Bible, the Gita or the Koran. It can be translated, nothing will be lost; it has no poetry in it. But when you translate poetry, much will be lost because each language has its own rhythm and each language has its own ways of expression. Each language has its own meter and music; it cannot be translated into another language. That music will be missed, that rhythm will be missed. You will have to replace it by some other rhythm and some other music. So it is possible...ordinary poetry may be translated, but when the poetry is really superb, of the other world...the more deep and great it is, the more difficult it is — almost impossible.

I treat Jesus as a poet. And he is. Van Gogh has said about him that he is the greatest artist that has ever been on this earth. He is. He talks in parables and poetry, and he means many more things than his words can convey. Allow me to give you the feeling of that infinity of meanings.

Poetry is not so clear — cannot be, it is a mystery. It is just early in the morning...all over you see a mist...fresh, just born...but clouds.... You cannot see far away, but there is no need: poetry is not for the far away. It gives you an insight in looking to the near and the close and the intimate.

Science goes on searching for the far away; poetry goes on revealing to you in a new way the intimate, the close, that which you had always known, that which is familiar. Poetry reveals the same path that you have been treading all your life, but with a new hue, a new color, a new light. Suddenly you are transported to a new plane.

I treat Jesus as a poet. He is a poet. And this has been very much misunderstood. People go on treating him as a scientist. You are fools if you treat him as a scientist. Then he will look absurd, then the whole thing will look miraculous. Then if you want to believe in him, you have to be very superstitious. Or you have to throw him completely – the baby with the bath water. Because either he's so absurd...you can believe, but then you have to believe very blindly and that belief cannot be natural, spontaneous; you have to force it, you have to believe for the sake of belief and you have to force it on yourself – or you throw him completely. Both are wrong. Jesus should be loved, not believed. There is no need to think of for or against.

Have you ever watched? – you never think for or against Shakespeare. Why? You never think for or against Kalidas. Why? You never think for and against Rabindranath. Why? Because you know they are poets. You enjoy them, you don't think for and against.

But with Jesus, Krishna, Buddha, you think for and against because you think they are arguing. Let me tell you: they are not arguing. They have no thesis to prove, they have no dogma. They are great poets – greater than Rabindranath, greater than Shakespeare, greater than Kalidas, because what has happened to Rabindranath, Kalidas and Shakespeare is just a glimpse. What has happened to Jesus, Krishna and Buddha is a realization. The same that is a glimpse to a poet is reality to a mystic. They have seen. Not only seen – they have touched. Not only touched – they have lived. It is a live experience.

Always look at them as great artists. A painter simply paints a picture; a poet simply writes a poem...a Jesus creates a human being. A painter changes a canvas: it was plain, ordinary; it becomes precious by his touch. But can't you see that Jesus touches very ordinary people – a fisherman, Simon called Peter – he touches, and by his very touch this man is transformed into a great apostle, a great human being. A height arises, a depth is opened. This man is no longer ordinary. He was just a fisherman throwing his net into the sea and he would have done that his whole life – or even for many lives – and would never even have thought, imagined, dreamed what Jesus transformed into a reality.

In India we have a mythology about a stone called *paras*. The stone paras is alchemical. You touch iron with the paras and it is transformed into gold. Jesus is a paras. He touches ordinary metal and immediately the metal is transformed, it becomes gold. He transforms ordinary human beings into deities, and you don't see the art in it. Greater art is not possible.

To me, the gospels are poetic. If I speak again on the same gospel, I will not speak the same, remember. I don't know in what mood, in what climate, I will be then. I don't know from which door I will enter then. And my house of God has many mansions. It is not finite.

The third question:

> Beloved Osho,
> Yesterday after the lecture I approached small Siddhartha by the drinking water. Having read what you said about him being one of the ancient ones, I crouched down, looked into his eyes and said, "Osho told me who you are." He smiled, looked deeply at me, and twice threw water on my head. He then softly hit me on the head and said quietly, "Shut up." There was silence. It was very beautiful.

It must have been. He baptized you by water. It was a baptism.

And he is very innocent, more than John the Baptist. His innocence is very spontaneous.

You should crouch more often before him. And you should allow him to throw water and hit you more. And when he says, "Shut up," then shut up and remain in silence.

He is a tremendously beautiful child.

The fourth question:

> Beloved Osho,
> When I reflect on Christ's persecution two thousand years ago, I feel that in the meantime nothing much has changed in people's attitudes towards a living messiah in their midst. Suspicion, cynicism and mistrust seem to be all around just as before. Could it be that you, too, one day will be persecuted by the establishment? Looking around the auditorium, I fancy that I can spot the Doubting Thomas, the John, the Simon Peter, Mary Magdalena, even Judas and the rest of the gang. Could this all be a live-action replay?

It is. They are all here. They have to be — because the gang leader is here! And nothing ever changes, all changes are superficial. Deep down, humanity remains the same. It is natural. I'm not condemning it, I'm not saying that anything is wrong in it. It has to be so, that's the way it is.

When Jesus comes, the Doubting Thomases are bound to be there. When people who trust come, people who can't trust also come. They create a contrast. And it is good, otherwise your trust will not be of much value. It becomes precious because of the Doubting Thomases around. You can compare, you can feel. You can see what doubt is, what trust is. The weeds will also come when you plant a garden. The weeds are also part. When a Jesus comes, a Judas is bound to be there because the whole thing is so tremendously significant that somebody is bound to betray it. It has such a great height that somebody is bound to feel very much hurt by it – the ego.

Judas was hurt very much. And he was not a bad man, remember. In fact, he was the only one amongst all of Jesus' disciples who was well-educated, cultured, belonged to a sophisticated society and family. He was, of course, the most egoistic. The others were just fishermen, farmers, carpenters – people like that, ordinary people from the ordinary rung of society. Judas was special. And whenever somebody feels special there is trouble. He wanted to even guide Jesus. Many times he tried. And if you listen to him, there is a possibility that you will be more convinced by Judas than by Jesus.

It happened: Jesus came to visit the home of Mary Magdalena. Mary was deeply in love. She poured precious, very precious, perfume on his feet – the whole bottle. It was rare; it could have been sold. Judas immediately objected. He said, "You should prohibit people from doing such nonsense. The whole thing is wasted, and in town there are people who are poor and who don't have anything to eat. We could have distributed the money to poor people."

He looks like a socialist – a forerunner of Marx. Mao, Lenin, Trotsky, all would agree with him.

What did Jesus say? He said, "Don't be worried about it. The poor and the hungry will always be here, but I will be gone. You can serve them always and always – there is no hurry – but I will be gone. Look at the love, not at the precious perfume. Look at Mary's love, her heart."

With whom will you agree? Jesus seems to be very bourgeois and Judas seems to be perfectly economical. Judas is talking about the poor and Jesus simply says, "It is okay. I will be gone soon, so let her welcome me as she would like. Let her heart do whatsoever she wants and don't bring your philosophy in. Poor people will always be there; I will not be here always. I am only here for a tiny while."

Ordinarily your mind will agree with Judas. He seems to be perfectly right. He was a very cultured, polished man of manners – sophisticated, a thinker.

And he betrayed. Only he could betray, because on each step his ego was hurt. He always felt himself superior to all of Jesus' disciples. He would always keep himself aloof, he would not move in the crowd. He always thought of himself as not part of the crowd. At the most he was second only to Jesus – and that too, reluctantly. Deep down he must have been thinking himself first. He could not say it, but it was in his heart.

He was madly hurt. Continuously Jesus was hurting their egos. A master has to, because if a master goes on pampering your egos then he will not be of any help, he will be poisonous. Then you can commit suicide through him, but you cannot resurrect. And of course Judas was the most egoistic, he was hurt more. And Jesus *had* to hurt him more. He took revenge. And he was a good man; there is no doubt about it. That is the problem with good men.

He sold Jesus for thirty rupees. He was so concerned with the perfume and its cost – look at the mind! – and he sold Jesus for thirty rupees, thirty silver pieces. Jesus was not even very costly. But then, when Jesus was murdered, crucified, he started feeling guilty. That's how a good man functions. He started feeling very guilty, his conscience started pricking him. He committed suicide. He was a good man, he had a conscience. But he had no consciousness.

This distinction has to be felt deeply. Conscience is borrowed, given by the society; consciousness is *your* attainment. The society teaches you what is right and what is wrong: do this and don't do that. It gives you the law, the morality, the code, the rules of the game. That is your conscience. Outside, the constable; inside, the conscience. That is the way that the society controls you.

If you go to steal, the constable is outside to prevent you. But you can deceive the constable, you can find ways. So the society has placed a deep electrode within you: the conscience. Your hand starts trembling, your whole inner being – you feel that your inner being is saying, "Don't do this; this is wrong." This is society speaking through you. This is just society implanted within you.

Judas had a conscience, but Jesus had consciousness. That was the rift. The man of conscience can never understand the man of consciousness because the man of consciousness lives moment to moment, he has no rules to follow.

Jesus was more concerned with the love of the woman Mary. It was such a deep thing that to prevent her would be wounding her love; she would shrink within herself. Pouring the perfume on his feet was just a gesture. Behind it, Mary Magdalena was saying. "I would like to pour the whole of the world on your feet. This is all that I have – the most precious thing. To pour water won't be enough; it is too cheap. This is the most precious thing that I have, but even this is nothing. I would like to pour my heart, I would like to pour my whole being...."

But Judas was blind towards it. He was a man of conscience: he looked at the perfume and he said, "It is costly." He was completely blind to the woman and her heart, and the expansion of consciousness and the gesture. Perfume looked too precious and love – love was completely unknown to him. Love was there. The immaterial was there and the material was there. The material is the perfume, the immaterial is the love. But the immaterial Judas could not see. For that, you need eyes of consciousness.

A man of conscience will always be in conflict with a man of consciousness because the man of consciousness sees things which the man of conscience cannot see. And the man of consciousness follows his consciousness: he has no rules to follow.

If you have rules you are always consistent because rules are dead. You are also dead with them: you are predictable. But if you have consciousness, you are unpredictable – one never knows. You remain a total freedom. You respond, you don't have any ready-made answers to give. When the question arises, you respond and the answer is born. Not only is the listener surprised by your answer – you are also surprised.

When I answer you, it is not only that you are listening to it, I am also a listener. It is not only that you hear it for the first time; I also hear it for the first time. I don't know what the next word or sentence is going to be. It can move in any direction, it can move in any dimension.

That's what I mean when I say that I remain a learner. Not only are you learning with me, I am also learning with you. I am never in a state of knowledge because a state of knowledge is dead. You have known something, it is ready-made. Now if somebody asks you can give it to him, it is already material.

I am never in a state of knowledge; I am always in the process of knowing. To be in the process of knowing is what I mean when I say I am learning. Knowledge is already past; knowing is present. Life is not a noun, it is a verb. God is also not a noun, god is a verb. Whatever the grammarians say, I am not concerned. God is a verb, life is a verb.

Knowing, learning, means that you always remain in a vacuum. You never gather anything. You always remain empty like a mirror, not like a photographic plate. A photographic plate immediately comes to a state of knowledge. Once exposed, it is already dead. Now it will never mirror anybody else; it has mirrored once, forever. But a mirror goes on mirroring. When you come before it, it mirrors you. When you are gone, it is again empty.

This is what I mean: a man of learning always remains empty. You raise a question. It is mirrored in my emptiness...an answer comes and flows to you. The question gone, the answer disappeared, the mirror is again in a state of not knowing – empty, again ready to reflect. It is not hindered by its past, it is always in the present and always ready. Not ready-made, but always ready to reflect, to respond.

When Jesus comes – a man of consciousness, a man of learning not of knowledge – Judas is bound to be there. He's the scholar, the man of knowledge. He must have felt many times that he knew more than Jesus. And maybe he was right also. He may know more, but he does not know the state of knowing. He knows only knowledge, dead information. He is a collector of dead information. He will betray Jesus. And of course, when Jesus is there, there will be women who will love him deeply: a Mary Magdalena, a Martha. They are bound to be there because whenever a man of the quality of Jesus arises, that quality has to be understood first by women and then by men. Trust is the door to it, and women are more trusting, more innocently trusting.

That's why it is so difficult to find a woman scientist. Sometimes a Madame Curie happens – that must be a freak of nature. Or the woman may not have been much of a woman.

Deep down, a woman is a poet – not that she writes poetry, she lives it. And she knows how to trust – it comes easy to her, it comes spontaneously to her. In fact, for a woman to doubt is a difficult training. She will have to learn it from a man, just like she will have to learn science from a man. She is illogical, irrational. Those are not good qualities as far as the world is concerned – they are disqualifications in the world – but as far as the inner kingdom of God is concerned, they are the qualifications.

And of course man cannot have both worlds. At the most he can have one where he's topmost: he can have the outer world. But then he will have to lose the other – there he cannot be the top, he will have to follow women.

Have you seen Jesus being crucified? No male disciple was near him – only women – because the male disciples started doubting. This man cured illnesses, this man revived dead people, and now he cannot save himself? So what is the point of believing and trusting in him? They were waiting for a miracle. They were hiding in the crowd and waiting for a miracle: something miraculous was going to happen. Then they would have believed because they needed proof. And the proof never happened; Jesus simply died like an ordinary man.

But the women were not waiting for any proof. Jesus was enough proof, there was no need for any miracle. *He* was the miracle. They could see the miracle that happened that moment – that Jesus died with such deep love and compassion. Even for his murderers he had a prayer in his heart. His last words were, "God, forgive them because they don't know what they are doing."

The miracle had happened, but for the male eye it never happened. The women around there understood immediately. They trusted this man and this man's innermost heart was opened to them. They understood that the miracle had happened. The man had been crucified and he was dying with love, which is the most impossible thing in the world: to die on the cross with a prayer for those who are killing you. But this was love. Only the feminine mind can understand it. They were close to him.

When Jesus revived, resurrected, after the third day, he tried to approach his male disciples. They could not see him because they had settled the fact that he was dead, and you see only things which you expect to see. If you don't expect, you don't see.

Your eyes are very choosy. If you are waiting for a friend, then even in a crowd you can see him. But if you are not waiting for him, if you have completely forgotten about him, then when he comes and knocks on the door, for a moment you are puzzled: who is he?

They had settled the fact that Jesus was dead, so when Jesus came across their path they could not recognize him, they could not see him. It is even said that he walked for miles with two disciples while they talked about Jesus' death. They were very miserable because of it – and Jesus was walking with them, they were talking to him! But they could not recognize him. Only love can recognize, even after death – because love recognized when you were alive. For love, death and life are irrelevant.

Jesus was recognized first by Mary Magdalena, a prostitute. She came running to the male disciples who were holding a great conference: What to do? How to spread the word to the whole world? How to create the church?

When they were planning for the future, she came running and said, "What are you doing? Jesus is alive!"

They laughed. They said, "Mad woman, you must have imagined it!" – man's mind always thinks that such things are imagination. They started talking to each other: "That poor woman, Mary Magdalena. She has gone mad. Jesus' crucifixion has been such a shock to her." They felt pity on her.

She insisted, "Don't feel pity on me. Jesus *is* resurrected!"

They laughed and they said, "We understand. You need rest, you are too shocked by the fact that he is dead. It is your imagination."

Around Buddha, around Krishna, around Jesus, Mahavira, there have always been a great number of women. They were the first-comers, they were the first disciples. It is natural. So don't be surprised.

Two thousand, or two million years... the human mind will remain the same. Humanity as a whole remains the same. The revolution is individual; you can be transformed as an individual. Then you go beyond the crowd. But don't be worried about such things.

This question is from Chaitanya Sagar. He's always worried about such things. I never answer him, but he's always worried: worried about others, worried about the world, he is worried about the organization, worried about the *ashram*, worried about my disciples, worried about me – never worried about himself. All these worries won't help. Time is short, life is very short. Use it.

Just the other night I was reading a play by Samuel Beckett: a small book, the smallest possible in the world – a short play. The name of the play is "Breath." The length of the whole play is only thirty seconds...thirty seconds! There is no actor in it, no dialogue. Just a stage.

The curtain opens. Many things are lying around. Rubbish – just as if somebody has left the house in a hurry. All sorts of things are jumbled, with no order. Just a disorder – rubbish. And from the background, a sigh is heard of a small child, just born. Then, after thirty seconds, the gasp of an old man who has died. This is all – but this is all life is. Thirty seconds: a sigh and a gasp. The first effort to inhale and the last effort to cling to the breathing... and everything is gone.

Life is short, not even thirty seconds. Use it. Use it as an opportunity to grow, use it as an opportunity to be, and don't be worried about other things; that is all rubbish. Only this is true: the sigh and the gasp, and all else is just rubbish. Forget about it – what do you have to do about it?

You should not be concerned with whether the world has changed or not. The world is the same, it has to be the same. Only *you* can be different; the world will never be different. When you become aware, conscious, you transcend the world.

The fifth question:

> Beloved Osho,
> What does Christ really mean when he says, "Come follow me"?

Exactly what he says: "Come follow me."

The sixth question:

> Beloved Osho,
> To follow Jesus a deep trust, surrender and love is needed, but today a deep skepticism is prevalent all over the world. What is the way?

This is from Swami Yoga Chinmaya. Think about yourself. Is deep skepticism within you? That is the question to be asked. "A deep skepticism is prevalent all over the world." Who are you to be worried about the whole world? This is a way to escape the real problem. Skepticism is deep within, the worm of doubt is there in your heart, but you project it; you see it on the whole world's screen.

Hmm? "The world is skeptical...what is the way out?" Now you are transferring the problem. Look within yourself. If there is doubt, then find it out. Then something can be done. The world won't listen to you, and there is no need, because if they are happy in their skepticism they have the right to be happy in their skepticism. Who are you?

Never try to think in terms of missionaries; they are the most dangerous people. They are always saving the world and if the world doesn't want to be saved, then still they are trying. They say, "Even if you don't like it, we will save you." But why the bother? If somebody is happy – eating, drinking, enjoying life – and is not in any way concerned with God, what is the point of forcing him? Who are you? Let him come to his own understanding. Some day he will come. But people are very much worried: How to save others? Save yourself! If you can, save yourself – because that too is a very difficult, almost impossible job.

This is a trick of the mind: the problem is inside – it projects it on the outside. Then you are not worried about it, then you are not worried about your own anguish. Then you become concerned with the whole world and in this way you can postpone your own transformation.

I insist again and again that you should be concerned with yourself. I am not here to make missionaries. Missionaries are the most mischievous people. Never be a missionary; that is a very dirty job. Don't try to change anybody. Just change yourself.

And it happens. When you change, many come to share you in your light. Share – but don't try to save. Many will be saved that way. If you try to save, you may drown them before they were going to be drowned by themselves.

Don't try to force God on anybody. If they are doubting, it is perfectly okay. If God allows them to doubt there must be some reason in it. They need it, that is their training; that is from where everybody has to pass.

The world has always been skeptical. How many people gathered around Buddha? Not the whole world. How many people gathered around Jesus? Not the whole world, just a very small minority – they can be counted on your fingers. The whole world was never worried about these things.

And nobody has the authority to force something on anybody else. Not even on your own child! Not even on your own wife! Keep whatsoever you feel is the goal to your life to yourself. Never force it on anybody else. That is violence, sheer violence.

If you want to meditate, meditate. But this *is* a problem: if the husband wants to meditate he tries to force the wife also; if the wife does not want to meditate, she forces the husband also not to meditate. Can't you allow people their own souls? Can't you allow them to have their own way?

This I call a religious attitude: to allow freedom. A religious man will always allow freedom to everybody. Even if you want to be an atheist, a theist is going to allow you. That is your way, perfectly good for you. You move through it because everyone who has come to God has come through atheism. The desert of atheism has to be crossed; it is part of growth.

The world will always remain skeptical, in doubt. Only a few attain to trust. Make haste so that you can attain.

The seventh question:

> Beloved Osho,
> Why do you always tell us to be happy
> if, before enlightenment, one has to
> reach a peak of pain and anguish?

If I don't tell you to be happy, you will never reach the peak of pain and anguish. I go on telling you to be happy, and the more I say, "Be happy," the more you become aware of your unhappiness.

The more you listen to me, the more you will find anguish arising. That is the only way to make you unhappy — to go on constantly forcing on you: be happy! You cannot be, so you feel the unhappiness all around you. Even what you used to think was happiness, even those points disappear and you feel absolutely hopeless. Even momentary happinesses disappear and the desert becomes complete. All hopes and all oases disappear.

But that's where the jump happens. When you are *really* unhappy, totally unhappy — not even a ray of hope — suddenly you drop all unhappiness. Why? — why does it happen? It happens because unhappiness is not clinging to you; you are clinging to unhappiness. Once you feel the total anguish of it, you drop it; there is nobody to carry it for you.

But you have never felt it so intensely; you have always been lukewarm. You feel a little unhappiness, but always there is a hope for the future: Tomorrow there is going to be happiness — a little desert, but the oasis is coming closer. Through the hope, you go on. Through the hope, the unhappiness remains.

My whole effort is to kill the hope, to leave you in such total darkness that you cannot allow any dream any longer. Once this intensity reaches to the hundredth degree, you evaporate.

Then you cannot carry it anymore, suddenly whatsoever you call it – unhappiness, the ego, ignorance, unawareness, or what have you: anything that you want to call it – drops.

I will tell you one story.

It happened.... A farmer had a pedigree ram. It was a beautiful animal, but sometimes it got mad and the shepherd who looked after the ram was very worried. He always wanted to get rid of it, but the farmer loved it.

One day it became too much, so the shepherd came and said, "Now you choose: either me or the ram. I resign... take my notice or this ram goes. This is a mad animal and continuously creating trouble. He gets so angry and so dangerous that sometimes one feels that he will kill."

The farmer now had to decide, so he asked his friends what to do. He never wanted the ram to be sold. They suggested an animal psychologist: "Ask...."

The psychologist was called. The farmer was skeptical, but he wanted to do anything so that the ram could be saved. The psychologist remained for four days: watched, observed, took notes, analyzed. Then he said, "There will be no trouble. You just go to the market, purchase a gramophone and bring Beethoven records, Mozart, Wagner – classical music. Whenever the ram gets mad, in a rage, just put on a classical record. Play it and it will soothe him, and he will be perfectly calmed down."

The farmer couldn't believe it, that this was going to be so – but it had to be tried, so he tried it. It worked! Immediately the ram would become silent and cool down.

For one year there was no trouble. Then one day the shepherd came running and said, "Something has gone wrong – I don't know what. The ram has killed himself! As usual, seeing that he was getting in a rage again, I had put

a record on. But he worsened. Then he became more and more mad and he simply charged into the wall. His neck is broken — he is dead."
The farmer went there. The ram was lying dead near the wall. Then he looked on the gramophone to see what record was there. There had been a terrible mistake: it was not classical music, but Frank Sinatra's record singing: "There Shall Never Be Another Like You."

That created the trouble. 'There shall never be another like you' — the ego is the cause of all madness, unhappiness, misery. That is going to be the cause of your death, that is going to break your neck.
You can cope with it if it is lukewarm. My whole effort is to bring it to a peak where you cannot cope with it. Either you have to drop it, or you will drop. And whenever such a choice arises — that you have to drop the misery or you have to drop yourself — you will drop the misery. And with the misery, the ego, the ignorance, the unawareness — they all disappear. They are names of the same phenomenon.

Enough for today.

Chapter 9

Let The Dead
Bury Their Dead

Let the Dead Bury Their Dead

Luke 9

57 And it came to pass, that,
as they went in the way,
a certain man said unto him,
"Lord, I will follow thee
whithersoever thou goest."

58 And Jesus said unto him,
"Foxes have holes,
and birds of the air have nests;
but the Son of man hath not
where to lay his head."

59 And he said unto another,
"Follow me."
But he said, "Lord, suffer me first
to go and bury my father".

60 And Jesus said unto him,
"Let the dead bury their dead:
but go thou and preach
the kingdom of God."

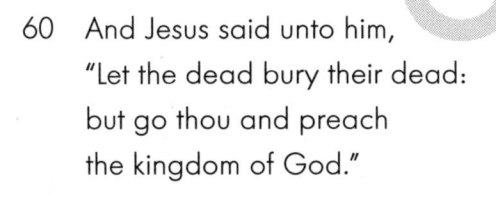

61 And another also said,
"Lord, I will follow thee;
but let me first go bid them farewell,
which are at my house."

62 And Jesus said unto him,
"No man, having put his hand
to the plough, and looking back,
is fit for the kingdom of God."

ONCE A MAN OWNED A VERY BIG POND. A SMALL LILY PLANT was growing in it. The man was very happy; he had always loved white flowers of lilies. But then he became concerned because the plant was doubling itself every day: sooner or later it would cover the whole pond. He had trout in the pond and he loved to eat those trout. Once the pond was covered by the lilies all the life from the pond would disappear, including the trout.

He didn't want to cut the plants, he didn't want his trout to disappear — he was in a dilemma. He went to an expert. The expert calculated and said, "Don't be worried. It will take one thousand days for the lily to cover the whole pond. The plant is very small and the pond is very big, so there is no need to worry." Then the expert suggested a solution which appeared almost absolutely right. He said, "Wait, and when half the pond is covered with lilies, then cut the plant. Always keep it only half-covered so that you will enjoy the white flowers and your trout will not be in danger. Fifty-fifty — half the pond for the lilies, half for the trout."

The solution looked perfectly right, and one thousand days — there was enough time, so there was no need to worry. The man relaxed. He said, "When the pond is half-covered, then I will cut the lilies."

The pond was half-covered — but it was half-covered on the nine hundred ninety-ninth day. Ordinarily you would think that it would be half-covered after five hundred days — no.

The plant used to double itself, so half the pond would be covered on the nine hundred ninety-ninth day and only one day would be left. But that would not be sufficient time to cut the plant or to keep it to the half.

And it happened. On the nine hundred ninety-ninth day the pond was half-covered and the man said – he was not feeling very well, a little sick – he said, "There is no hurry. I have waited nine hundred ninety-nine days and there was no trouble. Now it is just a question of one more day. After one day I will do it."

The next morning the whole pond was covered and all the trout were dead.

This is the puzzle of life. It is a dilemma; one has to choose. If you go on accumulating things and possessions, the plant is doubling on the pond. Every day your things go on growing and your life is suffocated. Life looks too long – seventy years, eighty years. There is no hurry. People think, "When we reach to the mid-point we will change."

People always wait to get old for religion; people go on saying that religion is for old people. Go into the churches, into the temples, and you will find old people – just on the verge of death. One foot is already in the grave: the nine hundred ninety-ninth day. The next morning, life is going to be suffocated. Then they start praying, then they start meditating, then they start thinking of what life is – what is the meaning of existence? But then it is too late.

Religion needs a deep urgency. If you postpone it, you will never be able to become religious. It has to be done right now. As it is you are already late, as it is you have already wasted much time – and wasted it in futile things, wasted it in things that are going to be taken away from you.

For all those things, you have to pay with life. Whatsoever you possess, you lose life for it. It is not cheap; it is very costly. One day you have many possessions, but you are no longer there. Things are there; the owner, dead. Great piles of things...but the one who wanted to live through them is no more.

People go on preparing for life, and they die before their preparation is complete. People prepare and never live. To be religious is to live life, not to prepare for it. You are doing a very absurd thing: your rehearsal goes on and on and the real drama never starts.

I have heard about a small drama company. They were rehearsing. The real drama was getting postponed every day because the rehearsal was never complete. One day the heroine was not there, another day some other actor was not there, one day something else happened – the electricity failed or something – and it went on being postponed. But the manager was happy for at least one thing: that the hero of the drama had always been present, he had never been absent.

The last rehearsal day he thanked the hero. He said, "You are the only person who can be relied upon. All these other people are unreliable. You are the only one who has never been absent. Summer or winter, cold or hot, you have always been here."

The hero said, "There is something I would like to say. I am going to get married on the day the real drama is going to be played, so I thought that I should at least attend the rehearsals. I will not be here on that day – that's why I have never absented myself."

Know well that exactly on the day when the real drama is to start, you will not be here. It is just a rehearsal: preparation and preparation.

Possessing things is simply preparing to live, arranging so

that you will be able to live. But to live, no arrangement is needed; everything is already ready. Everything is absolutely ready; only you are needed to participate. Nothing is lacking.

This is what I call the religious attitude: this urgency that you have to live now and there is no other way to live. Now is the only way to live and to be, and here is the only home. There and then are deceptions, mirages...beware of them!

Now try to understand these very significant sutras in the gospel:

> And it came to pass, that,
> as they went in the way,
> a certain man said unto him,
> "Lord, I will follow thee
> whithersoever thou goest."

When you come across a man like Jesus or Buddha, something suddenly strikes. They have a magnetism, a presence which attracts you, which surrounds you, invokes you, invites you, becomes a deep call in the heart of the hearts. You simply forget yourself; you forget your way of life. In the presence of a Jesus, you are almost absent. His presence is so much that for a moment you are dazzled, for a moment you don't know what you are saying, for a moment you utter things you never meant to utter – as if you are hypnotized.

It *is* a hypnosis. Not that Jesus is hypnotizing you – his very presence becomes a concentration of your being. It becomes such a deep attraction that the whole world is forgotten. You must have been going somewhere to do something: you have forgotten it. You must have been coming from somewhere: you have forgotten about it. Suddenly, in his presence, the past and future disappear.

Suddenly you are here and now and a different world opens: a new dimension is revealed.

And it came to pass, that, as they went in the way, a certain man said unto him, "Lord, I will follow thee whithersoever thou goest." This man doesn't know himself what he is saying. It is an urge of the moment. After a moment he will repent for it, after a moment he will start looking backwards, after a moment he will start thinking about what he has done.

When you come to me, sometimes you say things which I know you don't mean, which I know you can't mean, because they are so irrelevant, they don't fit — as if you are raised to a higher level of being, as if you are in a new state of consciousness and you utter strange things. Later on, when you fall back to your ordinary state, either you will forget what you said or you will shrug your shoulders — you will not be able to believe that you said this.

You come to me: you bring a thousand and one questions, but when you are near me, suddenly you forget. You start mumbling. I ask you for what you have come and you say, "I have forgotten." You think that I am doing something to you. Nothing — I am not doing anything to you. The questions and problems belong to a lower state of mind. When your state is changed, those questions and problems disappear, they are not there. Back home, when you settle down, they are there waiting for you again. Again you will come and you will forget.

This is something deep within you. When you are near me, you start looking at things through me. You are no longer in the dark, you are in my light, and the problems that were relevant in your darkness are no longer relevant. To ask them looks foolish, silly. You cannot articulate your problems because they are no longer there, but when we depart — you on your way, I on mine — again the suddenness of darkness. And now the darkness is even more than before, and those problems are multiplied.

This man...the gospel doesn't mention his name, knowingly. It simply says 'a certain man' because it is not a question of a particular man. It is not a question of a particular man: a certain man. Every man is implied in it.

Many people will meet Jesus on the way and it is *always* on the way. That too has to be understood. Jesus is always moving. That is the meaning: that he is always on the way. Not that he was continuously moving and never resting, but the meaning of 'on the way' is that Jesus is a river.

You may know it or you may not know it, but the river is flowing. The river is in its flowing: to conceive of the river as nonflowing is not possible because then it will no longer be a river. A Jesus is a flow, a tremendous flood: it is always on the way, it is always moving.

You had come to me yesterday, but I am no longer there. That land is already lost in the past, those banks are no longer anywhere. You may carry them in your memory, but the river has moved. And if you carry the past in your memory you will not be able to see the river: exactly where it is now, at this point of time.

And it came to pass, that, as they went in the way.... Jesus is a wanderer, because once your consciousness is freed, once your consciousness has entered the eternal, it is going to remain an eternal wandering. Then 'the whole' is the home; then the home is nowhere.

Then you will be continuously flowing. There will never come a moment of knowledge; you will only be knowing and knowing and knowing. It will never be completed because once knowing is completed, it is dead. You will be learning, but you will never become a man of knowledge. You will always remain empty.

That's why a man like Jesus is so humble. He says, "Blessed are the poor in spirit." What does he mean by 'poor in spirit'?

He means exactly what I am saying: people who don't attain to knowledge — because knowledge is 'the riches of the spirit'. You accumulate things outside, around the body; and you accumulate knowledge inside, around the soul.

A man may be poor as far as things are concerned and he may be rich as far as knowledge is concerned. Jesus says that just to be poor in body won't help; that is nothing much, that is not authentic poverty. The authentic poverty is when you don't accumulate things inside, when you don't come to the point where you declare that "I know!" You are always knowing, you remain a process — always on the way.

Many times we will come across the expression 'Jesus on the way'. He is a wanderer, but this wandering is an indication of the innermost flow. He is dynamic, he is not static. He is not like a stone, he is like a flower — always flowering, a movement, not an event.

...A certain man... that certain man can be you, can be anybody. He has no name. It is good that the gospel has not mentioned a name. Knowingly it has been done, because if you mention a name then people think that it must be about this certain man. No, it simply says that it is about the human mind — any man will be quite representative: *...a certain man said unto him, "Lord...."*

When you come across, when you encounter Jesus, suddenly you feel something of the divine. When you have lost contact with Jesus you may start thinking about whether this man was a god or not, but in his presence he's so much, he's so powerful in his inner poverty, his humbleness has such a glory.... His poverty is a kingdom: he's enthroned. He's in the highest of consciousnesses. He suddenly surrounds you — is your environs — wraps you from everywhere like a cloud. You forget yourself in it.

"Lord" — that's the only expression that can be used for Jesus —

"Lord, I will follow thee whithersoever thou goest." And in that moment of awakening, in that moment of exhilaration, in that moment of intensity, you utter something which you may not be aware of.

That certain man said: *"Lord, I will follow thee."* He doesn't know what he is saying. To follow Jesus is very arduous, because to follow Jesus only means to become a Jesus. There is no other following. It is to risk your all and all — for nothing. It is to risk all for nothing; it is to risk your life for a death. The resurrection may be or it may not be — who knows? You can never be certain about it and no guarantee can be given. It is just a hope.

To sacrifice all that you have for just a hope? The man is not in his senses — what is he saying? He is intoxicated by Jesus, he has drunk too much of his presence. He is no longer in his mind, in his common-sense mind. Back home he will think, "What happened? Why did I say this? Is this man a sorcerer, is this man a hypnotist, a mesmerizer? This man must have played a trick upon me; I was almost deceived. What have I said?"

No, Jesus is not a sorcerer and he is not a magnetizer. He is not a mesmerizer, he is not a hypnotist, but his presence …and you become poetic. In his presence something rises to a peak in you and you assert something from your innermost core of being. Even your surface, your peripheral self is surprised.

"Lord…." This man may not have said 'Lord' to anybody else before. But suddenly, when a Jesus comes you have to call him 'Lord'. When you encounter Buddha you have to call him 'Bhagwan'. It has to be so, because you cannot find any other expression. All other words seem to be insignificant — only 'Lord', 'God'…. *"Lord, I will follow thee…."* And when you say to somebody 'Lord', it immediately follows that "I have fallen in your love."

"...I will follow thee whithersoever thou goest." What a commitment! – made in a moment of ecstasy. You may repent for it forever, but this happens. Jesus knows it well:

> And Jesus said unto him,
> "Foxes have holes..."

Jesus is saying, "Poor man, think again – what are you saying? Don't commit yourself so deeply, don't get involved with me. Watch, wait, think, ponder – and then come back to me."

> "...Foxes have holes,
> and birds of the air have nests;
> but the Son of man hath not
> where to lay his head."

Whom are you going to follow? Even foxes have holes – if you follow a fox, at least you will have a hole in which to lay your head. Even birds of the air have nests, *"...but the Son of man hath not where to lay his head."* The greatest, the highest, the sublimest, are homeless. This has to be understood. This is one of the very penetrating sayings. It has tremendous meaning.

Watch...trees, animals, birds, all have deep roots in nature. Only man is without roots. Birds don't need families, they can survive without families – nature itself protects. The trees are not in need of anybody: if there was nobody, then too trees would be there, and flowering. Nature itself protects; they have a home.

But think of a small child, a human child. If the family was not there to look after the child, can you conceive that he would survive? He would be dead. Without society, without the family, without the artificial home, he would not be able to survive. Upon this earth only man is homeless, only man is the outsider – everybody else is an insider.

Hence, religion. Religion is nothing but the search for a home. This earth doesn't seem to be a home. If you think about it, you will feel yourself a stranger here. Sooner or later you will be thrown out – this life is momentary. You don't feel that you are welcome: you have to force yourself upon it.

The trees are welcome; it seems the earth is happy through them. The earth goes on giving, sharing. The birds are singing – as if the earth sings through them. Look at the animals – so alive and vital. Only man seems to be an intruder, as if he has come from somewhere else.

This earth may be a sojourn, but it is not a home. Maybe we are staying here for a time being – a *caravanserai*, but not a home: in the morning, we have to go.

Jesus' saying has many meanings, and I would like you to enter them all.

One, man is not rooted. Because he is not rooted he is always in search: where to find a home? God is nothing but the search for a home where we can feel at ease and relaxed, and where we can feel that there is no need to struggle. We are accepted – not only accepted, welcomed. There is no need to fight your way. You can be whatsoever you are and relax, and you know the love will continue flowing, life will continue flowing. There is no fear of punishment and no greed for any reward. You are at home. You are not a stranger in a foreign land.

This is the search of religion. That's why animals don't have religion. Birds don't have religion; they make nests, but they don't make temples. Otherwise, a temple is not very difficult: they can make a big nest and gather together and sing together and pray. But they don't pray; they don't need to. Man is the only animal who makes temples, churches, mosques. Prayer is a very strange phenomenon. Just think if somebody comes from some other planet and watches humanity....

If you are making love to a woman, the watcher will be able to understand. Something like it must be happening on the other planet also. He may not be able to understand what you are saying, but he will know what you must be saying. He may not understand the language, but he will understand what lovers say to each other. When you kiss and embrace each other, he will understand the gesture.

When you are doing business he will understand; when you are reading a book he will understand; when you are doing some exercise he will understand. But when you are praying, if something like religion does not exist on his planet, he will not be able to understand at all. What are you doing? Just sitting alone? Looking at the sky, talking? To whom? What are you saying?

And if he comes on a certain day, like a religious day of Mohammedans, Christians or Hindus – all over the earth, millions of Mohammedans praying, not talking to each other, talking to the sky – he will simply feel that something has gone wrong: "Humanity has gone mad – what is happening? What are these people gesturing about, why are they gesticulating? To whom are they talking, who are they calling 'Allah'? To whom are they bowing their heads? – because nobody seems to be there."

God is not visible, God is somewhere in the mind of man. Prayer is a monologue; it is not a dialogue. A man from another planet would think that something had gone wrong in the nervous system of humanity. He would think that it is a failure of the nerves: millions of people gesticulating to nobody, talking to the sky, looking at the sky, crying "Allah! Allah!" Something is wrong: the whole of humanity has gone mad, it seems.

Prayer will not be understood because prayer is absolutely human. That is the only thing that only man does; all other things animals are doing also. Love – yes, they also make love. Search for food – they also do that. Singing they do, dancing they do, talking they do – there is communication. They are sad, they are happy – but prayer? That is nonexistential.

Jesus says, *"Foxes have holes, and birds of the air have nests; but the Son of man hath not where to lay his head."*

Man is a stranger. That's why we go on creating the fiction that we are at home and not a stranger. The home is a fiction: we create a togetherness with people. We create communities, nations and families so that we are not alone and we can feel the other is there, somebody who is familiar, somebody who is known – your mother, your father, your brother, your sister, your wife, your husband, your children – somebody who is known, familiar. But have you ever thought about it? Is your wife really known to you? Is there really a way to know the wife or the husband or the child?

A child is born to you – do you know him, who he is? But you never ask such uncomfortable questions. You immediately give him a name so that you know who he is. Without the name he will create trouble: without the name the child will move in the house and whenever you will encounter him, the unknown will be looking at you.

To forget that some stranger has come, you label him; you call him some name. Then you start managing his character – what he should do, what he should not do – so that you know and you can predict him. This is a way to create false familiarity. The child remains unknown: whatsoever you do will be on the surface; deep inside he is a stranger.

There are moments, some rare moments, in which you suddenly become aware of this. Sitting by the side of your beloved, suddenly you become aware that you are far apart.

Suddenly you look at the face of your beloved and you cannot recognize who she is or who he is. But you forget such moments immediately. You start talking: and you say some thing, you start planning, you start thinking. That's why people don't sit in silence — because silence creates a restlessness. In silence, the fiction of familiarity is broken.

That's why if a guest comes to your house and you don't say anything, you simply sit silently, he will be very angry, he will be in a rage. If you go on sitting, just looking at him, he will get mad. He will say, "What are you doing? Has something gone wrong with you? Say something! Have you gone dumb? Why are you keeping silent? Speak!"

Speaking is a way of avoiding, avoiding the fact that we are unfamiliar. When somebody starts speaking, everything is good. That's why, with foreigners, you feel a little uneasy — because you cannot speak the same language. If you have to stay in the same room with a foreigner and you cannot understand each other, it is going to be very difficult. Continuously he will remind you that 'we are strangers'. And when the feeling comes that somebody is a stranger, you immediately feel danger. Who knows what he will do? Who knows if he will not jump on you suddenly in the night and cut your throat? He's a stranger!

That's why foreigners are always suspected. There is nothing in fact to suspect — everybody is a foreigner everywhere. Even in your own land you are a foreigner, but there the fiction is settled: you speak the same language, you believe in the same religion, you go to the same church, you believe in the same party, you believe in the same flag — familiarity. Then you just think you know about each other. These are tricks.

Jesus says, "The son of man is homeless."

Jesus uses two words again and again for himself: sometimes he uses 'son of God' and sometimes he uses 'son of man'.

'Son of God' he rarely uses, 'son of man' more often. It has been a problem for Christian theology. If he is the son of God, why does he go on saying 'son of man'?

Those who are against Christ say, "If he is a son of man, then why does he insist that he is the son of God also? You cannot be both. If you are the son of man...everybody is the son of man. But if you are the son of God, then why use the other expression?"

But Jesus insists on both because he is both. And I tell you, everybody is both: from one side son of man, from another side son of God. You are born to man, but you are not born only to be man. You are born to man, but you are born to be a god. Humanity is your form, divinity is your being. Humanity is your clothing, divinity is your soul. Jesus goes on using both expressions. Whenever he says 'son of man', he says that "I am joined with you. I am just as you are – plus. I am just as you are, and more." To indicate that *more*, sometimes he says 'son of God'. But rarely does he use that – rarely, because very few people will be able to understand it.

When he says 'son of man', he is not saying something only about himself. Just look at this sentence – he is saying something about every man, that the essential man is homeless. If you think you are rooted, if you think you have got a home, you are below humanity – you may belong to animals. *"Foxes have holes, birds...have nests... the Son of man hath not where to lay his head."*

If you think that you are rooted and you are at home in this world, you must be living below humanity, because anyone who is *really* human immediately becomes aware that this cannot be the life. It may be a passage, a journey, but this cannot be the goal. And once you feel homeless in this world, then the search starts. That certain man had said, *"Lord, I will follow thee whithersoever thou goest."*

He may be thinking that Jesus is going to the east, or the west or the south or the north. "I will follow him," but he does not know the direction where Jesus is going.

Jesus is going god-ward, and that is not north, that is not east, that is not west, that is not south; that is neither up nor down – it is none of these. To go god-ward is to go within. In fact, that is not a direction at all. It is to lose all directions: north, east, south, west, up, down – to lose all directions. To go within-ward means to move in the dimensionless, directionless.

He does not know what he is saying: *"Lord, I will follow thee whithersoever thou goest."* In his 'whithersoever', the god-wardness is not implied. He does not know what he is saying. Jesus is not going anywhere. He is going within himself – which is not a point in space.

To go within is to go beyond space. That's why the soul can never be found in any experiment. An experiment can find anything which belongs to space. You can kill a man, cut and dissect him, and bones will be found, blood will be found, everything else will be found – only the soul, only the essential man, will not be found. It does not exist in space. It touches space, but it doesn't exist in it. It is only touching it…and if you destroy the body, and cut the body, the touch is lost. That fragrance flies into the unknown.

That is where Jesus is moving. And he knows that this man is committing too much, and he will not be able to forgive himself for it. And when you commit too much, you will take revenge. This happens.

I come across many people who – in a moment, like lightning – say to me, "We would like to surrender. Now, whatsoever you will say, we will do." I know that if I accept them, they will take revenge because they will not be able to fulfill what they are saying. They don't know what they are saying and they don't know in what dimension I am moving. They will not be able to keep pace with me, and then there are only two possibilities: either they will become angry against themselves, which is not the usual way of the mind, or they will become angry with me.

That's simply the normal course: whenever you are in trouble, somebody else is responsible. Whenever they feel that trouble has arisen.... And it is going to arise. From the very first step it is going to be arduous, it is going to be a razor's edge. Then they will take revenge, then they will be against me, because that will be their only way to protect themselves. That will be the only way: if they can prove that I am wrong they can take their commitment back.

Jesus knows. He says, "I am homeless. With me, you will never find rest; with me, you will always be on the way. I am a wanderer, a vagabond. With me, you will always be on the road. And my journey is such that it starts, but never ends. "You don't know where I am going. I am going towards God. I am moving away from things and the world of things: I am moving towards consciousness. I am leaving the visible, moving towards the invisible."

You can't understand what the invisible is, because at the most you can think about it negatively – you can think it is that which is not visible. No, the invisible is also visible, but you need different eyes to see it.

It happened:

Mulla Nasruddin had opened a small school and he invited me. I looked around the school; he had gathered many students. I asked him, "Nasruddin, what are you going to teach these students?"

He said, "Two things, basically: to fear God, and to wash the back of the neck."

I couldn't see the relationship: to fear God and to wash the back of the neck? I said, "It is okay as far as teaching them to fear God goes, but I cannot see the relevance of why to wash the back of the neck!"

He said, "If they can do that, they can then cope with the invisible!"

The back of the neck is the invisible because you cannot see it. " If they can do that, they can cope with the invisible." Your 'invisible' can be just like the back of your neck: it is also part of the world. Your God is also part of the world; that's why your temples become part of your market and your scriptures become commodities. Your doctrines are just like things you purchase and sell.

The God of Jesus or Buddha is not your God. Your God is not Jesus' God. His God is a withinness, a beyondness; his God is a transformation of your being, a mutation, a birth of a new being with a new consciousness. Your God is something to be worshipped; Jesus' God is something to be lived. Your 'God' is in your hands; Jesus' God is one to whom you leave yourself, in whose hands you surrender. Your God is just in your hands; you can do whatsoever you want with your God. Jesus' God is one to whom you surrender – and surrender totally.

That man did not know what he was saying. Jesus prohibited him by saying this.

>   And he said unto another, "Follow me."

To the one who was ready to follow, he said, "Wait, please. You don't know what you are doing, you don't know what commitment you are making, what you are getting involved in."

The first man acted in a moment of inspiration, in a moment of enthusiasm, in a moment of intoxication. He's not reliable, he's influenced – and if you do something under influence, it's just as if you are drunk and you say something and the next day you have forgotten it.

And he said unto another, "Follow me." To one who has not said anything he says, *"Follow me."*

> But he said, "Lord, suffer me first
> to go and bury my father."

To the other man Jesus said, *"Follow me"* – and the man had not asked. But the man was more ready, the man was more prepared, the man was more mature.

Just a few days before, a Dutch woman came to me – a very simple and good-hearted woman, in fact too good-hearted. Even good-heartedness can become a disease if it is too much. She comes to me again and again, and she writes notes and letters that she cannot tolerate poverty. When she goes to her hotel she meets beggars on the road and she cries and weeps, she feels guilty and she suffers much. She cannot meditate – even in meditation those beggars' faces come. She thinks that it is selfishness to meditate while there is so much poverty. A very good-hearted woman, but not mature: simple, good – but childish.

I told her, "You do either of two things. Go and first remove the poverty from the world and then come – if time is left and I am here. First remove the poverty and then come and meditate so you don't feel guilty. Or, if you think that is impossible, then drop the idea. Meditate, and out of your meditation, whatsoever help you can give to people, give."

Then she became worried about sannyas. She wanted to take it and yet was afraid – the Christian upbringing. Then she came again and she said, "There is a problem. My father has been very good to me. He has taught me how to be.

Now if I take sannyas I will be betraying my father, his teachings. But if I don't take sannyas it is a constant haunting around me that I should move into it so I can be transformed."

I said, "You decide either way."

That too she couldn't decide. Then one day she came and she was very worried so I told her, "One thing is certain now: that even if you ask for sannyas, I am not going to give it to you. So you be at rest now. I'm not going to give you sannyas."

Since then I have seen her – she has not come to see me, but she is here. Now she seems to be worried – I can watch her face – that if she comes to me for sannyas, I will not give sannyas to her.

Good, but immature. Commitment can only be out of maturity. A certain ripeness is needed.

And Jesus *...said unto another, "Follow me."* But that man's father had died. He could not contain himself; that's why he may have come to see Jesus on the road. He was passing by the village, his father was lying dead, and he said, *"Lord, suffer me first to go and bury my father."*

This is a very symbolic situation: the father is dead, one who has given birth to the body, and another father is present who can give birth to the soul. The question is between the soul and the body the question is between life and death. From a worldly father you don't attain to life. In fact, you are born to die, you are born to death.

The father is dead. The man said, "Suffer me, Lord, to go and bury my father – a formality, but let me do it."

Jesus said unto him – one of the most poignant, penetrating utterances of Jesus – *"Let the dead bury their dead: but go thou and preach the kingdom of God."*

It looks a little harsh, it does not show compassion. The father is lying dead and the son is expected to bury him. It is a formality, a social mannerism and a duty. But Jesus said, *"Let the dead bury their dead."* Jesus said, "In the village there are many dead people. They will do that. You don't be worried about it. There is no need for you to go."

The symbolic meaning is that one who moves into religion need not bother about duties, morality, formalities, because morality is a lower religion, duty is a lower religion, formality is of the personality. When you attain to a higher religion, you can drop all morality because now you will be fulfilling something deeper and higher. Now there is no need to carry mannerisms, no need to carry social etiquettes: "There are enough dead people in the town who will do it, and who will do it happily. You don't be worried about it. Let the dead bury their dead; you go and preach the kingdom of God."

What manner of man is this Jesus? Some man's father is lying dead and he wants to make him a preacher of the kingdom of God? Is this the moment to go and become a preacher of God?

But it is symbolic. He's saying, "Don't be worried about death, be worried about God. And don't be worried about the father who gave birth to your body; think about the father, go and preach about the father who has given your soul to you."

"...But go thou and preach the kingdom of God." In a way, if you watch the death of anybody who has been so intimate to you – a father, a mother, a wife, a husband, a friend who has been very intimate to you and is dead – only in that moment is conversion towards God possible. If you miss that moment, you will again be in the mess of the world.

Death gives you a shock. Nothing can give you a shock like that – death is the greatest shock. If that shock does not make you awake then you are incurable, impossible. Jesus used that moment. He is one of the greatest artists who has ever walked on the earth, the greatest alchemist.

The situation is death. The father is lying dead in the home, the family must be crying and weeping – this is no time to go and preach the kingdom of God. It looks absurd, looks harsh. Jesus looks too hard. He is not. It is because of his compassion that he says this. He knows that if this moment of death is missed – in burying the dead body – then there will be no possibility to awaken. Maybe that's why he turned to this man and said, "Follow me." He must have seen death in his eyes, he must have felt death around him. Of course, it was bound to be so – the father was dead. But still the man could not contain himself. He had to come to see this man, Jesus. Maybe because of death Jesus became significant, maybe because of death he became aware that everybody is going to die. Maybe because of that he had come to Jesus in search of life.

The first man is just an onlooker; the second man is ready. Death prepares you. If you can use death, if you can use pain and anguish, if you can use suffering, misery, that can become a step towards the divine.

Shocked, this man must have been standing there almost as if he himself was dead. Thinking must have stopped. In such a shock you cannot afford thinking. If the shock is really total, even tears cannot flow. For tears to flow, the shock has to be not total. If the shock is total, one is simply shocked. Nothing moves: time stops, the world disappears, thoughts drop. One is dazed, one just looks with empty eyes – hollow. One simply looks, not looking at anything. Have you seen that type of look sometimes in madmen's eyes, or sometimes immediately after somebody has died who was very intimate?

Jesus must have watched: this man was ready. Let me tell you, unless you have experienced death, you are not ready.

Life is very superficial; it is just on the periphery, just on the surface. Death is deep – it is as deep as God – so only from death is the conversion possible. Only in the moment of death do you change, your outlook changes, your attitudes change, the old world becomes irrelevant. Buddha was transformed by seeing a dead man.... Jesus must have looked – *And he said unto another, "Follow me."* Only one who has known death can follow Jesus.

If you have known death, only then can you follow me. If you have known suffering and the cleansing that comes out of suffering, if you have known pain and the shock that is a by-product of pain, then and only then can you be with me. Otherwise sooner or later you disperse because life goes on calling you back; there are a thousand and one things yet to be fulfilled. You will continually be going backwards.

Only when death cuts the bridge, breaks all the ties with life, is there a possibility that you will turn – turn your back to the world and you will face God. That's why, in one sentence, Jesus says two things which on the surface look very irrelevant: *"Let the dead bury their dead: but go thou and preach the kingdom of God."*

This man is not even a disciple – he is a stranger standing by the side of the road – and Jesus says, "Go and preach the kingdom of God." This is my observation also: that the best way to learn a thing is to teach it.

The best way to learn a thing is to teach it, I repeat it, because when you start teaching, you are learning. When you are simply learning you are too self-centered and that very self-centering becomes a barrier.

When you start teaching you are not self-centered: you look at the other, you look at the need of the other. You watch and observe *his* problem. You are completely aloof, detached – a witness. And whenever you can become a witness, godliness starts flowing from you. There is only one way to learn great things and that is to teach them. That's why I go on saying to you that if you have shared my being in any way, go and spread, go and teach, go and help other people to meditate, and you will suddenly be surprised one day: the greatest meditation will happen to you when you are helping somebody to go into meditation.

While meditating, things will happen. While you yourself are meditating many things will happen, but the greatest will happen only when you are able to teach meditation to somebody else. In that moment you become completely detached – in that detachment, you are completely silent. You are so filled with compassion – that's why you are helping the other – that something immediately happens to you. Jesus said, *"...but go thou and preach the kingdom of God."*

> And another also said,
> "Lord, I will follow thee;
> but let me first go bid them farewell,
> which are at home, at my house."

And another said, "I would also like to be with you. I'm ready to follow you, but I would have to go back, at least just to say good-bye to my family, friends, to those who are at home."

> And Jesus said unto him,
> "No man, having put his hand
> to the plough, and looking back,
> is fit for the kingdom of God."

No man who looks back is fit for the kingdom of God – why? Because no man who looks in the past can be capable of being in the present.

A Zen seeker came to Rinzai, the great master. He wanted to meditate and he wanted to become enlightened, but Rinzai said, "Wait, a few other things first. First things first. From where are you coming?"

The man said, "I always break my bridges which I have passed over."

Rinzai said, "Okay, from wherever you are coming is not the point. But what is the price of rice there these days?"

The disciple laughed and he said, "Don't provoke me, otherwise I will slap you."

Rinzai, bowing down to the seeker, said, "You are accepted."

Because if a man still remembers the price of rice from where he is coming, he is not worthy. Whatsoever you carry from the past is a burden, a barrier; it will not allow you to open to the present.

Jesus said, *"No man, having put his hand to the plough, and looking back, is fit for the kingdom of God.* If you want to follow me, follow me. There is no way of going back. There is no need: what is the point of saying good-bye? What is it going to serve? If you want to follow me," Jesus says again and again in the gospel, "then you will have to deny your father, your mother; you will have to deny your family."

Sometimes he looks almost cruel. One day he was standing in the village market and a crowd was surrounding him. Somebody said, "Lord, your mother is waiting outside the crowd." Jesus said, "Who is my mother, who is my brother, who is my father? Those who follow me, those who are with me – they are my brother, they are my father, they are my mother."

Looks really cruel – but he was not. He's not saying anything to his mother: he's saying to those people, if you're clinging too much to the family the inner revolution will not be possible, because the family is the first imprisonment.

Then the religion you belong to is the second imprisonment...then the nation that you belong to is the third imprisonment. One has to break them all, one has to go beyond them all. Only then can one find the source – the source which is freedom, the source which is godliness.

"No man, having put his hand to the plough, and looking back, is fit for the kingdom of God." One has to renounce all that is futile to gain that which is meaningful.

Once it happened that a group of friends were sitting and talking about what the most essential thing is that cannot be renounced. Somebody said, "I cannot renounce my mother. She has given birth to me; I owe my life to her. I can renounce everything, but not my mother."

Somebody else said, "I cannot renounce my wife because mother and father were given to me – they were never my choice – but my wife I have chosen. I have a responsibility towards her, I cannot renounce her. But I can renounce everybody else."

This way they went on. Somebody said he could not renounce his house, somebody else said something else. Mulla Nasruddin said, "I can do without everything except my navel."

Everybody was puzzled – just a navel? So they pressed him to explain it. He said, "Whenever there is a holiday and I am at ease, I have leisure time, I lie down on my bed and eat celery."

They said, "But how is that concerned with the navel? You can eat celery...."

He said, "You don't understand. Without the navel I have nowhere to put the salt." He puts the salt in his navel when he eats celery!

But all your attachments are just that absurd. Except for your innermost consciousness, everything can be renounced. Not that I say, "Renounce it," but deep down one should live in renouncement – be in the world, but one should remain in renouncement.

You can live in the family, not being part of it; you can live in the society and yet out of it. It is a question of inner attitude. It is not a question of changing places, it is a question of changing the mind.

The things that you are too attached to are not bad in themselves, remember. Father, mother, family, wife, children, money, house – they are not bad in themselves. The attachment is not bad because these things are bad, or these persons and these relationships are bad: attachment is bad. It can make you very stupid.

Mulla Nasruddin suddenly became rich, he inherited a great treasure. And of course, what happens with newly rich people happened with him also: he wanted to show it, exhibit it. He called the greatest painter in the country to make a portrait of his wife.

The painter started working. Nasruddin said that there was only one condition. "Remember it, don't forget it: the pearls must be in the painting." His wife was wearing many pearls and diamonds: they must be there. He's not worried about the woman – what she looks like in the painting is not the question – but the pearls and the diamonds should be there.

After a while when the painting was ready, the painter brought the painting. Mulla Nasruddin said, "Quite good, quite good. Only one thing: can't you make the breasts a little smaller and the pearls a little bigger?"

The mind of an exhibitionist, the mind of showing that you have something precious, valuable, the mind of the ego....

The question is not of living in a palace: live in a palace, that's not the point; or live in a hut or live just by the side of the road, that is not the point. The question is of the ego.

You can be an exhibitionist in a palace; you can be an exhibitionist on the road. If your mind is wanting somebody to know that you possess something, or have renounced something, then you are in a deep darkness that has to be broken.

Jesus says that one should not be attached and one should not look backwards. Looking back is an old habit with the human mind; you go on looking back. Either you look back or you look in the future – and this is how you miss the present.

The present is divine. The past is dead memory; the future is just hope, fiction. Reality is only in the present. That reality is God, that reality is the kingdom of God.

Jesus said, *"No man, having put his hand to the plough, and looking back, is fit for the kingdom of God."* Just this is to be understood; nothing else has to be done. Just listen to me: you know well that the past is past; it is no more, nothing can be done about it. Don't go on ruminating about it, wasting time and energy. That rumination about the past creates a screen around you and you cannot see that which is already here.

You have been missing it, and it has become a habit. Whenever you are sitting, you are thinking about the past. Become aware! I'm not saying to try to stop it, because if you try to stop it you will still be engaged with it. I am saying: be disengaged with it!

So what will you do? – because whatsoever you do will be an engagement with it. You just have to be aware. When the past starts coming in the mind just relax, quiet yourself, still yourself. Just remain alert, not even verbalization is needed. Just know that the past is gone; there is no use chewing over it again and again.

People use the past as a chewing gum; they go on chewing it. Nothing comes out of a gum – it is not nutritious, it is just futile – but just through the exercise of the mouth one feels good. Just the exercise of the mind and one feels as if one is doing something worthwhile.

Just remain alert. And if you can be alert about the past you will become aware, by and by, that the future has disappeared automatically. The future is nothing but the projection of the past. The future is the desire to have the past that was beautiful, again and again, in more beautiful ways – and not to have the past which was painful, to never have it again.

This is what future is. You are choosing a part of the past, glorifying it, decorating it, and imagining that in the future you will again and again have those moments of happiness – of course more magnified, more inflated. And you will never have the pain that you had to pass through in the past. This is what future is.

Once the past disappears, it does not disappear alone. It also takes the future with it. Suddenly you are here, now – time stops. This moment which is not of time I call meditation …this moment which is not of time Jesus calls 'the kingdom of God'.

Just remember it more and more. Nothing is to be done, only remembrance – a deep remembrance which follows you like breathing whatsoever you are doing – which remains somewhere in the heart. Just a deep remembrance that the past has to be dropped – and future goes with it.

Here-now is the door; from here-now you pass from the world into God, you pass from the without to the within. Suddenly, in the marketplace, the temple descends: the heavens open and the spirit of God descends like a dove.

It can happen anywhere. Every place is holy and sacred; only your ripeness, your maturity, your awareness, is needed.

The word 'awareness' is the master key.

We will come across many situations in the gospel where Jesus goes on saying: "Awake! Be alert! Be conscious! Remember!" Buddha goes on saying to his disciples: "Right mindfulness is needed." Krishnamurti goes on saying: "Awareness." Gurdjieff's whole teaching is based on one word: 'self-remembering'.

This is the whole of the gospel: self-remembering.

Enough for today.

Chapter 10

Open
The Door

THE FIRST QUESTION:

> Beloved Osho,
> Do you ever cry?

Yes, whenever I look at you. You may not see my tears, you may not hear my cry, but always when I look at you the cry is there. Because of that, I go on working on you. It is not only to help you to come out of your misery, it is to help myself also. If you come out of your misery, I will come out of my misery that is created by your misery.

It is said that when Buddha reached to the Ultimate's door, he stopped there, he wouldn't enter in. The door was open, the *devas,* the gods, were ready to welcome him in, but he wouldn't enter. The devas asked him, "Why are you standing there? Come in. We have been waiting for you since ages. You are welcome. You have returned home."

Buddha said, "I will stay here, I will have to stay here. Until the last human being passes by me and enters the door, I cannot enter."

This is a beautiful parable. Don't take it literally.... But it is true. Once you become aware, once you become a being – once you *are* – infinite compassion arises in you. Buddha has made compassion the criterion of enlightenment. Once you have attained you don't suffer for yourself, but you suffer for others: seeing the misery all around, seeing the whole absurdity of it; seeing the possibility that you can come out of it immediately, right now, and still you go on clinging....

By one hand you push it away, by another hand you pull it close. You go on creating your own prisons and still you would like to be freed. Your whole effort is contradictory. You want to come to the east and you go towards the west. Seeing you...yes, I always cry.

The second question:

> Beloved Osho,
> For ten years I have identified myself as
> a poet. But since I took sannyas ten days
> ago it has become unimportant to me
> whether or not I ever write another verse,
> even though I have often heard you
> praise the poet. What has happened?

The first thing: you cannot be identified as being a poet, because poetry is something that happens only when you are not there. If you are there, it will just be rubbish. It happens only when you are absent. That's why it is so beautiful. It comes into your emptiness: it fills you – your vacuum. You become pregnant with the unknown, with the strange.

The poet is just a mother. The mother is not going to produce the child. The child has been conceived: at the most the mother is tending it, caring for it deep within her heart, trying to give it a body – not the soul. Poetry comes to you just like a child is conceived – in deep love. In deep receptivity you become a womb and the poetry is conceived. It is a pregnancy. And one has to be very careful because miscarriage is always possible: you can abort; you can be too much in a hurry and you can destroy it.

Allow it to settle within your being. It will take its own time, it will grow by and by. It will grow in your unconscious. Your conscious is not needed; your conscious will be an interference. Forget about it, let it grow.

You will feel heavy...your whole being will be as if carrying a burden – nice, pleasant, but still a burden. And then one day the child is born. In that moment not only the child is born...the mother is also born. When the poetry is born, then the poet is born. It is not the poet who writes the poetry. In fact, it is the birth of poetry which creates the poet. You were not a poet before it – only by its birth.

A woman becomes a mother. A mother is a totally different category from an ordinary woman. A woman is a woman – a mother is totally different. She has conceived something of the beyond; she has carried the beyond into her womb and she has given it a body.

The poet is born when the poetry is born. It is a shadow of the poetry, a consequence of the poetry. It succeeds poetry, it does not precede it. There was no poet before, there was no mother before. There was a man, there was a woman – but there was no poet, there was no mother. The mother comes into existence after the poetry has happened.

Ordinarily, whatsoever you call poetry is not poetry. It is just a mind thing. You think it; you write it. Whatsoever you write is prose and whatsoever God writes through you is poetry. It may have the form of prose – it doesn't matter. Whatsoever Buddha says or Jesus says is poetry. The form is prose, that is not the point. It is poetry because God writes it: the whole writes through the part; the ocean tries to give you a message through the drop. Whenever *you* write, it is prose – ordinary prose. Whenever God writes through you, it is poetry. It may be prose...it is still poetry.

You cannot be identified with being a poet. That will be a disturbance, that will destroy the whole music and the whole harmony. It is good, good that the identification has dropped, good that you have forgotten about poetry, good that it doesn't seem to affect you in any way now whether you write or not. This is the right situation. Now for the first time there is a possibility that poetry may happen.

I cannot say, "It *will* happen," because poetry cannot be predicted. If you predict it, again the mind will start functioning and waiting and trying and doing something about it. No, you completely forget about it. It may take months, it may take years, it may take your whole life, but some day, if you have really completely forgotten your identification, you will become the medium. Something will flow through you. It will come through you, but it will be of the beyond. Then you will be a watcher, a witness to it. You won't be a poet, you will be a witness. And when it is born, a different quality of being will come in its wake. That's what a poet is. All great poets are humble, they don't claim.

The Upanishads are not even signed – nobody knows who wrote them. The greatest of poetry, and the poets have not even tried to sign it; they have not left their signatures. That would have been profane. They have left it, they have not claimed. They were just vehicles.

A real poet is a vehicle, a medium. That's why I praise poetry so much – because it is very close to meditation, very close to religion – the closest neighbor. The politician works with the practical, the scientist with the possible, the poet with the probable, and the mystic with the impossible. The probable is the closest neighbor of the impossible – that's why I praise poetry.

But when I praise poetry, I am not praising your poets. Ninety-nine percent of them are just writing junk. They are doing a mind thing, an ego-trip. They manage, that's all – but poetry doesn't come through them.

You can write poetry. Technically it may even be correct, but it may be dead. Sometimes it happens that a poem is technically not correct, but it is alive. Who bothers about whether a thing is technically correct or not? The real thing is whether it is alive or not.

If you are going to become a mother, would you like a child who is technically correct, but dead? A plastic child: technically, absolutely right; you cannot find a fault.... In fact, if you want technically correct human beings, then only plastic beings are possible, only they can be absolutely correct. A real, alive child has so many defects – bound to be so, because life exists in danger and death. Only a dead thing is out of danger. Life is always a hazard: there are a thousand and one difficulties to be crossed, riddles to be solved. The very phenomenon that life exists is a miracle, with so many imperfections....

Life is imperfect because life is a growing phenomenon. Anything that is growing will be imperfect, otherwise how will it grow? Anything that is perfect is already dead: it is good for the grave – you cannot do anything else with it.

Ninety-nine percent of your poets are just writing junk; they give birth to dead children. Sometimes – and only sometimes, rarely – a poet is there. And whenever such a phenomenon as the poet exists – which is a miracle on this earth – just next to him is the mystic. One step more and he will become a mystic. If the poet tries to be on his wings a little more, he will become a mystic. And if the mystic, in his compassion, descends a step towards you, he will become a poet.

Poetry is a communication of the mystery of life. Unless you have felt it, how can you communicate? Poetry is a relationship between you and the whole. Something transpires between the drop and the ocean, between the leaf and the tree. Something transpires between the whole and the part, and the part starts dancing. The part is so overflowing with joy that it sings...so delighted that its movements become poetic. It no longer walks on the earth – it flies.

Prose is just walking on the earth; poetry is a flight into the sky. Prose is just walking, poetry is dancing. The movements are the same, but the quality is tremendously different.

Good – you are blessed if the identification is gone. And that's what I'm trying to do through sannyas, so that when your old identification is gone, you are left in a vacuum. Only in the vacuum can the hands of God descend in you and create something out of the mud that you are, create something beautiful. It will not be yours – it will come through you. Rejoice that the identification is gone; don't try to bring it back. Forget all about it, forget all about everything that you know in relation to poetry, poetics. Forget everything – just rejoice in being yourself.

One day, suddenly you will fall in line with the whole – a turning in, a tuning in – and a song will descend like a dove. Then you will be, for the first time, a poet. You will not claim it, but you will be it. Those who are, don't claim. Those who are not, only they claim.

The third question:

> Beloved Osho,
> I feel like an actor in a play and
> I don't always like my role in it.
> Just when I feel it is dropping, you push
> me back in it – defining it, defining me.
> It appears you give me a form,
> while my being is bursting at the seams.
> I want to explode and spread.
> Why do you mold me so?

The first thing: if you really feel that you are an actor in a play then there is no question of your like or dislike. Then you cannot say, "Sometimes I don't like my role in it," because like and dislike come only when you think of yourself not as an actor but as a doer.

To the actor, all roles are the same. What difference does it make whether you become Jesus or Judas in a drama? If you really know that this is a drama, and Judases and Jesuses are all the same behind the curtain, behind the stage – it is just an act – then what is wrong in being a Judas? How can you dislike it? And what is good in being Jesus? How can you like it?

Like and dislike exist only when you think you are the doer. Then good and bad come in; then judgment, evaluation; then condemnation, appreciation. Then the duality enters. Only with the doer, the duality enters. If you are an actor it is all the same whether you are a Judas or a Jesus. Once you understand the point that life is just a great drama you are finished with likes and dislikes. Then whatsoever the whole wills, you do it. You are not the doer: you fulfill the desire of the whole.

That is one of the greatest teachings of all religions: to become an actor in life. Then like/dislike disappears. When like/dislike disappears, choice disappears – and when you are choiceless, you are free. *Moksha,* nirvana, is attained.

Become an actor. Play the role, play it beautifully...because when one has to play it, why not play it beautifully? You are a Judas – perfectly okay. Be a Judas – enjoy the role and let the audience also enjoy the role. Behind the stage, Judas and Jesus are meeting and having tea. They are friends there, they have to be.

In fact, without Judas, Jesus cannot be. Something in the story will be missing, something very essential will be missing. Just think of Jesus without Judas. Christianity will not be possible. There might not have been any record of Jesus without Judas. Because he betrayed, Jesus was crucified, and because Jesus was crucified, the event stuck hard in the heart of humanity.

Christianity is born not because of Christ, but because of the cross. So I would prefer that Christianity be called 'Crossianity'. It should not be connected with Christ, but with the cross.

If you go and look at the church, you will see the cross raised higher than Jesus, and the bishops and the popes wearing the cross. Christianity is born out of the cross. But if you think that, then who is the author of this crucifixion? – Judas, not Jesus.

At the last moment on the cross, just before he died, Jesus hesitated. The part hesitated to dissolve into the whole, the river hesitated to fall into the ocean. It's natural, it is human: Jesus is son of man *and* son of God.

Every river must be tremendously apprehensive and afraid when it comes to the ocean. It was coming all the way – it may have journeyed thousands of miles to meet the ocean – but whenever the river falls into the ocean, a deep turmoil is bound to be there in the heart. She is going to disappear. The ocean is so vast – where will she be? She will be lost, her identity gone: the name, the form, the dreams, the desires – all gone. The ocean is so vast, she will simply disappear. Falling into the ocean is death, there is the cross. When a river falls into the ocean, there is a cross.

Jesus, at the last moment, looked at the sky and said, "God, have you forsaken me? Why is this happening to me?" – a deep cry of anguish. "Why have you forsaken me?" shows the humanity of Jesus. That is where Jesus is tremendously beautiful, incomparably beautiful.

Buddha is more inhuman. You may call it superhuman, but he

is inhuman. If he was going to die on the cross, he would not have cried toward the sky, "Why have you forsaken me?" He knows that there is nobody to cry to, he knows no God exists, that that is all human foolishness. He knows that all that is born is going to die; he has understood it totally. He will not cry, he will simply dissolve. The river of Buddha will not hesitate, it will not hesitate for a single moment. There will not be a cross.

Buddha is inhuman, very far away from the human heart. Mahavira is still even more inhuman. They are not of this world at all; they are very abstract, as if they are not concrete human beings. They look more like disembodied ideas. They look fictitious, they look mythological – but not real.

Jesus is very real. He's as real as you are. And this cry.... Buddha must have laughed. If he had been there he would have laughed at how foolish this man was: "What are you crying about? To whom are you crying?"

In Lewis Carroll's beautiful book, *Alice in Wonderland*, there is a small dialogue:

Tweedledum says to Alice. "Why are you crying? You are unreal – just a dream of the king."
Alice looks at him and says, "But I am *real*."
Tweedledum laughs and says, "You are foolish. If he, the king, stops dreaming, where will you be?"
Alice says, "I will be here of course."
Tweedledum laughs again and says, "You fool! If he stops dreaming, you will simply disappear. You are a figment of his dream. Don't cry. How can you cry? – you are unreal."
Alice goes on crying. She says, "If I am unreal, then who is crying? If I am unreal, then what about these tears?"
Tweedledum says, "You fool, do you think these tears are real or your crying is real?"

Buddha would have laughed, Shankara would have laughed: "What are you doing? This whole world is *maya*: the dream of the king. You are just part, a figment of it; you are not real, you are unreal. Just disappear. Why are you saying, 'You have forsaken me?' Who is there to forsake you?"

But not Jesus. He cries – tears may have flowed through his eyes. He is human, as human as you are, rooted in the earth as you are. He is very earthly…but not just earthly, not merely earthly. He is more.

He cried. For a moment he even became angry and annoyed. He said, "What are you doing to me? Have you forsaken me?" And then he understood. The river hesitated, then understood and moved into the ocean.

Then he said, "I understand. Thy will should be done, not mine." The part was ready to fall into the whole.

He is earthly and he is heavenly – both. He is a great bridge. At the last moment he understood the whole thing as just a role to be played. "Thy will should be done, not mine" – then it becomes acting. If it is your will, then it becomes doing. This is the difference.

You say to me, "I feel like an actor in a play." You must be just *thinking* of yourself as an actor in a play because the next part of the sentence denies it – "…and I don't always like my role in it." If it is just a play, then why bother? Be a Judas or be a Jesus – it is all the same. From where does the evaluation of like and dislike come? The ego exists in your likes and dislikes. In your choice exists the ego; when you don't choose, the ego disappears. That is what I'm doing to you: "Just when I feel it is dropping, you push me back into it."

Yes, I will go on pushing you until the choice disappears completely. Don't resist me because if you resist then you will not be able to understand for long. Don't get annoyed and don't say, "What are you doing to me?"

"It appears you give me a form, while my being is bursting at the seams. I want to explode and spread...." That 'I want' is the barrier to exploding and spreading. The 'I' cannot explode and cannot spread. It can only think, it can dream.

My whole effort is so that you can drop the 'I' and just be. Then you will spread; then there will be no barrier for you, then you can become infinite. You *are* infinite: the ego won't allow you to see it, the ego won't allow you to see the truth.

"Why do you mold me so?" I will go on molding you from one form to another, and again from one form to another, so that you can understand that you are formless. Only the formless can be molded into form. If you have a form, then you cannot be molded into another form; you are already fixed.

If you want to mold steel it will be difficult, but you can mold mud easily. Why? Why not steel? Steel has a more fixed form. You can say it in this way: steel believes in a more fixed form, the steel is deceived by a more fixed form. The mud is not so deceived.

Then there is water: formless, fluid. You put it in a jar; it takes that form. You move it into another jar; never for a single moment does it resist – it takes another form. It is fluid.

Allow me to mold you in many forms because only in changing from one form to another – somewhere in between – will you become aware of the formless. There is no other way to become aware of the formless. Moving from one form to another – just in the middle somewhere, when the old form has gone and the new has not arisen – in that interval, some day you will become aware.

That's what God himself is doing – goes on changing your forms. Sometimes you were a plant...then you were a bird ...then you became an animal.... Then you became a man: sometimes a woman, sometimes a man; sometimes black, sometimes white; sometimes stupid, sometimes intelligent. He goes on changing your form because that is the only opportunity.... By changing the form, somewhere in the middle, one day you will become aware.

The whole thing is an acting; then you will be able to say: "Thy will should be done, not mine." That moment you are freed. When you can say with your whole heart, "Thy will should be done, not mine," you have disappeared. The river has fallen.

The fourth question:

> Beloved Osho,
> I feel that I have been dishonest and insincere in all my relations throughout my life. I have not done justice to my parents, my wife, nor my children, nor my friends and neighbors, and so on. And now I feel I am not just and sincere to my Master and my sannyas also. This is the cause of great agony to me, to my mind. What should I do?

If you start thinking in terms of doing, you will again be insincere because in whatsoever you have done, you have been insincere. Your doing has become corrupted.

So the first thing is: resist doing! Just remain alert, alert to your insincerity. Don't be in a haste to do anything because that will be done again by you; your whole past will be involved in your doing. Resist! Just remain with this feeling that you have been insincere, that's enough. It is purifying, it has a tremendous capacity to purify and cleanse you. Just remain with the feeling that "I have been insincere," that

"I am insincere" and don't try to do anything about it. That is again trying to make a good image of yourself: that you are not insincere, that you are a sincere man. Your ego is hurting because you have been insincere.

Try to be aware of the fact; don't try to do anything about it. Anything that you do will be immature and too early. Just remain with the idea, live with it. Live with the idea that you are insincere. If you can live with it, the very idea, the very awareness will kill your ego completely. The ego cannot remain alive if you think you are insincere. The ego needs a good image: that you are a sincere man – very honest. That's what the ego is saying to you: "Do something so you can repaint the image, renovate the image."

You have been insincere. This has been revealed through meditation. Now the ego is in danger of death. The ego says, "Do something." Through doing it will try to again reclaim the fallen image, resettle with the old so you can feel again that "I am good, I am beautiful. I am sincere, I am moral, I am this and that."

The first thing – very difficult, arduous, but this has to be done: just remain alert to the insincerity, live with the idea and don't be bothered to change it.

It will change of its own accord because once you understand that you are insincere, you cannot remain insincere. It is impossible, it has never happened. It cannot happen, the very thing is impossible. If you know that you are insincere, it will drop. If you want to save it, then do something to create the feeling that you are sincere.

If you know that you are a liar, the lying will stop of its own accord. If you feel you are immoral, don't try to do anything: don't repent, don't feel guilty – those are tricks. Remain with the idea, the naked fact of who you are. Don't move, don't get occupied in doing something. Remain naked, with the naked idea, the naked reality, and you will see a change is happening...not by your doing. When a change comes to you not by your doing, it comes from God. Only God can make you moral, sincere; only God can make you religious; only God can make you pure. It is *prasad*, it is his gift; you cannot do it. All your doing will be an undoing. Please, remind yourself again and again that you are not to do anything.

You say, "This is the cause of great agony to my mind." Yes, it is a great cause of agony to your mind – and to the ego which is the same; mind or ego – because the ego feels hurt. *You* – and so insincere? You had always believed that you were a very sincere man, you had always believed that you were a pinnacle of a man, a crescendo of humanity, the purest gold. You had always believed that.

Now meditation has broken a window into the falseness. You have been able to look into yourself, the reality. You have come across a mirror. Now don't try to escape from it, remain with the fact. Whosoever you are, that is your reality. Remain with the fact. If you can remain with the fact, you will change. But that change will not be your doing, it will happen.

When a transformation comes to you, it has a totally different grace. Whatsoever you do will always be tiny, mediocre and finally useless. Whatsoever God does to you is infinite. Only that can be infinite which comes from the infinite. Don't try to do anything. Accept the fact, remain with it, relax, and suddenly there will come a transformation.

I teach sudden transformation, and I teach transformation by God, not by you. You are just to allow him. That is all that you have to do on your part. Open the door, wait. Just open the door – that much you have to do. Allow...so that when he knocks at the door you can welcome him, when he comes you can recognize him, when he comes you can call him in. Just don't sit with closed doors, that's all.

Meditation is nothing but that: opening the door.

Meditation will not give you enlightenment, remember. No technique can ever give you enlightenment; enlightenment is not technical. Meditation can only prepare the ground, meditation can only open the door. Meditation can only do something negatively; the positive will come. Once you are ready, it always comes.

Please don't try to do anything. Just be.

The fifth question:

> Beloved Osho,
> You said that the family is the first thing
> to renounce. I don't understand
> why we were served prasad
> on the day of your father's initiation.

The family has to be renounced, that's true. I have renounced my family, but my family is rare: they haven't renounced me. And it is rare, I say, because it has not happened before.

Jesus' father never came to Jesus to be initiated. John the Baptist initiated many, but his own father never came to be initiated. Krishna's father was not a disciple of his.

My father is rare – not because he is my father: he is simply rare. There was every possibility....

As human nature goes, there is every possibility that a father cannot come and bow down to his own son. It is almost humanly impossible. He has done that. You will not find a parallel in the whole history of man. And it may not happen again.

But you are blind and you cannot see the fact, so even the *prasad* became a problem to you. Just think of bowing down to your own son, coming to the feet of your own son, being initiated. A tremendous humbleness, a tremendous innocence is needed.

That is one of the most difficult things in human relationships. It is not accidental that Jesus' father never came to him. It is simple: to believe in the son to whom you have given birth, whom you have seen from the very first day, from his first cry – how can you believe that he has become enlightened? Your own son? – impossible. Your own blood and bone? – impossible. How can you think that he has become something, someone from whom you have to learn?

A son remains a son…and to a father he remains a child always, because the distance is always the same. If my father was twenty when I was born, that twenty years' distance has remained the same; it will always remain the same. If I am forty-five, he will be sixty-five. I cannot come closer to him in age. He will always be twenty years more experienced than me.

And to come back to me and to surrender…. You cannot realize the significance of it! That is why you ask such foolish questions. It is one of the rarest moments.

I again repeat: my father is rare – not because he is my father. He's simply rare.

The sixth question:

> Beloved Osho,
> Did Jesus become the Christ on the cross,
> or when he came out of the River Jordan?
> Are there stages of christhood also?

There are no stages. Enlightenment – or christhood or buddhahood – happens in a single split second, there are not gradual stages. But when Jesus was baptized by John the

Baptist in the River Jordan, the journey started – not christhood. The seed started moving towards being a tree. The seed was broken in the soil, now the tree and its coming is only a question of time. You cannot say that when the seed has broken in the soil the tree is there – you cannot say it because the tree is *not* there.

You cannot say that the tree is. You cannot say it because where can you see the tree? You cannot rest under the tree, you cannot pluck the fruits, you cannot have the fragrance of the flowers. The tree is nonexistential. Yes, in one way you cannot say the tree is. But in another way the tree is, because the seed is broken. The tree is on the way, it is coming; now it is only a question of time. It has come, in a way, because it has started.

The day John the Baptist initiated Jesus the seed was broken. The heavens opened and the spirit of God, like a dove, descended. This was the beginning – not of christhood, the beginning *towards* christhood; the seed moving towards the tree.

Jesus became Christ on the cross, when he said, "Thy will be done. not mine." That day he became a tree; he became a big, vast tree. Thousands could take shelter under him now. It bloomed, it filled the whole earth with fragrance.

So in a way you can say that in the River Jordan, when he was initiated, the first glimpse was achieved; on the cross, the last. It depends how you want to express it. But I think I have conveyed the meaning to you: he started on the journey towards being a Christ on that day.

You can also call him Christ on that day; it is just a question of how to express it. But my emphasis is that he moved towards christhood. He became Christ on the cross.

Christhood or buddhahood, nirvana, moksha, enlightenment – they happen in a split second, they have no gradualness about them. They are sudden transformations.

The seventh question:

> Beloved Osho,
> The return is entirely a personal affair.
> Even a very near one cannot understand.
> It is actually easily possible only for those
> who have suffered. But you are calling
> all. Is it possible for them to hear your
> call of love?

That is not the point. Whether they hear it or not is not the point: I should go on calling. They may be deaf, but I am not dumb. If they don't listen I will have to call more loudly, that's all.

And when you call a thousand, only a hundred will listen. One can never know who the hundred will be. You call a thousand, a hundred will listen. The very nature of the call is such that only those who are just near awakening can listen to it. Only those whose sleep is almost complete, who are nearing the morning and are getting ready to wake – only they can listen. But you cannot see who those will be. Call a thousand: a hundred will listen and only ten will start moving. Ninety will listen and still will not move; they will listen but they will not understand, or they will understand something else, or they will misunderstand. Ten will start moving. And when ten move, only one reaches; nine will be lost on the way. Call a thousand and you have called only one. But this is how things are, so one has to go on calling.

So I don't bother a bit whether you listen or not – I go on calling. One is bound to come and that's enough. If you call a thousand and one comes, if you call ten thousand and ten come, that's enough. One should not ask for more, that is already too much.

This is right that only those who have suffered will be able to understand me...because pain purifies, suffering gives understanding. Suffering gives a certain crystallization. Unless you suffer you don't know what life is. Unless you suffer you don't know how difficult it is to get out of life.

I was reading the life of a great Japanese poet, Issa. He suffered. He must have been a very, very sensitive man: he was a great poet, he's one of the greatest *haiku* poets.

When he was only thirty he had already lost his five children; five children had died by the time he was thirty – almost every year a child died. Then his wife died and he was almost completely mad – in anguish, in suffering.

He went to a Zen master. The Zen master asked, "What is the problem?" The Zen master must have been almost like a buddha – not like Jesus – one who has attained, but one who has completely forgotten human misery.

Issa said, "My five children are dead and now my wife is dead. Why is there so much suffering? I can't see the reason for it. What is the explanation? I have not done anything wrong to anybody, I have lived as innocently as possible. In fact, I have lived very much aloof. I'm not very related to people – I'm a poet, I live in my own world. I have not done anything wrong to anybody.

"I have lived a very poor life, but I was happy. Now suddenly my five children are gone, my wife is also gone – why is there so much suffering, and for no reason? There must be an explanation."

The Zen master said, "Life is just like a dewdrop in the morning. It is the nature of life that death happens. There is no explanation; it is the nature of life. There is no need for any special reason to be given. Life's nature is like a dewdrop: it hangs for a while on a leaf of grass, a small breeze and it is gone, the sun rises and it evaporates.

That is the nature of life. Remember that."

Issa was a man of deep intelligence. He understood it. He came back and he wrote a haiku. The haiku means: Life, a dewdrop? Yes, I understand. Life is a dewdrop. Yet... and yet....

In that "Yet...and yet..." he's saying something superbly human. "Life is a dewdrop; I understand. And yet...." The wife is gone, the children are gone and the eyes are full of tears: Yet...and yet....

"Yes, life is a dewdrop, but...." And that 'but' is great. Only those who have suffered can understand that life is a dewdrop, and even then "Yet...and yet..." remains. Even when you understand, understanding is difficult.

And those who have not suffered, what to say of them? They live a superficial life. Happiness is always superficial, it has no depth in it. Only sadness has depth. Life is superficial, only death has depth. Life is very ordinary: eating, earning, loving – very ordinary. Suffering has a depth; it awakens you, it shocks you out of your sleep.

Yes, only those who have suffered will understand what I'm saying: Yet...and yet.... Even they may not understand. But this is so, this is how life is. If one becomes despondent because of this and thinks not to call, not to say anything....

It happened:

When Buddha became enlightened, for seven days he remained silent. He thought, "Who will listen?" He thought, "What am I going to say? Who will understand?" He thought, "The things that have happened to me, if somebody had told them to me when they had not happened to me, even I would not have understood. So who will understand? Why bother?"

For seven days he sat and sat and sat under the Bodhi Tree. Tradition says that the *devas* in heaven became very disturbed. "Why is he keeping quiet? Only after thousands of years does one become enlightened. Why is he not calling people?"

They came – a beautiful story – they bowed down to Buddha and said, "You should say something. You have attained; you should give the call. The word should spread to people – why are you keeping quiet? We waited and waited. Seven days looked like seven centuries. What are you doing? Don't waste time. You will only be for a little while more and then you will disappear for ever and ever. Before you disappear, give a call."

Buddha said, "Who will listen? Who will understand?"

But those devas were very cunning. And it is good that they were cunning. They argued, they persuaded. They said, "Yes, you are right. Rare – rare is the possibility of someone's listening, and rarest is the possibility of someone understanding. But it is there.

Call a thousand – a hundred will listen, ninety will not understand; ten will walk, nine will be lost on the way. Somewhere or other they will think that they have achieved; they will sit by the side and they will think they have come home. Only one will arrive – but one is more than enough."

Buddha understood and he started preaching.

I know it is a very hopeless effort. Knowing well that you will not understand, I go on talking to you. It is as if one is talking to walls.

When Bodhidharma became enlightened he was sitting near a wall, his back to the wall. Immediately he turned and faced the wall. For nine years he would not sit in any other way. Whenever he would sit, he would face the wall. If somebody was there – an inquirer, a seeker – he would have to ask his questions from the back.

People asked, "What foolish posture have you chosen? There have been many buddhas in the world, but nobody has sat facing the wall. Why are you sitting this way? Why are you so crazy?"

Bodhidharma said, "As far as I know, all the buddhas have been facing walls" – because wherever you look, there is a wall. That's not the point.

Bodhidharma would say, "They all have faced walls, but they were a little more polite." He would say, "I'm not so polite, that's all. I don't bother a bit what you think of me. I will turn my face towards you only when I see that someone is there who can understand me."

For nine years he faced the wall. Then one man came. The man said, "Turn towards me otherwise I will kill myself" – he had a sword in his hand. Still Bodhidharma would not turn. He cut off his hand and said, "Look, the hand is gone. The second thing will be the head."

Then Bodhidharma turned. He said, "Wait! So you have come" – because only those who are ready to behead themselves can understand.

Enough for today.

About Osho

Osho defies categorization, reflecting everything from the individual quest for meaning to the most urgent social and political issues facing society today. His books are not written but are transcribed from recordings of extemporaneous talks given over a period of thirty-five years. Osho has been described by *The Sunday Times* in London as one of the "1000 Makers of the 20th Century" and by *Sunday Mid-Day* in India as one of the ten people – along with Gandhi, Nehru and Buddha – who have changed the destiny of India.

Osho has a stated aim of helping to create the conditions for the birth of a new kind of human being, characterized as "Zorba the Buddha" – one whose feet are firmly on the ground, yet whose hands can touch the stars. Running like a thread through all aspects of Osho is a vision that encompasses both the timeless wisdom of the East and the highest potential of Western science and technology.

He is synonymous with a revolutionary contribution to the science of inner transformation and an approach to meditation which specifically addresses the accelerated pace of contemporary life. The unique Osho Active Meditations™ are designed to allow the release of accumulated stress in the body and mind so that it is easier to be still and experience the thought-free state of meditation.

ABOUT OSHO

Osho International Meditation Resort

Every year the Osho International Meditation Resort welcomes thousands of people from over 100 countries who come to enjoy a holiday in an atmosphere of meditation and celebration. The 40-acre resort is located about 100 miles southeast of Mumbai (Bombay), in Pune, India, in a tree-lined residential area set against a backdrop of bamboo groves and wild jasmine, peacocks and waterfalls.
The basic approach of the resort is that of "Zorba the Buddha": living in awareness, with a capacity to celebrate everything in life. Many visitors come to just be, to allow themselves the luxury of doing nothing. Others choose to participate in a wide variety of courses and sessions that support moving toward a more joyous and less stressful life by combining methods of self-understanding with awareness techniques. These courses are offered through Osho Multiversity and take place in a pyramid complex next to the famous Osho Teerth zen gardens.
You can choose to practice various meditation methods, both active and passive, from a daily schedule that begins at six o'clock in the morning. Each evening there is a meditation event that moves from dance to silent sitting, using Osho's recorded talks as an opportunity to experience inner silence without effort.
Facilities include tennis courts, a gym, sauna, Jacuzzi, a nature-shaped Olympic-sized swimming pool, classes in zen archery, tai chi, chi gong, yoga and a multitude of bodywork sessions.

The kitchen serves international gourmet vegetarian meals, made with organically grown produce. The nightlife is alive with friends dining under the stars, with music and dancing.

Make online bookings for accommodation at the new Osho Guesthouse inside the resort through the website below or drop us an email at guesthouse@osho.com

Take an online tour of the meditation resort, and access travel and program information at: www.osho.com

The daily meditation schedule may include:

OSHO Dynamic Meditation™: A technique designed to release tensions and repressed emotions, opening the way to a new vitality and an experience of profound silence.

OSHO Kundalini Meditation™: A technique of shaking free one's dormant energies, and through spontaneous dance and silent sitting, allowing these energies to be redirected inward.

OSHO Nadabrahma Meditation™: A method of harmonizing one's energy flow, based on an ancient Tibetan humming technique.

More Osho Books

Satyam Shivam Sundaram
Truth Godliness Beauty
A much-loved, all-time classic, and a must for those new to meditation and to Osho's vision. It is an invitation to discover that the more comfortable we are with being ourselves, the easier it is to go beyond ourselves – to be able to relax, meditate, laugh at ourselves and enjoy our lives each and every moment.

Osho responds to questions such as: Why is it so difficult to be in a state of let-go? Are men responsible for women feeling fed up? How can I love better? What is it to give and what is it to receive? Why do enlightened masters criticize each other? Are there real differences in races? Why am I scared to accept myself as I am?

There are also many classic talks on subjects such as the mystic rose, how watching leads to no-mind, how hypnosis can help meditation, running away from ourselves, jealousy, boredom, sex, loving ourselves, relaxation, getting older, music, creativity, politics and war, dropping our masks, fear of the new...

ISBN 81-7261-192-7

Beyond Psychology
Talks in Uruguay
In this book Osho shows us that the real meaning of "taking responsibility" is to go beyond the narrow confines of the

mind. Showing us why psychological answers to our self-made miseries will never work, Osho gives many techniques to help us step beyond our psychology. He answers our most personal and existential questions, and takes a radical new look at a variety of esoteric subjects.

ISBN 81-7261-195-1

Ancient Music in the Pines

Osho introduces the book:
Zen is the way of the spontaneous – the effortless effort, the way of intuition.
A Zen Master, Ikkyu, a great poet, has said: "I can see clouds a thousand miles away, hear ancient music in the pines."
This is what Zen is all about. You cannot see clouds a thousand miles away with the logical mind. The logical mind is like glass, too dirty, too covered with the dust of ideas, theories, doctrines. But you can see clouds a thousand miles away with the pure glass of intuition, with no thoughts – just pure awareness. The mirror is clean and the clarity supreme. You cannot hear ancient music in the pines with the ordinary logical mind. How can you hear the ancient music? Music once gone is gone forever.
But I tell you, Ikkyu is right. You can hear ancient music in the pines – I have heard it – but a shift, a total change, a change of gestalt, is needed.... You can hear the ancient music in the pines because it is eternal music; it is never lost.

ISBN 81-7261-079-3

Further Information

Osho International Meditation Resort
17 Koregaon Park
Pune 411001 MS, India
Tel: +91 (0) 20 6601 9999
Fax: +91 (0) 20 6601 9990
resort@osho.net

www.osho.com
A comprehensive website in different languages with an online magazine, audio and video webcasting, an Audio-book Club, the complete English and Hindi archive of Osho talks and a complete catalog of all Osho publications including books, audio and video. Includes information about the active meditation techniques developed by Osho, most with streaming video demonstrations.

For information regarding Osho worldwide publishing, please contact:
Osho International, New York
oshointernational@oshointernational.com

Osho books are available worldwide through your local bookstores and in India through Sadhana Foundation at distrib@osho.net